Contemporary Perspectives on Capital in Educational Contexts

A volume in
Contemporary Perspectives on Capital in Educational Contexts
RoSusan D. Bartee, *Series Editor*

Contemporary Perspectives on Capital in Educational Contexts

Edited by

RoSusan D. Bartee

University of Mississippi

Foreword by M. Christopher Brown II

IAP

INFORMATION AGE PUBLISHING, INC.

Charlotte, NC • www.infoagepub.com

Library of Congress Cataloging-in-Publication Data

Contemporary perspectives on capital in educational contexts / edited by
RoSusan D. Bartee ; foreword by M. Christopher Brown II.
p. cm. – (Contemporary perspectives on capital in educational
contexts)
Includes bibliographical references.
ISBN 978-1-61735-363-5 (pbk.) – ISBN 978-1-61735-364-2 (hardcover) –
ISBN 978-1-61735-365-9 (e-book)
1. Education–United States–Finance. 2. Capital–United States. I.
Bartee, RoSusan D.
LB2825.C616 2011
371.2'06–dc22
2010052697

Printed and bound by CPI Group (UK) Ltd, Croydon, CR0 4YY

To my beloved nephews,
Howard Bartee, III and Davis Lamar Bartee . . .
May you always enjoy the pursuit of academic excellence.

CONTENTS

PART II

EDUCATIONAL CONTEXT AND THE PRODUCER ASPECTS OF CAPITAL

PART III

EDUCATIONAL CONTEXT AND THE REGULATOR ASPECTS OF CAPITAL

FOREWORD

MAKING IT ON THE BROKEN PIECES OF CAPITAL AND CONTEXT

In 2009, I accepted the appointment to serve as Executive Vice President and Provost of the historic Fisk University in Nashville, Tennessee. After nearly two decades of employment in large, predominantly white, research universities, I chose to return to the South and serve at one of the nation's preeminent bastions of black intellectual thought and one of the epigenetic paragons of excellence in curriculum, faculty, and student success among historically black colleges and universities. This migration to the "black Harvard" was conjoined to delusions of academic and social grandeur regarding the "talented tenth," the black intelligentsia, the Cosby-era bourgeoisie, and high-cotton, silk-stocking, fair-complexioned students of old black money—the kind garnered in century-old funeral homes and legacied medical or dental practices. What a wonderfully ethereal and ebullient set of expectations.

While Fisk and her sister schools certainly have their share of the above, I was struck by the panoply of heterogeneity on the campus—black and white faculty, Latino and Caribbean students, tuition paid by cash and by loan, debutante-like arrivals by Mercedes and pauper-like appearances by taxi. Fisk, for all its grandeur, was not an academic resort for the elite, but it was an educational factory for the aspiring. The average statistics for a

Contemporary Perspectives on Capital in Educational Contexts, pages ix–xiii regularly admitted student at Fisk is a 3.3 GPA and a 22 on the ACT. Despite the academic readiness of our student population, there are host of other dynamics confounded by the psychosocial, economic, environmental, and familial realities from which our student population is derived.

Just last week, I met in my office with a family presenting a series of concerns that delimited the likelihood of enrollment for their child. During the conversation, I realized that while content knowledge was a critical component capacity for any collegian, even more was the need for resilience, fortitude, and tenacity. The hurricane like climate of the family and neighborhood structures of so many of the nation's youth remind me of the tortured lives detailed in my earlier work *The Children Hurricane Katrina Left Behind: Schooling Context, Professional Preparation, and Community Politics* (Robinson & Brown, 2007). More recently, I have been giving thought to the epic storm Euroclydon narrated in the biblical book of the Acts of the Apostles.

In Acts 27 (KJV), the narrator recounts a mortally catastrophic storm in which a group of prisoners, military guards, naval seamen, and the Apostle Paul are engulfed. After a litany of events, we encounter two verses of miraculous deliverance. In verses 43 and 44, these words are written:

> But the centurion, willing to save Paul, kept them from *their* purpose; and commanded that they which could swim should cast *themselves* first *into the sea,* and get to land: and the rest, some on boards, and some on *broken pieces* of the ship. And so it came to pass, that they escaped all safe to land.

Wow! The story in Acts details a huge storm with no apparent safety, and then the resilient act of survival based on individual resolve. What I now realize is that all students are simply *making it on broken pieces.*

Many of the difficult realities grown in school settings emerge from a deep, dark soil—mixed and mired with social problems, economic influences, and community realities (Brown & Davis, 2000). The students who arrive in our nation's pre-kindergarten through postgraduate classrooms are not true "tabula rasa" as antiquated educational philosophy would posit. They are not unscripted tablets or blank slates, but rather they are complex and complicated novels, epic musical scores, and cryptic paintings. Therefore, it is within this context of "broken pieces" that the education profession must confront the challenges and controversies of understanding the role(s) of social, cultural, economic, and human capital in the educational context(s). In this seminal compendium, *Contemporary Perspectives on Capital in Educational Contexts,* RoSusan Bartee and her compeers engage the consumer, producer, and regulator dimensions of this foreground.

A thorough reading of this text forces a reconsideration of the tenets of capital and currency in both school settings and institutions of higher learning. Even more, *Contemporary Perspectives on Capital in Educational Con-*

texts interrogates the ways in which individuals and institutions navigate the broken pieces of capital in all of its forms from birth through adulthood. The book provides a new form, structure, and lens for excavating the old territories of student achievement, differential performance, and academic success so critical to improving our understanding of schools and colleges, as well as for framing interventions to promote educational attainment for all students. To this end, the book does not build a new model, program, or fad for educational improvement, but rather lays bare the materials, parts, and tools needed to construct real and relevant pedagogy and practice responsive to the unique nuances of individual learners, classroom communities, and academic environs.

In fact, in spite of some valiant and occasionally heroic efforts, American education continues to be plagued by pendulum-like paradigm shifts that proffer inconsistent and unsustained outcomes for the nation's youth. Nationally, many educational initiatives are fettered by inattentive engagement of the complex consideration necessary to design meaningful schemes and/or strategies that can insure the success of all students. There are troubling trends in the national student performance data on reading, composition, mathematics, and critical thinking. Despite this nationwide scatter-plot of proficiency, schools still have the power to teach, inspire, and transform (Brown & Land, 2005).

The time has come for educators to begin telling the truth about the conditions and contexts requisite to promoting student success. There is unquestioned agreement in the international literature base that a teacher's experience level, subject matter knowledge, and pedagogical knowledge have direct correlations to student attainment (Brown & Bartee, 2007). The data are consistent and undisputed that there is a high correlation between the learning outcomes of a student and the efficacy of the academic environment. We must reify the importance of social, cultural, human, and economic capital to both understanding and improving educational contexts. Even more, we must acknowledge the integral role of difference and resilience in order to assist students with their uniquely "broken piece" of the educational structure.

In an earlier project, Dr. Bartee and I explored the importance of the varied forms of capital in facilitating educational excellence for students in the book, *School Matters: Why African American Students Need Multiple Forms of Capital* (Bartee & Brown, 2007). Our nascent treatment of student success as a correlative of academic rigor and ambition failed to fully assert the more complicated and intersectional "third space" or nexus of capital and educational context. In every sense imaginable, *Contemporary Perspectives on Capital in Educational Contexts* is an expansion and extension of *School Matters.* Bartee's new project advances the initial exploration of different forms of capital as producer (*improve the status quo through inputs*), consumer (*par-*

ticipant based upon outputs), and regulator (*maintain the status quo through the process*) within the educational system. The intentional examination the academic pipeline results in a more substantive knowledge base on the multifaceted role that the various forms and dimensions of capital manifest for institutional and individual capacities within educational contexts.

Contemporary Perspectives on Capital in Educational Contexts is timely in its unique and appropriate analyses of the prevailing internal and external dynamics of capital as indicative of the type of currency within institutional structures or the currency among individual stakeholders of education. The intersection of capital and currency emerges similarly and differently within the American *compulsory-based* system of K–12 and the *choice-based* system of higher education. More specifically, this book disentangles the particularistic student challenges from the universal opportunities of myriad school and university contexts to proffer emergent insights and informed analysis of the intellectual landscape inclusive of human, social, economic, and cultural capital.

RoSusan Bartee and her colleagues' new book, *Contemporary Perspectives on Capital in Educational Contexts* provides clear guidance on how the forms of capital manifest within the institution of education and among individual stakeholders for public schools and higher education. Understanding the implications associated with capital within these contexts are paramount for (1) an individual to understand how to navigate and negotiate the academic pipeline and (2) an institution's ability to effectively facilitate the process. The quest to fulfill the national mandate that "no child be left behind" depends on the capacity to meaningfully engage the role of capital in educational planning, delivery, assessment, and outcomes (Brown & Bartee, 2009).

To the extent that we are successful, parents, business leaders, policymakers, and the students we serve may one day rewrite the last two verses of Acts 27. My personal prayer is that it will one day read:

> But the educators, willing to insure that *no child was left behind*, accounted for the unique educational context; and commanded that with resolve *each learner* engage their unique portfolio of human, social, cultural, and economic capital, in order to pursue their ambitions and *achieve the best education attainable*: and each student, some with excellence and others with proficiency, engaged the task of learning *on their individually broken pieces*. And so it came to pass, that all students attained their highest aim and *achieved their intended goal*.

—M. Christopher Brown II, PhD
Former Executive Vice President and Provost
and University Professor (2009–2010)

Current President of Alcorn State University
(2011–present)

REFERENCES

Bartee, R. D. & Brown, M. C. (2007). *School matters: Why African American students need multiple forms of capital.* New York: Peter Lang.

Brown, M. C., with Bartee, R. D. (2007). *Still not equal: Expanding educational opportunity in society.* New York: Peter Lang.

Brown, M. C. & Bartee, R. D. (2009). *The broken cisterns of African American education: Academic performance and achievement in the post-Brown era.* Charlotte, NC: Information Age.

Brown, M. C., & Davis, J. E. (2000). *Black sons to mothers: Compliments, critiques, and challenges for cultural workers in education.* New York: Peter Lang.

Brown, M. C., & Land, R. R. (2005). *The politics of curricular change: Race, hegemony and power in education.* New York: Peter Lang.

Robinson, S. P., & Brown, M. C. (2007). *The children hurricane Katrina left behind: Schooling context, professional preparation, and community politics.* New York: Peter Lang.

CHAPTER 1

INSIGHTS INTO DIFFERENT FORMS OF CAPITAL

RoSusan D. Bartee
University of Mississippi

M. Christopher Brown II
Fisk University

Distribution of capital in home and school settings affects the types of educational outcomes and the quality of lifelong opportunities that individuals are able to enjoy. Resource availability and accessibility influence the success levels at which teaching and learning is experienced. Capital possession or acquisition impacts the ability to navigate the academic pipeline and to recognize the appropriate tools by which to do so. Given the relative nature of capital, the know-hows of navigating the pipeline reflect the ideologies of the respective context. There are four types of capital: economic, human, cultural, and social. The ways in which these forms of capital emerge as consumer, producer, and regulator demonstrate how educational processes occur within a mutually interactive relationship. Understanding the nature of the different roles of capital provides more informed perspectives about the complexities of education and schooling.

Contemporary Perspectives on Capital in Educational Contexts, pages 1–59

Economic capital is generally considered a form of financial currency. Individual possessions determine the amount of exchange and assets, both material and nonmaterial, that is involved. Human capital is viewed as the likelihood of "return" from the investment of resources in the academic potentials of individuals. Human capital increases according to the quantity and quality of educational degrees. Cultural capital refers to certain kinds of acquired knowledge, value systems, language patterns, and/or visible dispositions. The type of activity participation and behavioral patterns that emerge are often associated with particular racial/ethnic groups and social classes. Social capital is linked to influential networks and associations. Affiliations with these organizations and/or institutions enable individuals to have access to useful material and nonmaterial resources.

Minimal attempts have been made to address different perspectives related to economic, human, cultural, and social capital. This chapter identifies the various tenets of capital as having shared similarities and/or differences. More specifically, this article reveals how the distribution of capital impacts educational settings. Both perspectives must be examined to understand the implications of capital within mutually interactive roles of the school and the home and the persisting influence upon academic outcomes and opportunities.

HISTORICAL PERSPECTIVES OF ECONOMIC CAPITAL

Capital's historic embodiment in physical assets connotes a sense of definitiveness about the term that may mislead most readers about the ambiguity of the term's uses in the research setting. Items such as cash and property, the commonly accepted manifestation of *economic capital*, are easily latched onto because of their centrality in the lives of the masses. This sense of ease with the term's meaning appears to cause many to take it for granted in the sense that when it is employed in the research setting it is rarely defined, suggesting that the author believes the reader to inherently understand its intended use. One of the many problems associated with using the term without explicitly defining its intended meaning is that "*economic capital*" has become a catchall phrase encompassing all types of capital not specifically designated as associated with another form of capital (e.g., cultural, human, and social). As such, authors have employed the term in a variety of manners (all centered on the general concept of assets), but often use different parameters for defining those assets.

Readers of literature in the fields of sociology, economics, and education will realize the grand assumptions, some contradictory in nature, when the term (and its surrogates *physical* and *financial capital*) is employed in both scholarly and administrative writings. The idea of *economic capital* can be found in educational research for at least the last century, but the term was not actively employed until the 1970s. While utilization of the term provided a scholarly codification for the concept of *economic capital,* such codification quickly became a handicap to understanding its usage. Those not using the term were forced to explain exactly the type of assets employed in their study, whereas those authors who utilize the term either fail to define it or do so in inconsistent manners.

Coherent and cogent use of the term throughout research does not exist. This is most likely because economic capital does not have the scholarly origins or defined field of inquiry that cultural, human, and social capital do. Economic capital has been a central aspect of civilization that is assumed to exist, but no one ever set forth to define it in a scholarly fashion as the others were. Its existence is, more or less, based on the existence of the other forms of capital and its necessity for validating those other species. In an attempt to inform ongoing and forthcoming research incorporating economic capital, this chapter reviews the various forms, utilizations, and definitions of the term. The piece begins with an etymology of the term "capital" and an epistemological discussion of how economic capital evolved into a de facto subcategory as the singular "capital" became a much more *in toto* concept. The concluding section guides the reader through the symbiosis of education and economic capital, specifically in terms of education as a consumer, producer, and regulator of economic capital.

ECONOMIC CAPITAL: AN EPISTEMOLOGICAL DISCUSSION OF ORIGINS

The earliest meaning of capital embodied what would now be termed physical assets (e.g., oxen, land, grain, and labor) and later financial assets (i.e., monetary wealth). Once the intelligentsia and businessmen of Europe recognized capital not just as cumulative wealth, but also its metaphysical and kinetic characteristics, it became possible to incorporate nonphysical properties under the "capital" umbrella. The first differentiation came in the form of human capital as the great thinkers of the nineteenth century (e.g., Edmund Burke, Karl Marx, Adam Smith, and Voltaire) identified an individual's ability to engage in labor as a capital asset because of the connected potential for producing more capital. Later, a nation's worth would be partially accounted for by the productivity of its labor force (i.e., human capital), and it was understood in an abstract sense that the value of that capital could be increased through investment (i.e., advanced education). The point here is not to encapsulate the historical origins of human capital (that is done later in the paper), but to demonstrate how capital began to splinter into variant species. In this case, labor did not resemble the traditional manifestations of capital, and, more importantly, was not as easily measurable as cash or land. To separate it from the traditional economic druthers of capitalistic notions, the term "human capital" evolved. A very similar evolutionary process can be witnessed of Bourdieu's (1986) other "species," except for economic capital.

Whether one subscribes to a neoclassical or postmodernist definition of economic capital, its existence is proven by the modern inclination to differentiate among multiple types of capital. At one point in time, the term *economic capital* would have been believed to be tautological as *capital* was grounded on economic principals. As the definition of capital broadened to incorporate the cultural, human, and social components, the traditional economic definition of capital became muddled and intermixed with other forms. Thus, capital became both a term to describe monetary wealth, physical wealth, and the collective wealth of all sub-capital categories. Moreover, the legitimacy of the newly developed forms was based their ability to create or be converted into economic capital (Bourdieu, 1977). Given the definitional dilemma that sub-capital categories were both the same as and different from capital, the term *economic capital* (along with financial and *physical capital*) was utilized to provide a more definitive conceptualization of the traditional uses of capital and to free the classical term to assume a more modern and holistic definition.

This rather convoluted history of economic capital creates two dilemmas for scholars in general and educationalists in specific. First, since economic capital evolved more out of necessity than any formal scholarly pursuit, the operationalization of the term differs both among and within the various academic fields in which it is utilized. Second, economic capital encompasses assets and practices that are such an inherent component of a market-based civilization that researchers often employ some variation of economic capital in their activities without specifically labeling it as such. Because of this ambiguity in research on education and educational institutions, the following provides an overview of the various uses of the term in research and summarizes some of the means in which economic capital has been used in the educational research.

ECONOMIC CAPITAL IN EDUCATION RESEARCH

The concept of economic capital has been a central theme in research on education since the turn of the century, although the term did not become widely used until the later half of the century. Therefore, to identify both the meaning and uses of economic capital, one must not just identify the uses of the term but also the manner in which financial and physical assets have been utilized in the analysis and assessment of educational institutions and practices. Moreover, *economic capital, financial capital,* and *physical capital* have been used interchangeably within scholarly writing.

The use of economic capital in education research was first popularized by Bourdieu (1977, 1984, 1986, 1989) and Bourdieu and Passeron (1979) in the analysis of the reproductive aspects of education. To suggest otherwise is to ignore not just the vast amount of scholarship produced by Bourdieu, but also the countless pieces (e.g., Anheier, Gerhards, & Romo, 1995; Brubaker, 1985; Pels, 1995) that have been dedicated to understanding and furthering his seminal contributions to sociology and the sociology of education. Bourdieu and Passeron (1979) suggested that schooling systems, which were built upon the morals and norms of the elite classes, acted as mechanisms for reproducing social classes and the associated distribution of economic capital.

Unlike his stoic attempts to define and categorize cultural and social capital, economic capital receives little attention from Bourdieu beyond mere acknowledgement of its twofold existence as a progenitor of cultural capital and the recognition that for social and cultural assets to be classified as capital they must be convertible into economic capital (Bourdieu, 1977). However, he does go so far as to suggest that economic capital "is immediately and directly convertible into money and may be institutionalized in the form of property rights" (Bourdieu, 1986, p. 242). It is likely the combination of Bourdieu's large influence over the sociological aspects of capital and his general lack of providing a concrete definition that cause the ambiguity and confusion of the term's uses to continue.

The embodiment of economic capital in physical and monetary assets is now the predominant use of the term (see Anheier et al., 1995; Keller, 2001; McDonough, 1994; Webb, 1982; Woolcock, 1998). In each of these cases, economic capital is explicitly stated as comprised of both fiscal and material wealth or implied through its operationalization. Anheier, Gerhards, and Romo (1995) propose that "Economic capital focuses on commercial success verse failure with money as the major currency and economic status as the major indicator" (p. 866). In terms of the educational setting, a family's financial assets and their ability to be converted into housing, clothes, cars, and other items that be used to improve the students' educational experience can be classified as *capital* (Keller, 2001).

Although Bourdieu has exhibited the greatest amount of influence over the term, others, and even those who attested to emulating some of Bourdieu's work, have used other definitions. Zhou and Logan's (1989) analysis of the political economy of communication based largely on the work of Bourdieu suggests that the Bourdieuian concept of economic capital merely represents money. While much of Bourdieu's scholarship would appear to negate this oversimplified definition, Zhou and Logan are not alone in paralleling economic capital with money. Portes (1998), in his historical assessment of social capital, described economic capital as that which "is in people's bank's accounts" (p. 7) and uses the terms *economic* and *financial capital* interchangeably.

In some cases (Gaudiani, 2000; Karen, 1990; McDonough, 1994; Persell & Cookson, 1987), the term is utilized by the author but no definition is supplied and the reader is left to infer the meaning from its usage within the text. To complicate matters even more, the American sociologist James Coleman (1988) employs the term *financial capital* and, while not recognizing Bourdieu's contributions, uses a similar definition as Bourdieu's economic capital. "Financial capital is approximately measured by the family's wealth or income. It provides the physical resources that can aid in achievement" (p. 109). The implication is that financial capital is measured by monetary wealth, but that the measurement includes the family's ability to acquire material goods. Financial capital has also been utilized to describe family wealth in college prediction models (Freeman, 1997) and as a predictor for an institution's ability to survive (Stetar, 1985). Velez (1989) suggests that immigrants moving to better neighborhoods may offset the loss of social capital with gains in financial capital. In each of these cases, the context of the term's usage implies that financial capital captures fiscal and not material wealth.

Physical capital has been incorporated in research in a fashion similar to economic capital and may enjoy a similar level of popularity in its usage. While often used interchangeably with economic capital, physical capital as a part of the common vernacular tends to connote more of a sense of material worth rather than financial, but this is not always the case in the research literature. Coleman (1988), Shultz (1961), and Becker (1964) described physical capital as material goods such as tools, machines, and other productive equipment that can be used to create additional capital. In other cases, *physical* is embodied in public assets such as new industrial plants, equipment, and infrastructure (Chandler, Hagstrom, & Solvell, 1998; Couch & Dunn, 1997) and the physical plants (i.e., buildings and grounds) of public institutions such as colleges and universities (Bradburd & Mann, 1993). Couch (1997), in addition to equating physical capital with public infrastructure, also employed a much more complex mathematical equation incorporating the value of a nation's currency and the education levels of the labor force. All of these works suggest a symbiotic relationship between public and private capital. Each relies on components of the other to facilitate the creation of new capital and enjoys the accompanying benefits. For example, an extensive national infrastructure facilitates efficiency of communication, travel of individuals, and transport of goods, which may not be possible in less developed countries. Growth in private capital equates to larger amounts of productivity and tax revenue, both important forms of economic capital for the development and defense of nation-states (Bourdieu, Wacquant, & Farage, 1994).

On the other hand, Bowman (1966) made a concerted effort to separate private physical capital from public infrastructure, suggesting that capital is that which is owned and utilized by individuals. In a similar fashion, other authors have equated physical capital with private assets, most through the summation of financial wealth. Woolcock (1998) references physical capital in conjunction with land and labor as the three primary factors driving economic development. Listing the terms independently of each other suggests that Woolcock separates land, unlike some authors above, from physical capital, but one is left wondering if the economic development capacity of physical capital is derived from physical assets, financial, assets, or some combination of both.

A new and potentially confusing development in the use of economic capital comes from the excerpt of a book from Gaudiani (2000). In the excerpt, Gaudiani (2000) posits that *wisdom capital* is another form of economic capital. The important aspect here is not that Gaudiani is believed to have uncovered a new form of capital—rather, that she connotes this new form with economic capital rather than the umbrella term *capital*. Such use of the term economic capital threatens to undercut the current conceptualization of capital. There are certain truths about economic capital embodied in the research literature. First, economic capital is embodied in physical and/or financial assets. The exact nature of these assets is still up for debate, but general parameters exist. Second, each species of capital was separate from the others. One does not suggest that cultural capital is economic capital; rather, one can be used to create the other. Third, the existence of the species is validated by its ability to be transformed into economic capital. To suggest that wisdom capital is economic capital completely negates everything previous scholars have come to acknowledge about capital.

SURVEY OF THE USES OF ECONOMICS OF EDUCATION

The study of economic capital within this context does not just involve understanding the various uses of the term, but also the characteristics of the nexus between said capital and education. The importance of education within society has been limited to modern society (Haller, 1970; Haller & Portes, 1973). Since that importance was first recognized, economists, educationalists, and sociologists have utilized both concepts in the study of the other. The following sections review the role of education as a consumer of capital, as a producer of capital, and as a regulator of capital. These sections are not intended to provide an exhaustive review of the field of economics of education, for that is not the purpose at hand; rather, the following is a survey of the different ways in which economic capital is used in the study of educational processes and institutions.

Education as a Consumer of Economic Capital

Within the field of the economics of education, Return on Investment (ROI) is one of the more pervasive research themes. The question revolves around the idea of proving the worth of education by determining whether the gains generated by pursuing an education offset the expectant costs. Some early scholars (e.g., Marx, 1867/1996; Smith, 1776/1953) acknowledged that educating or training individuals can positively affect productivity, but it was not until the 1910s that economists began to derive equations for measuring the monetary return (through increased wages) for justifying educational costs (Mennell & Goudsblom, 1998). While a great deal of discussion revolves around that which constitutes returns, there seems to be a general level of consensus about what constitutes the costs. Economists inform us that there are two types of costs: direct and indirect. Direct costs are those that are easily attributable to the task at hand. In terms of the education enterprise, the standard direct costs are tuition and fees, books, and commuting and travel costs (Arai, 1998; Atkinson, 1983; Cohn, 1972; Sheenhan, 1973; Thomson, 1952; Walsh, 1935). The one historical aberration in the debate is the accounting of living expenses such as room and board, clothes, and recreation. Older works (such as Walsh, 1935) incorporate such costs into their assessment methods. However, more recent scholarship excludes such costs from input parameters as such costs would be incurred regardless of whether one was attending school or pursuing some other activity and thus are not directly attributable to educational pursuits (Arai, 1998; Atkinson, 1983; Cohn, 1972; Sheenan, 1973).

Indirect or opportunity costs are a bit more abstract and difficult to account for, but are at least theoretically important to include in this discussion. Costs such as foregone earnings by not working during school and sacrifice of a higher standard of living are the most direct, measurable, and private form of opportunity costs in education (Arai, 1998). Not all opportunity costs, however, are private in nature. By encouraging individuals to pursue advanced education, communities forego short-term economic gain through a loss of taxes and labor productivity as an investment in long-term gain (Arai, 1998; Atkinson, 1983; Cohn, 1972; Sheenhan, 1973; Thomson, 1952; Walsh, 1935). Brownell (1946) provided an interesting and extensive critique of the societal costs of advanced education by suggesting that colleges and universities destroy the economic and social vibrancy of rural communities. This destruction occurs slowly by siphoning off the best and brightest of a rural community's students, educating them in cosmopolitan environments and shipping them off to urban environments. While few have included such a cost in their assessments, it demonstrates the potentially broad range of intended and unintended societal costs attributable to higher learning. It should also be noted that Brownell's assessment appears to have become a remnant of the past as many now recognize the university as a catalyst for economic development and job growth in their communities (Chandler et al., 1998; Institute for Higher Education Policy, 1998).

Education as a Producer of Economic Capital

Scholars and philosophers have long attempted to validate the worth of education through assessment of its pecuniary aspects. What does an individual gain by pursuing a higher education? How does society benefit by subsidizing the cost of education? These two questions have pervaded the scholarship of education almost since its inception (see Chandler, 1998; Clark, 1930; Engel, 1984; Haddad, 1981; Institute for Higher Education Policy, 1998; Litten, 1980; Smith, 1776/1953; Walsh, 1935). While it has become widely accepted that education has positive effects on both the individual and society, this has not always been the case and there continues to be debate about whether society or the individual benefits more (Chandler, 1998; Institute for Higher Education Policy, 1998). The importance of these questions to both practitioners and scholars is that the answer largely impacts governmental policy, which subsequently impacts the individual through the concomitant issues of cost and access (Key, 1996; Thomson, 1952). For example, Key (1996) argues that Congress approved the Morrill Land Grant Act not because of the desire to increase educational attainment, but to encourage economic development in the frontier. Furthermore, Haddad (1981) says that education contributes to economic development through the creation of a similar base of knowledge, attitudes, and norms; supporting the development of social services; and training a skilled and flexible labor class.

Assessment of the impact of education on the long-term increase in earnings is one of the longest-run lines of inquiry in the field of education. One of the first pieces of literature discussing the return on investment in education was produced during higher education's transition from a social institution for the elites to that of the masses. As an attempt to demonstrate the economic value of education, the U.S. Bureau of Education commissioned a study comparing the lifetime earnings of those with a college education to those without. Using the data available at the time, the report concludes that each additional day in school adds $9.02 to an individual's lifetime earning (Mennell & Goudsblom, 1998). Shortly after researchers began assessing this line of inquiry (Mennell & Goudsblom, 1998; Lord, 1928), others were quick to critique and demonstrate methods for improving the original analytical methods. One of the first articles to appear in the new *Journal of Higher Education* was such a critique that suggested the statistical analysis of education's impact on earning previously employed could be improved by accounting for variables such as variant occupations (Clark,

1930). Since that time, statistical models have continued to be refined and advanced, and a number scholars have found positive correlations between educational attainment and increased earnings (e.g., Blaug, 1972; Clark, 1930; Cohn, 1972; Eckaus, 1973; Mennell & Goudsblom, 1998; Gorseline, 1932; Hartog & Oosterbeek, 1998; Levin, 1979).

It should be noted that there has been debate over the type of relationship that exists between education, productivity, and earnings (Atkinson, 1983). Some scholars suggest that the value of an education may lie more in the academic credential than in the lessons learned (Berg, 1971; Bourdieu, 1984, 1989). In these arguments, the academic degree serves as a mechanism for signifying that an individual has the capacity to be productive rather than connoting any type of academic knowledge base. Others argue that the worth of the credential depends upon the academic environment and experience. Karen (1990) and McDonough (1994) both suggest that an Ivy League education advantages graduates over those without such degrees. Similarly, women benefit economically from unisex institutions because of the increased opportunities to create social and cultural capital (Riordan, 1994). While the exact nature of the production of education's ROI is still hidden in the black box, the output almost always outweighs the input from both the societal and individualistic aspects.

The introduction of mass education at the basic level in the 19th century and at the post-secondary level in the early 20th century triggered a capitalist revolution throughout the world (Thurow, 1999). Within the first wave of capitalism, the labor classes were largely viewed as interchangeable and expendable parts. Education, however, made it possible for individuals to acquire a more central role in the capitalist process by making themselves unique through advanced training. This advanced training through education made it possible for children of the proletariat classes to make economic gains regardless of their family background, and this created a situation of continuously increasing wealth. As indicated above, numerous reports have proven that lifetime wealth is positively correlated with the person's level of academic achievement. The value of these gains diminishes over time as a larger percentage of the public pursues an education (Atkinson, 1983), but the gains exist nonetheless. From a societal aspect, higher education contributes to local economies be creating jobs, increasing productivity, and generating a larger tax base (Chandler et al., 1998; Institute for Higher Education Policy, 1998).

Gatekeepers of Economic Capital

One last arena of critical import to the discussion of the nexus of education and economic capital is the role of educational institutions in the creation, maintenance, and reproduction of wealth. There exist two primary and competing hypotheses about education's role in these processes. The first suggests that colleges and universities act as socially constructed institutions for reproducing preexisting social classes and the corresponding levels of economic capital (Bourdieu & Passeron, 1979). The second theory posits that such institutions provide opportunity for upward mobility and a partial deconstruction of the stratification of the social classes (Thurow, 1999).

While a full theoretical treatise on the intricacies and dynamics of this complex relationship is not possible in this limited space, a brief overview of the general parameters of the relationship of these two aspects of the social and economic hierarchy is important for understanding the two aforementioned mentioned perceptions. As discussed above, there is a widely accepted belief that there exists a positive correlation between the level of education and an individual's earnings. In other words, the more time one spends in school, the higher their lifetime earnings are likely to be. The compounding phenomenon is that enrollments in colleges and universities in the United States have exponentially increased over the past eighty years.

There is little doubt that education increases earnings and productivity of the individual and, as these individuals pervade society, the economic development of the community. The research (as discussed above) largely supports this concept, and the media and popular belief largely reinforce it. Business, media, and government leadership are dominated by those with college degrees. Much as the high school degree of a hundred years ago, the collegiate diploma has come to be viewed as the key needed to gain access to opportunities for economic success. As suggested by Goldin (2001) in a report from the National Bureau of Economic Research, the production of a large group of educated citizens and workers "did not, by and large, reinforce 'class' distinctions, but rather enabled social and geographic mobility and a large decrease in inequality in economic outcomes" (p. 26).

If education increases access to the upper echelon of society and access to these educational opportunities increases, then one could logically assume that education deconstructs socialized stratifications, *ceteris paribus.* One of the problems some scholars face about this assumption of logic is that educational institutions are neither objective nor equal for all students. These institutions are socially constructed institutions and based upon the principals of the elites who tend to dominate the public sphere (Bourdieu & Passeron, 1979; Labaree, 1986). Therefore, the children of the elite have an inherent advantage in the educational system over their peers from the lower and middle classes. Children of the elite classes enter school with an understanding of the social cues needed for success while children from other classes must learn these cues after entering the academic setting (Bourdieu & Passeron, 1979). Along similar lines, Zweigenhaft (1993) found that college students from private high schools and more academically challenging high schools were more concerned with pursuing studies to gain *cultural capital*, but that private school students were more concerned with social networks needed to utilize and maximize *economic capital* because they already possess the *cultural capital* poorer and less prepared students are still pursuing. To reference a popular metaphor, the children of social elites are able to hit the ground running, while the others are still looking for the starting line.

Even as faculty, administrators, and policy makers have made noble efforts to diversify student demographics and equalize educational opportunity, members of the elite classes continue to possess inherent advantages (Bowles, 1972; Hauser & Daymont, 1977; Keller, 2001). Prior to education being recognized as an important social institution for upward mobility, families passed their economic capital on to children either through the inheritance of deeds to the business or providing opportunities for the children to establish their own business (Labaree, 1986). The problem is that while education has become a mechanism for increasing the *economic capital* of all segments of society and subsequently society as a whole, some scholars suggest that the social constructs on which many of our educational institutions were founded continue to benefit the upper classes (Bourdieu & Passeron, 1979).

While some have acknowledged that education has diminished the importance of the family to imbibe the next generation with economic capital (Thurow, 1999), some evidence suggests that families with economic capital incorporated education into their equations for reproducing and sustaining the family's economic capital. In a longitudinal study of 15,000 individuals in Sweden between 1938 and 1971, Fagerlind (1975) found that family background had little correlation with future earnings independent of educational attainment, suggesting that the family's ability to transfer wealth is largely dependent on the education system. (The reader should not confuse education's impact on an individual's ability to generate future earnings and an individual's wealth contingent on private inheritance.) Bourdieu and Saint Martin (1974) advise that parents convert their economic capital to cultural capital by sending their children to the best colleges and universities. The children then reconvert their newly developed cultural and social capital back to economic dominance. Following historic patterns of valuing the family as a social institution, the family continues to act as a bank or venture capital fund, enabling more wealthy students to pursue academic or leisure interests not available to socially independent or poorer students (Coleman, 1988; Keller, 2001).

Moreover, as egalitarianism has become the driving force behind academic principals, the historic norms of the nation's more elite institutions continue to pervade decision making and the wealthy have identified new ways to leverage their *economic capital* to ensure the success of their offspring. As admission to Ivy League institutions has become increasingly difficult due to increased competition, parents are utilizing their *economic capital* to higher private counselors to assist students in successfully navigating the admissions process (McDonough, 1994). On the opposite side of the admissions process, selection of students remains contingent upon the value of the economic capital of a student and his or her family, regardless of claims otherwise. In a case study of the Harvard admission process, Karen (1990) found that even though the process did not directly factor in financial worth of a family, students who had attended a private high school, were an athlete or whose family had contributed to the athletic program, or were a Harvard legacy had significantly higher likelihood of acceptance than other applicants. Karen suggests that one of the reasons that the move toward an objective meritocratic selection process has not been as successful as intended is that the dominant classes, those who possess and control capital, define the standards for being meritorious.

While Bourdieu is largely held to be the father of the study of the social reproduction aspects of education, Thorstein Veblen (1899/1994) may have been the first to point out the rationale behind the sustainability of such a system. One could certainly wonder why the masses continue to support and participate in a system that is inherently biased toward the elite classes. Veblen suggested that the ability of the elites to maintain their status is strengthened by the tendency of the "servile" classes to emulate those of higher income, status, and power than to organize and create different societal constructs. While not directly referring to education, the idea is certainly applicable. The academic credential is the embodiment of the property and economic capital of the wealthy and the question then becomes, why change a system, even though it is inherently biased toward the elites if it allows the masses to also obtain that credential? The difference is that not all credentials are the same, and the system was designed that way to continue the reproduction of the elite classes.

HISTORICAL PERSPECTIVES OF HUMAN CAPITAL

Adam Smith, the 18th century philosopher-economist, first introduced the concept of humans as capital in his classic work, *Wealth of Nations* (Baptiste, 2001; Hornbeck & Salamon, 1991; Schultz, 1961). Smith included "all of the acquired and useful abilities of all of the inhabitants of a country as a part of capital" (Schultz, 1961, p. 2), stating that a crucial part of the nation's wealth lies in its people. Other individuals such as Alfred Marshall and Irvin Fisher continued Smith's work; however, the theory of humans as capital remained relatively undeveloped well into the 20th century. What became the focus instead was economic thought focused on the role of land, capital stock, and hours of labor as the crucial ingredients of economic growth (Baptiste, 2001; Hornbeck & Salamon, 2001).Three distinguished individuals who looked at human capital are Adam Smith; H. Von Thiinen, who argued that "the concept of capital applied to man did not degrade him or impair his freedom and dignity" (Schultz, 1961, p. 2); and Irving Fisher, who argued that it is not "appropriate or practical to apply the concept of capital to human beings" (Schultz, 1961, p. 3).

Several factors influenced the delay in the development of human capital theory (Baptiste, 2001). First, there were differences of opinion regarding the relationship between earnings, capital, labor, and humans. As a result, three different camps emerged. John Stuart Mill and Alfred Marshall distinguished between the "acquired capacities (skills and knowledge) of human beings, which are classed as capital and human being themselves" (Baptiste, 2001, p. 185). In addition, they had a deep-seated philosophical and moral commitment to human dignity and freedom and found the thought of humans as capital offensive. They thought that "humans were the purpose for which wealth and capital existed: the end to be served by economic endeavor.... [A]lthough it is quite possible and ethical for people to sell their labor, there ought not to be a market in human beings" (p. 185).

The second camp that emerged was that of Adam Smith, Irving Fisher, and the Chicago School. This camp believed that "human beings are themselves capital, that the notion of humans as capital is not incompatible with freedom and dignity, and that to the contrary, by investing in themselves, people enlarge the range of choices available to them and so enhance rather than limit their freedom" (Schultz, 1961, as cited in Baptiste, 2001, p 186). In addition, they believed that earnings are tied to educational expense (capital investment) and not just to productivity. The third camp, espoused by Karl Marx, however, agreed with Smith "that greater productivity does not account for the higher earnings of educated workers, but that the cost of education (investment) also enters into the equation" (Marx, 1867/1976, as cited in Baptiste, 2001, p. 186). Marx agreed with Mill that workers sell their labor and not themselves; however, the main difference in Marx' beliefs was that he "argued that the capacity to labor itself is not a form of capital, but that a worker's labor power become capital only when it is used in the process of production" (Marx, 1867/1976, 1894/1981, as cited in Baptiste, 2001, p. 186).

In addition, the human capital theory remained largely undeveloped because of the widespread use of the Keynesian definition of investment and consumption, which viewed them as categories that were mutually exclusive. The Keynesian definition "regarded education as largely a household expenditure and therefore treated it as pure consumption with no investment component" (Blaug, cited in Baptiste, 2001, p. 186). Lastly, the nature of economic production before World War II led to the lack of development of human capital theory. It has been argued that prior to World War II, highly skilled workers were not needed due to the industrial and agricultural economy. As a result, there was no need for human capital theory (Briggs, cited in Baptiste, 2001).

Schultz (1960) further articulated the notion of human capital by treating "education as an investment in man and to treat its consequences as a form of capital" (Schultz, 1960, p. 571). Because education becomes a part of the person who receives it, it is referred to as human capital. Even though it cannot be bought, sold, or treated as property, it is a form of capital because it "renders a productive value to the economy" (Schultz, 1960, p. 571). He hypothesized that "underlying this treatment of education is that some important increases in national income are a consequence of additions to the stock of this form of capital" (p. 571).

In the past, human capital was omitted from the conversations about capital in economic analysis. Many viewed it as "degrading to man and morally wrong to look upon his education as a way of creating capital" (Schultz, 1960, p. 572). Many criticized the term human capital because they viewed it as treating "people as slaves or machines" (Becker, 1993, p. 10). On this point, Schultz (1960) argues, "some kinds of education may improve the capabilities of a people as they work and manage their affairs and that these improvements may increase the national income" (p. 572).

USES OF HUMAN CAPITAL

There appears to be a consensus on what constitutes human capital – the "knowledge, attitudes, and skills that are developed and valued primarily for their economically productive potential" (Baptiste, 2001, p. 185) and the "acquired skills, knowledge, and abilities of human beings" (Hornbeck & Salamon, 1991, p. 3). These "skills and knowledge increase human productivity... and they do so enough to justify the costs incurred in acquiring them" (Hornbeck & Salamon, 1991, p. 3). Human capital takes many forms, which includes the "skills and abilities personality, appearance, reputation and appropriate credentials" (Becker & Tomes, 1986, p. 56). The expenditures on improving human capital are thought of as human capital investments: "As the authoritative *Palgrave's* puts it 'human capital refers to the productive capacities of human beings as income producing agents in the economy'" (Rosen 1987, p. 681, as cited in Hornbeck & Salamon, 1991, p. 3).

Education as a Consumer of Human Capital

Investments in human capital include expenditures on education, training, medical care, and the like, and these investments produce human capital as opposed to physical or financial capital because a person cannot be separated from his knowledge, skills, or health (Becker, 1993). "Topics as diverse and 'sociological' as schooling attainment; childbearing and child care; housework; worker training, productivity, and earnings; geographic mobility; and health can be unified as *human capital investment* and assigned to economists for study" (Farkas, 1996, p. 9). This idea is further reinforced as both ideological and practical components of human capital: "Present consumption and competing investments are forgone in order to reap a later reward, much as with investment in capital equipment" (Farkas, 1996, p. 9). Using investment and consumption principles, human capital becomes critical toward forging deliberate outcomes for the consumer.

Similar to the ideas espoused by human capital economists, the functionalism/human capital paradigm has a similar approach to schooling, occupational, and earning attainment. It focuses on "atomistic individuals and their families, with relatively little attention to group and contextual social structure" (Farkas, 1996, p. 9). According to Collins (1971, 1979 as cited in Farkas, 1996), regarding educational and earnings stratification, the functionalism/human capital paradigm is "open competition in which individuals invest in their own skill and productivity, so that those achieving greater educational performance simply receive their just deserts" (p. 10). Regarding differential school success of groups defined by ethnicity and poverty status, the functionalism/human capital paradigm argues that there is a "meritocratic competition based upon skill and performance. Here atomistic individuals assess their own tastes and naturally endowed skills, and invest in themselves accordingly" (p. 10).

Education as a Producer of Human Capital

"Education and training are the most important investments in human capital" (Becker, 1993, p. 17). High school and college education raise a person's income, and the earnings of those who are more educated are usually above average (Becker, 1993). By investing in themselves, people can enlarge the range of choices available to them. It is one way free men can enhance their welfare (Schultz, 1961, p. 2). "Human capital analysis assumes that schooling raises earnings and productivity mainly by providing knowledge, skills, and a way of analyzing problems" (Becker, 1993, p. 19). Investments in human capital such as formal education and on-the-job training raised the earnings at older ages and lowered them at lower ages (Becker, 1993).

Education as a Regulator of Human Capital

Human capital theorists see the world as an "educational meritocracy in which a person's socioeconomic status is limited, presumably, only by his or her educational investment" (Baptiste, 2001, p. 195). As a result, those who have access to education have the ability to increase their human capital. Some argue that human capital theory treats humans as lone wolves who are "radically isolated hedonists, creatures of habit (not intentions) who temper their avarice with economic rationality" (p. 197), whereas educational programs that are wedded to human capital theory treat learners as "rugged individualists indebted to no one and requiring nothing of anyone" (p. 198). Human capital theorists "assume that the world is an educational meritocracy in which a person's socioeconomic status is limited, presumably, only by his or her educational investment: More educated people are always more productive than less educated people, and this differential productivity is sufficient to explain all social inequalities" (p. 195).

HISTORICAL PERSPECTIVES ON CULTURAL CAPITAL

Cultural capital assumes a number of different meanings than its original definition by Bourdieu and Passeron (1977). A review of Bourdieu's meaning of cultural capital denotes the concern with "the contribution made by the educational system [and family socialization] to the reproduction of the structure of power relationships between classes, by contributing to the reproduction of the structure of distribution of cultural capital among these classes" (p. 487).

In late 1970s and early 1980s, several scholars (Collins, 1987; Cookson & Persell, 1985a; DiMaggio & Mohr, 1985; DiMaggio & Useem, 1978; Gouldner, 1979; Lamont & Lareau, 1988; Martin & Szelenyi, 1987; Robinson & Garnier, 1985) interpreted the term in regards to how they "make meaning" of cultural capital. Lamont and Lareau (1988) succinctly sum up Bourdieu's meaning of cultural capital as an "informal academic standard, a class attribute, a basis for social selection, and a resource for power which is salient as an indicator/basis of class position" (p. 156). Further, Lamont and Lareau point out that the forms of cultural capital mentioned in Bourdieu's definition are not stand-alone characteristics. They propose their own definition of cultural capital as "institutionalized, i.e., widely shared, high status cultural signals (attitudes, preferences, formal knowledge, behaviors, goods and credentials) used for social and cultural exclusion, the former referring to exclusion from jobs and resources, and the latter, to exclusion from high status groups" (p. 156). In offering their definition, Lamont and Lareau acknowledge the limitations to their definition, which they did not address in their research.

DiMaggio and Useem (1978) associate cultural capital to the knowledge of those individuals with "high culture." DiMaggio and Mohr (1985) operationalize the term to an individual's participation in "high-cultural interests and activities." DiMaggio (1992) further states that cultural capital can be defined as "the mastery of elements of a prestigious status culture" (p. 191). Still other scholars view cultural capital as "educational attainment" (Robinson & Garnier, 1985), as "symbolic practices" (Martin & Szelenyi, 1985), and offer a definition associated with curricular concerns of "elite schools" (Cookson & Persell, 1985).

Progressing through the 20th and 21st centuries, other scholars (Isserles & Dalmage, 2000; Mohr & DiMaggio, 1995; Throsby, 2001) continue to offer their view on what the term "cultural capital" means. Mohr and DiMaggio (1995) define cultural capital as "prestigious tastes, objects, or styles validated by centers of cultural authority, which maintain and disseminate societal standards of value and serve collectively to clarify and periodically revise the cultural currency" (p. 169). While Isserles and Dalmage (2000) define cultural capital as "a set of tools and skills acquired through experience that includes knowledge about how to present oneself vis-à-vis relations of power. . .[it] is information necessary to get ahead; knowing how to present oneself for certain rewards" (p. 160).

Throsby (2001) defines cultural capital as "an asset which embodies, stores or provides cultural value in addition to whatever economic value it may possess" (p. 46). He further discusses that cultural capital exists in two forms: "1) tangible—occurring in the form of buildings, locations, sites, precincts, artworks, artifacts etc.... it includes but is not limited to cultural heritage...and 2) intangible—occurring as intellectual capital in the form of ideas, practices, beliefs and values which are shared by a group" (p. 46). Throsby notes that the concept of cultural capital "can provide a common basis from which the analysis of both economic and cultural goods, services, behavior, and other phenomena can proceed" (p. 44).

Arnold (2002), however, interprets Bourdieu (1973, 1974, 1984) in distinguishing cultural capital as "characteristic of dominant groups in society, such as verbal facility, knowledge about high-status institutions, and preference for so-called 'high-culture' forms of art and leisure, results in ways of perceiving and presenting oneself ('habitus') that are rewarded in formal education" (p. 9). Furthermore, Tierney and Hagedron (2002) shed light on the contradictory meanings of cultural capital. They assert that "cultural capital is not unidimensional... [it] is convoluted and consists of multiple denominations that cannot be interchanged" (p. 5).

Education as a Consumer of Cultural Capital

The purpose of education centers on the issues of: who is being educated, how they are being educated, and what the expectations are of those being educated. Public K–12 schools and higher education institutions face the daily demands of its students—consumers of education. Students enter schools having different class status of cultural capital (Bourdieu & Passeron, 1977; DiMaggio, 1992). One's existing cultural capital is important in acquiring more education and property that "families transmit to their offspring which substitutes for or supplements the transmission of economic capital as a means of maintaining class status and privilege across generations" (McDonough, 1997, p. 8).

Bourdieu (1973, 1974, 1984) professes that "individuals are socialized into the cultural capital of their families and social milieu, including modes of expression, aesthetic tastes, general cultural awareness, and facility with symbols and objects (like books and scientific instruments)" (Arnold, 2002, p. 9). McDonough (1997) infers that Bourdieu's cultural capital concept plays an important role in understanding "how and why class status plays a role in educational achievement" (p. 8). Arnold (2002) further remarks that "students from privileged social backgrounds are able to exchange their cultural capital for high grades, superior verbal SAT scores, prestigious educational credentials and ultimately, entrance into high-level professional circles" (p. 9).

Education as a Producer of Cultural Capital

Higher education institutions emphasize the "rewards" of a post-secondary degree. In applying Bourdieu and Passeron's (1977) cultural capital concept, a post-secondary degree amounts to an increase in one's cultural capital. Higher education institutions look to increase enrollment through market tools to attract students to their campuses. Higher education institutions appeal to the potential employment opportunities that would be available to students who earn a college degree (Pascerella & Terenzini, 1991). Karen Arnold (2002) writes about the enhancement of students' cultural capital as a "bonus" role that prestigious colleges play in the education of its students: "Although selective admission processes favor students with abundant cultural capital, one role that prestigious colleges play is to help student acquire this cultural capital. Prestigious institutions... reinforce and increase cultural capital and provide bridges to post-college circles where cultural capital can be converted into high-status careers" (p. 10).

McDonough (1997) refers to cultural capital as the "knowledge that elites value yet schools do not teach" (p. 9). She goes further to state that "a student's disposition toward school is important because to maximize or conserve cultural capital one must be willing to consent to the investments in time, effort, and money that higher education requires" (p. 9). Bourdieu and Passeron (1977) link individuals with high cultural capital to having clear objectives of "how much and what kind of schooling each generation should have" (McDonough, 1997, p. 9). Olneck (2000) comments that "the most familiar way in which education institutions determine or reproduce the value of cultural capital is by establishing and making known hierarchies of knowledge and students" (p. 322). He further notes that higher education institutions play an important role in allocating culture capital and it is in higher education where competition over who is to be regarded as "culturally authoritative" begins to take form (p. 322).

Education as a Regulator of Cultural Capital

In applying Bourdieu and Passeron's terminology introduced earlier in the writing, a distinction to make is that education takes the form of markets. According to Olneck (2000), "interchanges between teachers and students... represent exchanges in which the cultural capital expended by both parties is positively and negatively sanctioned, which may or may not yield symbolic profits" (p. 320). Moreover, Olneck points out that cultural capital produces distinctions among individuals while reproducing its own value. Bourdieu (1984) refers to schools as agents of education where "cultural consecration and conservation" classifications are objectified as a means to validate cultural capital (Olneck, 2000).

Other researchers shed light on the issue of education as a regulator of cultural capital. Lauglo (2000) says, "one influential social reproduction argument concerns the special importance of cultural capital, that the odds in school are stacked particularly heavy in favor of those students whose parents are the well-placed insiders in a society's educational and cultural institutions, the cultural elite" (p. 144). Lauglo comments that cultural capital serves as the prerequisite for one's success and that the further one's origin is from a country's cultural elite, the fewer are one's chances of doing well in school. Lauglo continues to state that students with limited economic resources, hence "low" cultural capital—often measured by the number of books in the home—are those who value school the most. However, research studies show that students from low socio-economic status families are often the ones that do not continue their education beyond the college years (McDonough, 1997; Nettles, Perna, & Freeman, 1999; Pascerella & Terenzini, 1991; Tierney & Hagedorn, 2002). According to Hagedorn and Tierney (2002),

> [M]any college preparation programs implicitly or explicitly accept the role of cultural capital in creating the appropriate environment for college attendance... one might think of college preparation programs as a structural response to low-income children's deficit of cultural capital – a response that simulates the conditions to deliver the social and academic capital necessary to succeed in college. (p. 4)

Hagedorn and Tierney (2002) propose that educational institutions and groups need to become more responsive to children with low cultural capital. They further encourage "the need for structural changes to take place to create closer working relationships between schools and postsecondary institutions" as a way to cultivate and not regulate "the kind of cultural capital that will not only sustain students to college, but will evolve and grow to nurture students through college" (p. 5). Olneck (2000) identifies ways in which multicultural education may transform cultural capital. He remarks that cultural capital produces distinctions among individuals and in doing so reproduces its own value. Mohr and DiMaggio (1995) relate schools as the "centers of cultural authority which maintain and disseminate societal standards of value and serve collectively to clarify and periodically revise the cultural currency" (p. 168). DiMaggio (1992) found that cultural capital impacts the kinds of grades high school students receive and may impact their educational attainment and college attendance. However, he clearly notes that "educational attainment is a very imperfect proxy for cultural capital" (p. 199).

DYNAMICS OF CULTURAL CAPITAL

Cultural capital contains dynamics that need to be considered in examining the educational processes. The dynamics associated with cultural capital emerge in different forms. Those forms revolve around institutional and individual capacities. The institutional capacities emerge in the purposes that schools serve for educating. Are schools serving in the capacity of credentialing students for certain levels of access and opportunities? Are schools obligated to provide a quality education only for the sake of a quality education? Bourdieu (1984) examines these dynamics very thoroughly in his analyses of schools. In addition, the individual approach seeks to reconcile the issues emerging from the home and school environment. The perspectives are primarily associated with the discussion surrounding the cultured and uncultured nature of particular activities and their resulting effects (DiMaggio & Ostrower, 1990; Kalmijn & Kraaykamp, 1996; Lareau, 1987; Lareau & Horvat, 1999; Olneck, 2000). The underlying arguments suggest that while differences may or may not exist in the home and school environments, expectations surrounding performance and achievement moderate the tensions.

Institutionalized Perspectives on Cultural Capital

Bourdieu (1984) reveals that the knowledge-base and experience of those participants who acquired their cultural capital primarily from educational settings are more transferable or valuable in those areas that accommodate high academic qualifications. This position suggests that students who attend the better quality schools are more likely to excel in scholastically inclined activities and those students who do not attend such schools are not as likely to excel academically. Students from both environments nonetheless understand the intricacies of their educational settings, and they become innately resigned to the ideological expectations of that climate. Bourdieu (1984) asserts the following perspectives regarding scholastic and status-based capital:

> The more the competences measured are recognized by the school system and the more academic the techniques used to measure them, the stronger is the relation between performance and educational qualifications. The latter, as a more or less adequate indicator of the number of years of scholastic inculcation, guarantees cultural capital more or less completely, depending on whether it is inherited from the family or acquired at school, and so it is an unequally adequate indicator of this capital. (p. 13)

The argument implies that inherited, family resources have greater impact upon academic performance than the traditional forms of education that are acquired in schools. Family resources contain a variety of networks that offer options and opportunities for individuals from middle, upper-class backgrounds. Bourdieu (1984) demonstrates how schools inherently prepare students for institutional arenas that are complimentary to their respective schooling culture in K–12 environments. Social background primarily influences the degree to which cultural capital gets maximized by either scholastic achievement or family resources. While the study provides a vivid analysis of the relationship between social background and the acquisition of cultural capital, Bourdieu (1984) uses a linear and rational approach that presupposes that certain inputs equate to certain outputs. The study does not consider the role of intrinsic and other less obvious factors upon educational performance.

More specifically, DiMaggio (1982) distinguishes between models of cultural mobility and cultural reproduction as they relate to cultural capital. The study situates the cultural reproduction model as containing greater returns for students from upper status backgrounds than from lower status families. The cultural mobility model, however, posits that the "impact of cultural capital will be greater on the grades of less advantaged youth, for whom the acquisition and display of prestigious cultural resources may be a vital part of upward mobility" (DiMaggio, 1982, p. 195). The differences of cultural reproduction and mobility resonate within the span of academic achievement and educational attainment. Academic achievement is primarily concerned with the immediate outcomes in school settings, whereas educational attainment focuses on the success trajectories of both school and career contexts as a long-term process.

DiMaggio (1982) contends that participation in high cultural activities significantly influences grade performance. Those students who participate in certain activities are more likely to get better grades. Particularly, females from high status families receive greater cultural capital returns than females from lower status backgrounds. These findings remain consistent with the positions related to the cultural reproduction model. Among males, however, the influence of cultural capital on grades is primarily restricted to students from lower status families. Sons of college graduates are no more likely than sons of non-college graduates to receive good grades if they are involved in high cultural activities. These findings align with the expectations of the model of cultural mobility.

The different findings of DiMaggio (1982) primarily point to a relatively low correlation between parental education and cultural capital. In many ways, the quality of opportunities that are afforded by schools compensates for the lacking family resources. The arguments thereby suggest that the cultural capital is not as strongly tied to parental background. The study dismisses the notion that the level of cultural capital is a sole determinant of educational attainment, although cultural capital does significantly impact the types of grades that are received in high school. These findings situate cultural capital as a form of status that contains a utilitarian, institutionalized purpose.

Individualized Perspectives of Cultural Capital

Bourdieu's *Distinction: A Social Critique of the Judgment of Taste* (1984) is a study based on a 1963 survey consisting of 692 males and females who reside in Paris. In 1967–1968, the sample is increased to 1,217 subjects to better analyze differences within racially identifiable, homogenous groups. Bourdieu (1984) examines how cultural practices are linked to educational capital and social status. The respondents' preferences in tastes and lifestyles reflect those entities (i.e., music, dress, food, mannerism, etc.) that are perceived as more commonly associated with their respective background. While the study does not negate the importance of particular forms of cultural capital within institutional settings, the study does not acknowledge the relative aspects of cultural practices that represent various meanings for different people in different settings. In effect, cultural capital only assumes value within those settings that recognize or accept its utility. The study also reveals that given the equivalent levels of educational capital, social origin assumes a more important role in determining cultural practices. The respondents revert to or subscribe to those practices that are more identifiable with their upbringing. Individuals from working class or lower socioeconomic backgrounds oscillate between cultural practices associated with their social origin and their acquired educational capital. The study does not seem to consider this fluctuation as natural ebb and flow that allows them to remain connected to their familiar roots and to maintain self-preservation. There is a degree of patronization and stigmatization imparted upon those in the study who continued to engage in perceivably uncultured activities.

Kalmijn and Kraaykamp (1996) examine the link between racial inequality in schooling and differences in cultural capital and the parents' socialization of their children into high-status culture. The study uses data from the 1982 and 1985 Survey of Public Participation in the Arts (SPPA), which contains questions on the consumption of arts, parental background, and cultural socialization. This particular survey is done in conjunction with the National Crime Survey. The total number of respondents is 6,248—of which 5,660 are non-Hispanic whites, and 588 are African Americans. The participants include men and women over the age of 25. The cohorts range from individuals born in 1900 to individuals born in 1960 and the schooling is measured in single years of completed schooling, ranging from 0 for no schooling to 20 years for PhDs. The study posits three different questions to explore the implications of cultural capital:

1. How have cultural resources changed across birth cohorts of blacks and whites?
2. To what extent can these changes be explained by changes in family background?
3. Have changes in family background and cultural resources contributed to the black–white convergence in schooling?

The study finds that schooling and family resources overall have increased for both African Americans and whites. More specifically, the study pinpoints that the growth has occurred at a faster rate for African Americans in these arenas, given the state of African Americans during the beginning of the 1900s, after the period of Reconstruction. In many of the cohorts, however, the mean of the acquisition of cultural capital for African Americans is below the acquisition of cultural capital of whites. According to Kalmijn and Kraaykamp (1996), these findings imply that cohorts born in 1960 did not have any differences in terms of involvement in high-brow cultural activities, thereby indicating the convergence of Blacks and Whites in their acquisition of cultural capital. Unlike DiMaggio's (1982) earlier study, this study reveals that the parents' level of education determines the child's participation in the arts. The argument suggests that by virtue of their educational attainment, parents are likely to have more knowledge and/or understanding of the kinds of activities in which their children should engage.

The study reveals that given the increases in the parental education or the cultural capital of African Americans, no significant changes have occurred in the number of years that African-American children attend schools. In other words, the number of years that African Americans attend schools is not predicated upon the number of years that their parents attend school. This finding remains consistent in terms of the sort of cultural capital that they are able to gain. However, the study does not address the issues of access and opportunity that are related to this phenomenon. For whites, the number of years that their children attend schools is more likely to be determined by the parents' education.

The study also reveals that declining racial differences or cross-selecting of cultural activities have positive, but modest impact on how racial inequality in schooling has changed. This study links this finding to "a relative decline in the cultural resources of Whites than from an improvement in the cultural resources of Blacks" (Kalmijn & Kraaykamp, 1996, p. 32). The argument is that white parents have not been participating in high-brow cultural capital activities at a rate proportionate to their education. However, the study reveals that cultural capital does assume a significant role in the transferal of advantages that stem from middle and upper level socioeconomic backgrounds.

DiMaggio and Ostrower (1990), using the 1982 SPPA, suggests that important differences exist in arts consumption of African Americans and whites. The study focuses solely on the racial implications associated with cultural capital. The study reveals that whites are more likely to attend classical music concerts, opera, and ballet performances as well as visit museums and other historical sites. The study also reveals that African-Americans are more likely to engage in the traditional forms of arts for their respective culture. Those art forms primarily revolve around musical engagement—listening to jazz and blues, attending jazz and blues concerts, and even watching these art forms on television. DiMaggio and Ostrower (1990) conclude that there are differences in the consumption of art forms between blacks and whites. Irrespective of parents' education, while these differences in art consumptions are somewhat linked to the differences in schooling outcomes between the two racial groups, the influence of race still remains significant.

The study also reveals that socialization into high-brow cultural activities is much more prevalent in white families than it is in black families (DiMaggio & Ostrower, 1990). This finding remains consistent even after the mother and father's education of both groups are taken into account. In some regards, this finding suggests that whites place more emphasis on the participation in cultural forms than African Americans. The reasons underlying these decisions are not as obvious, although it is easily inferable that school curricula subscribe to the ideological dispositions of these traditions. The study further reveals that there has been little or no convergence between African Americans and whites in high-brow cultural activities. African Americans may participate in such exclusive activities but they do not integrate and assume them as part of their cultural associations or identity. DiMaggio and Ostrower (1990) refer to this phenomenon as "cultural resistance." While African Americans have increased their socioeconomic status, they still remain associated with or attached to their cultural art forms, unlike the finding of Bourdieu (1984), who reveals that poor whites who climb the socioeconomic ladder most often disconnect with any associations related to their background. In particular, Bourdieu (1984) pinpoints that if this particular group does not break its familiar ties, they are likely to be ridiculed for not doing so. However, for African Americans, this form of attachment to their background is used to maintain association with their cultural identity. As a result, if African-Americans break these particular familiar ties, they are more likely to be ridiculed for doing so within their community.

More importantly, DiMaggio and Ostrower (1990) reveal that Whites, over a period of time, have subscribed to the traditional, cultural forms associated with African-Americans. Whites are increasingly listening to jazz, blues, and other soul music as well as becoming performing artists in these traditions. This form of integration has not occurred in these same regards for African-Americans that are in contrast to the behavior of Whites. This finding does contradict with Kalmijn and Kraaykamp (1996) who reveal that convergence of cultural activities has occurred between African-Americans and Whites. These researchers suggest that the analysis of DiMaggio and Ostrower (1990) focus on the respondents' cultural socialization at a specific state in their life cycle, age 15, whereas their analysis focuses on the respondents' cultural capital at one point in time, particularly during 1982. Kalmijn and Kraaykamp (1996) reveal that cohort comparisons of are not impacted by age-related factors in their analyses. The arguments of Kalmijn and Kraaykamp (1996), however, do not reveal the implications of this integration that whites undergo into African-American traditions upon their children's educational achievement. Such discussion would provide a model for better understanding the transferal processes of different types of cultural capital across racial groups upon educational outcomes.

Olneck (2000) posits that multicultural education can redefine the implications of cultural capital for minority students. Olneck (2000) basically identifies cultural capital as a form of power and privilege that is used to define and locate individuals within certain positions of the social ladder. One position suggests that multicultural education seeks to redefine what constitutes as cultural deficit behavior within school settings. The cultural capital model, as it is currently defined and arranged, does not accommodate the individuals' experiences (i.e. language, cultural associations, etc.) that are not from traditions associated with middle and upper echelons. Olneck (2000) asserts the following statements:

> The incorporation of students' cultural repertoires reorganizes school practices in ways that dissolve dichotomies by which minority students had been classified negatively. For example, it can have effect of redefining as 'relevant' rather than 'tangential' or 'off the point,' the perspectives that students bring to the classroom. It recognizes what students, their parents, and community members know as being school-worthy 'funds of knowledge' rather than being mere everyday or 'knowledge.' It may also diminish the extent to which disengagement from academics provides a means to express an oppositional identity. (p. 324)

The use of multicultural education provides a means to expand the definitions of culture to become more inclusive of other groups and their experiences. Multicultural education, in effect, contributes to the reordering of social identities. However, from a different viewpoint, Olneck (2000) very carefully points out that multicultural education is not likely to transfer into cultural capital. The undergirding idea is that cultural capital is gained from a traditional curriculum. These demands are ones that students must meet in order to become successful within educational arenas. The fundamental argument that Olneck (2000) seeks to promote is the position that multicultural education serves to propel the educational achievement and attainment rates for minority students through its accommodation of cultural differences within school settings.

Lareau (1987), however, examines how class-related cultural factors influence the relationship between parents' compliance with teachers' requests for parental participation in schools. The qualitative study involved two first-grade classrooms that were located in two different communities. The participants include a white working-class community and a professional, middle-class community. The study reveals that both sets of teachers at the different schools considered parental involvement as indicative of the value that parents placed on education. Differences emerge within this study as it pertains to the level of educational aspirations that the parents have for their children. For the working-class community, a high school diploma is identified as an ultimate indication of success in education. The professional, middle-class individuals in this study promote the importance of getting a college and/or advanced degree. The working and middle classes also viewed the role of the school toward education differently. The working class parents primarily placed the responsibility of education upon the teachers, whereas the middle class parents consider the process of educating to be a shared, collective experience. These particular parents are more likely to read to their children, initiate contact with their children's teachers, participate in school activities, and so on. These varied approaches speak to the link between social class and educational and material resources.

The differences in cultural capital, as having a negative impact, emerge particularly during the teachers' requests for parental involvement in schooling activities. The working class parents in this study are more likely to decline participation in activities that require higher levels of educational skills. The working class parents view intelligence in terms of educational degrees and as a result, they do not feel capable or qualified even to read books to their children. The professional, middle class parents are more eager and anxious to participate in activities to show their support of teachers and dedication to education. In addition, participation in parent–teacher conferences and other school events are most often held during the afternoons. The professional, middle class parents are able to take advantages of these particular activities, given the greater flexibility within their work schedules. These observations address the implications of cultural capital for family–school relationships. The arguments further promote the notion that while class provides social and cultural resources, these "resources must be invested or activated to become a form of cultural capital" (Lareau, 1987, p. 84).

In a later study, Lareau and Horvat (1999) conduct a very thorough case study regarding the implications of parental involvement with their third-grade children; the study also explores this perspective of activation. The study is conducted in a small, Midwestern city where 52% of the students are white, 44% of the students are African-American, 3% of the students are Asian, and 1% of the students are Hispanic; 40% of the students are considered low-income. The number of participants in this study is 24. The breakdown is 12 white children (5 girls and 7 boys) and 12 African-American children (7 girls and 5 boys). The study results in a comparison between the white middle-class families and the African-American working class and poor families.

The study is framed using Bourdieu's theory of cultural capital. The authors challenge the various components of this theory, particularly as it relates to a deterministic approach toward educational outcomes. This approach suggests that given the forms of cultural associations within lower socioeconomic backgrounds, individuals from such status are not as likely to perform well in school. Lareau and Horvat (1999), however, suggest that researchers need to pinpoint how cultural resources are valued within the respective environments. From this perspective, arguments can be made to understand how particular forms of cultural ideologies gain their legitimacy in school settings. These specific findings can then be articulated to groups whose capital does not always receive the same value.

The study reveals that socioeconomic background influenced the ways in which African-American parents address issues within this school. Working-class African-American parents are more likely to be considered confrontational and combative in their approach toward school officials. For example, the study highlights one couple that challenged the school about the academic track in which their daughter was placed. This particular couple is conscious of the prevalence of racial discrimination. The teachers refer to this particular mother as angry and hostile as she questions their motives. Even after the mother's efforts, her daughter is still denied being placed in a higher track. Lareau and Horvat (1999) classify this phenomenon as a moment of exclusion that is defined as the "coming together of various forces to provide an advantage to the child in his or her life trajectory.... [T]hese moments may include placement in an academically gifted program, enrollment into a suburban school, encouragement and preparation for applying to college" (p. 48).

Another case reveals that a middle-class African American couple expressed the same concern for their daughter. The study indicates that the teachers consider this couple to be more supportive and respectful in their approach. This couple is successful in enrolling their child into an academically gifted class, although they, too, share the same concern about the effects of racial discrimination as the former couple. The authors refer to this phenomenon as a "moment of social inclusion" that may include "placement in a low reading group, retention, placement in remedial course, and the failure to complete college-preparation requirements" (p. 48). Lareau and Horvat (1999) assert the following:

> The most important point, however, is that social class appears to mediate how parents with similar types of concerns about racial discrimination seek to mange their children's school careers. The results point to the influence of social class on how families manage their concerns about racial injustice at school. (p. 46)

These same scenarios with different players demonstrate how the acquisition of cultural capital influences the style of communication. Lareau and Horvat (1999) reveal that this scenario identifies the implications for the possession and activation of cultural capital. The former couple does not possess the habitus of cultural capital to enable them to draw or pull from different approaches. By virtue of their educational or social background that has afforded them cultural capital, the latter couple, however, possesses the knowledge about communication styles and is able to activate this knowledge in ways that are considered non-confrontational. Therefore, the study suggests that academic success of individuals (i.e., whites, African Americans, Hispanics, Asians, etc.) is significantly influenced by the ability of the parent(s) to intervene in ways that are conducive to and acceptable within that environmental context.

Zweigenhaft (1993) argued that Harvard students in the 1960s graduated with more cultural capital than they did social capital. More focus was placed on the accumulation of cultural capital via academic achievement as opposed to participating within the influential networks and clubs that the acquisition of social capital demands. The public school graduates were also more likely to earn advanced degrees that allowed them access to graduate and/or professional degrees. Many of these students, however, were not from socioeconomically affluent backgrounds, and their fathers had less formal education than any other groups that were analyzed (i.e., fathers/mothers of the children who attended private, elite schools, fathers/mothers of the children who attended non-elite private schools, fathers/mothers of children who attended boarding schools). The argument about these Harvard graduates nonetheless does infer that individuals who subscribe to perhaps the lowest considerable form of legitimate cultural capital increases the likelihood of access to vast opportunities for educational credentials.

Katsillis and Robinson (1990) examine the relationship between social background inequalities and educational attainment. Their study uses data from a national sample of Greek high school seniors who come from a range of socioeconomic backgrounds. The study reveals that individual ability and effort significantly influence educational achievement. The individualized components of ability and effort, however, do not prohibit the reproduction of the social hierarchy through schooling. The argument suggests that while cultural capital is a necessity for educational achievement, the sole operation of cultural capital is not sufficient to produce higher levels of educational outcomes.

DeGraaf, DeGraaf, and Kraaykamp (2000) conducted a study on the influence of parental cultural resources upon the educational attainment of their children. The study is based on data from the Netherlands Family Survey in 1992–1993 that included 1,653 participants, all of whom were over the age of 25. The study found that the participation of parents in their children's education, particularly in reading, influences the educational achievement more so than the parents' participation in culturally stimulated activities. This finding supports DiMaggio's cultural mobility theory suggesting that there is no relationship between socioeconomic background and cultural capital. Therefore, cultural capital cannot mediate the effects of parental socioeconomic background. In terms of Bourdieu's cultural reproduction theory, the study does reveal that children from high socioeconomic backgrounds perform better in schools than do children from lower socioeconomic backgrounds. For this group of students, this success occurs despite their parents not reading to them.

The study concludes that in the Netherlands the reading behavior of the parent increases the likelihood that children advance in their educational performance. Parents who read to their children have comparable linguistic and cognitive skills that are comparable to the curricular demands of the schools. More specifically, the type of environment that these parents provide for their children also is very educationally stimulating. In addition, the study reveals that the acquisition of cultural capital seems to be primarily an issue for students who come from lower socioeconomic backgrounds. While the results suggest that children from higher socioeconomic backgrounds perform well in schools and the impact of their parents' cultural habits is little, the study does acknowledge that research cannot negate its importance. However, the study urges that researchers specifically identify direct measures of parental cultural capital in order to validate their argument.

Farkas (1990) argues that the possession of cultural resources or the appropriate behaviors exhibited within social interactions often influences how teachers assign grades to students. Students whose disposition mirrors those traditions associated with middle and upper echelons often receive better grades in their course work. The study reports that the informal standard with which teachers reward these particular skills, habits, styles, and other cultural forms leads to grade inflation and creates differentiating results among the categories of race, class, and gender. This form of gatekeeping serves to reinforce the idea that cultural capital is only limited to an exclusive group.

Roscigno and Ainsworth-Darnell (1999) examine the differences in the cultural capital and educational resources of black and white students and the role that these factors assume in mediating the relationship between family background and racial disparity. The study uses the National Education Longitudinal Survey (NELS) database to draw random samples of about 25 eighth graders in each of about 1,000 middle schools. The participants include black and white students, 83.6% of whom are white and 16.4% of whom are black. The study finds that cultural capital and educational resources vary among races primarily as a result of disparities within socioeconomic status. From a macro-based perspective, Roscigno and Ainsworth-Darnell (1999) assert that socioeconomic backgrounds greatly impact the level of access to resources. This position, however, differs from the work of Lareau and Horvat (1999), which argues that racial discrimination propels socioeconomic disparities.

Roscigno and Ainsworth-Darnell (1999) consider the effects of racial discrimination to emerge within the micropolitical contexts of schools. The idea is that while cultural capital and educational resources do affect educational outcomes, the relationships between teachers and students and student placement have a greater influence upon the performance of African-American students:

> Disparate racial and class returns for cultural and educational resources appear to be partially explained by micropolitical processes that are tied spe-

> cifically to teachers' evaluations of students' efforts and more systematic relegation associated with tracking... Race remains an influential and easily identifiable status in this society, and race-based micropolitical processes occurring in the school and classroom may be, as the findings suggest, important in the evaluation and rewarding of background attitudes. (p. 171)

The argument suggests that increased cultural capital does not necessarily connote increased academic performance. Closing the achievement gap between African-Americans and Whites remains an issue about resource distribution (Heubert & Hauser, 1999; McNeil, 2000). Closing the achievement gap also speaks to factors associated with the conditions of schooling in magnet schools. Whether directly or indirectly, in effect, the *acquisition of* or *possession of* cultural capital via institutional and individualized perspectives influences these processes.

HISTORICAL PERSPECTIVES OF SOCIAL CAPITAL

Evidence of social capital can be traced back to the early works of Emile Durkheim (Portes, 1998). Durkheim was instrumental in creating the language that currently defines the field of sociology. He coined the term *anomie,* for example, which refers to a condition of weak regulation or the breaking down of social norms among any given society (Bellah, 1973). This state of being was particularly problematic for Durkheim because he was an advocate for social justice and his scholarly writings centered on the idea of maintaining social order and stability. He focuses on the importance of group behavior and solidarity; therefore, anomie threatens the future of cohesion among individuals and weakens the collective conscience (Pope, 1998). Although Durkheim did not specifically use the term *social capital,* his work is credited as being the foundation to understanding the value of group dynamics. Cohen and Prusak (2001) too suggest that social capital first appeared in print in 1916. They acknowledge the writings of Jane Jacobs, John Seeley, and George Homans as initiators of the social capital conversation. However, the concept has been given academic credentials by the writings of Pierre Bourdieu, Glen Loury, James Coleman, and Robert Putnam (Cohen & Prusak, 2001; Dekker & Uslaner, 2001; Portes, 1998; Schuller, Baron, & Field, 2000; Smith, 2001).

USES OF SOCIAL CAPITAL

The discourse surrounding social capital extends across various disciplines including sociology, education, anthropology, and economics (Castle, 2002; Grootaert & Van Bastelaer, 2002). Although the concept is not a new one, the current resurgence of interest in social capital (along with cultural, human, and economic capital) has recently become prevalent among faculty, administrators, and policy makers. Perhaps this is due to the universal curiosity about and concern with understanding interpersonal communication and exchange among members of society. Notwithstanding, due to the varied interest in social capital, various interpretations emerge, and according to Portes (1998), "the point is approaching at which social capital comes to be applied to so many events and in so many different contexts as to lose any distinct meaning" (p. 2). Furthermore, "social capital is so much a part of the fabric of people's working lives that it tends to be invisible, as the things we see every day and take for granted often go unnoticed" (Cohen & Prusak, 2001, p. 11). As a result, due to the multidisciplinary appeal of social capital, it is difficult to find a common definition. Notwithstanding, the presence of this variety found throughout the literature is not to provoke a state of confusion regarding the meaning of the term. Rather, it serves as a means to better understand social capital by exposing different perspectives and interpretations.

According to Portes (1998), Pierre Bourdieu produced the first systematic analysis of social capital. Bourdieu (1986) defines social capital as "the aggregate of the actual or potential resources which are linked to possession of a durable network of more or less institutionalized relationships of mutual acquaintance or recognition" (p. 248). His approach highlights the value of group membership and the need for creating and maintaining social networks. Although Bourdieu discusses other forms of capital throughout his work, social capital is uniquely situated in the sense that it capitalizes on the other recognized forms. Portes (1988) makes the following observation:

> Through social capital, actors can gain direct access to economic resources (subsidized loans, investment tips, protected markets); they can increase their cultural capital though contacts with experts or individuals of refinement (i.e., embodied cultural capital); or alternatively, they can affiliate with institutions that confer valued credentials (i.e. institutionalized cultural capital). (p. 4)

In this regard, social capital represents an intangible necessity that is keen for survival and upward mobility.

While Bourdieu views social capital through the lens of a social theorist, Glen Loury interprets the concept from an economic standpoint. His work recognizes racial and economic disparities that coexist and contribute to the detriment of collective prosperity. More specifically, he investigates the epidemic of poverty among African Americans and reveals its power in hindering future opportunities regarding employment and education (Loury, 1977). Loury argues against the individualistic character of conventional economic theory and suggests that success is only achieved through the commitment of individuals bonding together to combat issues of inequalities (Portes, 1998).

Robert Putnam is regarded as the most cited author of recent social capital research (Schuller, Baron, & Field, 2000). According to Putnam (1995), social capital refers to features of norms, trust, and social life networks that facilitate coordination and cooperation among participants for mutual benefit. In his landmark book, *Making Democracy Work,* Putnam discovers the importance of social capital as he conducts a systematic study of civic life in Italy in order to identify sources of wealth differentiation among various regions (Putnam, 1995). He finds that social capital is the distinguishing factor that enables certain communities to thrive. Regions that lacked in cooperative efforts, shared goals, and trust among its residents did not flourish economically.

In his later studies that focus on the United States, Putnam uses the activity of bowling as a means to show the decline of social capital. In *Bowling Alone* (Putnam, 2000), he suggests that while bowling tends to be a communal activity, marked by group connections, interdependence, and interpersonal exchange, more people are choosing to bowl in isolation. According to Smith (2001), Putnam saw a fundamental shift in political and civic engagement, informal social ties, and tolerance and trust. Possible explanations for this decrease include change in family structure, suburban sprawl, and electronic entertainment (Smith, 2001). Individuals are more prone to not have children and live alone, and this limits their ability to interact fully. Suburban sprawl reflects the substantial distance that individuals travel away from their homes. This hinders them from making meaningful connections with other members of the community. Similarly, electronic entertainment lures individuals into private spaces. Television, for example, consumes a great deal of time and takes individuals away from the collective body. As a result, their social networking skills slowly diminish, and this contributes to further decline of social capital.

Although the literature covering social capital is diverse, all unite in the possession of two key components: trust and networks (Schuller, Baron, & Field, 2000). Additionally, Grootaert (2001) identifies the following common features of social capital:

1. All link the economic, social, and political spheres. They share the belief that social relationships affect economic outcomes and are affected by them.
2. All recognize the potential created by social relationships for improving development outcomes but also recognize the danger for negative effects.

3. All focus on relationships among economic agents and how the formal or informal organization of those can improve the efficiency of economic activities.
4. All imply that "desirable" social relationships and institutions have positive externalities. Because these cannot be appropriated by any one individual, each agent has a tendency to underinvest in social capital; hence, there is a role for public support of social capital building (p. 12)

Education as Producer of Social Capital

James Coleman is responsible for bridging the inquiry between social capital and education. He defines social capital in terms of its function and suggests two key elements: "they all consist of some aspect of social structures, and they facilitate certain actions of actors—whether persons or corporate actors—within the structure" (Coleman, 2000, p. 16). Educational settings are ideal for producing high levels of social capital because they embody daily interactions among various groups including students, faculty, administration, and staff. While most analysis of social capital refers to individuals, communities, and cultures, Cohen and Prusak (2001) explore the concept in regard to functioning organizations. Drawing from this particular literature, academic institutions, therefore, clearly fit within the identifying characteristics of such structures based on the nature of their composition. Cohen and Prusak (2001) assert the following:

> Social capital makes an organization, or any cooperative group, more than a collection of individuals intent on achieving their own private purposes. Social capital bridges the space between people. Its characteristic elements and indicators include high levels of trust, robust personal networks and vibrant communities, shared understandings, and a sense of equitable participation in a joint enterprise- all things that draw individuals together into a group. This kind of connection supports collaboration, commitment, ready access to knowledge and talent, and coherent organizational behavior. (p. 4)

Not only are educational institutions producers of social capital because of the overall makeup, but they are also producers because of their goals and functions. The uniting theme across different institutional types regarding students is the commitment to preparation. Most students engage in schooling in order to equip themselves. The intent is to acquire all of the skills deemed necessary to secure future success and fulfillment. Although on the surface it appears to be a selfish act, maneuvering through the educational system proves to transform this individualistic attitude. Schools bring together different individuals possessing diverse personalities, backgrounds, and aspirations. While the journey begins selfishly, students eventually begin to interact and rely on one another. Through study groups and social, academic, and athletic organizations, students are able to develop friendships and establish networks of support.

In a seminal study, Brown and Davis (2001) identify historically black colleges and universities (HBCUs) as purveyors of social capital for African Americans. Building upon Bourdieu's theory, the authors contend that black colleges allow African American students the opportunity to create networks and relationships that prove beneficial to their future success.

> The transferal of the social information, achievement, and credentials needed for African Americans to enjoy full participation in the larger society remain a primary role of the black college. This purveyance of social capital sustains the equalization of African Americans in the nation and the world. Indeed, Black colleges are important mediators in the pursuit of African Americans for both equality of opportunity and equity in outcomes. (Brown & Davis, 2001, p. 44)

The arguments clearly demonstrate that the relationships that develop within the contexts of HBCUs are a form of social capital. This type of capital has long-term effects. Knowing the right kinds of information can lead to the right kinds of job opportunities. The privileged networks transcend into a higher quality of life which these individuals are able to enjoy.

Education as Consumer of Social Capital

While education produces social capital, it is also a consumer of it. The campus environment is enhanced based on the way in which participants engage with one another. If a campus welcomes ideas, encourages discourse, and ultimately creates a space of free exchange, it is rewarded. It reaps the benefits of acquiring a positive reputation that potentially impacts student enrollment and attracts quality faculty. In addition, educational institutions are also held responsible for the lack of social capital accrued within its structure. In Coleman's research, he studied social capital as a way of understanding the relationship between social inequality and educational underachievement (Schuller, Baron, & Field, 2000). By conducting a longitudinal study of high school sophomores, he discovered disparities between Catholic and state schools. Coleman found that Catholic schools students have higher levels of academic attainment due to the expectations of teacher responsibility. These findings suggest that state schools are missing a critical tool that has proven to be an effective strategy toward improving academic achievement.

In institutional settings, the possession of social capital is somewhat like having a two-edged sword. Acquiring much of it proves to be beneficial to students by helping them in regard to socialization and academic success. On the other hand, low levels of social capital serve as a detriment to their ability to progress and effectively function in society. As consumers of social capital, however, it is imperative for educational centers to find ways to increase the dosage of social capital that is absorbed by the student body. Evidence of education as a consumer can further be drawn from the writings of Bourdieu. As previously mentioned, Bourdieu proposes that institutional affiliations provide individuals with valued credentials, and as a result, social capital increases. This is particularly true in regard to higher education. Students often choose schools based on their perceived level of prestige. Consequently, Ivy League schools such as Harvard and Yale enjoy a certain sort of social capital that is unavailable at other types of institutions. In a sense, these elite schools have fixed social capital. Due to their acquired reputations, schools of this caliber do not have to work toward maintaining social capital because it is inherent in the fabric of the university.

Education as Regulator of Social Capital

The regulation of social capital among learning institutions is reflected in the selection process of students. Colleges and universities require certain standards to be met in order for admission to be granted. Applications, interviews, and standardized test scores serve as regulators; they greatly influence the decision making process and ultimately represent the type of characteristics that are valued by the college or university. In this respect, institutions recognize the importance of social capital and use this process as a step toward building and sustaining it. World Bank (1999) has developed statistical research surrounding social capital and shows that it has both economic and social value. Based on their findings with regard to education, schools are more effective when parents and other citizens are active participants (Smith, 2001). Education thus becomes a regulator of social capital because the greater the influence of others, the better students will perform in the classroom.

Social capital is a multidimensional concept. It does not fit within the confines of a box, but rather takes on new meaning as different authors approach it. Dekker and Uslaner (2001) reveal the following:

> It is depicted as a treatment for the disruptive consequences of social disintegration and disappearing cohesion; it is expected to stimulate cooperation, well-being, and economic growth; it is considered to be both a prerequisite and a result of democratic societal processes simultaneously; and it refers to the potential for developing social skills and attitudes. (p. xvii)

Social capital is an essential ingredient to sustaining a productive communal society. The way in which individuals interact with one another will continue to occupy the minds of researchers and policy makers. And while there has been a recent interest in various forms of capital, social capital maintains its intangible uniqueness. "Whereas economic capital is in people's bank accounts, and human capital is inside their heads, social capital inheres in the structure of their relationships" (Portes, 1998, p. 7).

NETWORKS OF SOCIAL CAPITAL

Social capital is highly predicated upon resource access and/or distribution. The networks that emerge from the availability of social capital for information prove relevant to educational processes. Although social capital is not contained in the sense that everyone has the same type, these perspectives do suggest that the legitimacy of social capital, like cultural capital, is relative to its environment. There are different forms of social capital, internal and external, that serve as resources for students matriculating through the academic pipeline. The quality of those networks of social capital significantly impacts the quality of the educational experience.

External Networks of Social Capital

Lee and Croninger (1999) examined the effects of school-based forms of social capital on adolescents' academic development. The study sought to understand the nature of social capital, its creation, and its use. More specifically, the study sought to distinguish between the mechanisms that shape students' access to social capital and the qualities that define the construct itself. Lee and Croninger (1999) identified social capital as a "resource embedded in a person's social network . . . the manner in which the structural characteristics of social groups facilitate or hinder helpful exchanges between members" (p. 6). Particularly at the individual or micro-based level, social capital is considered a resource to which students have direct access to maximize their personal interests. The macro or structural level locates social capital as those norms, traditions, behavioral patterns, and social organizational characteristics that influence the goals that individuals choose to pursue and the opportunities to do so. The comparative case study examined six high schools, particularly those comprised of students from racial minority and lower-income backgrounds. The study included 210 respondents from urban, parochial, and rural schools. Interviews were conducted with key administrators and teachers while focus groups were conducted with teachers, parents, and students. Both inductive and deductive methods were used to analyze the qualitative data.

The results of the study were distinguished according to the qualities of social capital and the mechanisms for generating and sustaining it. The qualities of social capital included subcomponents—the uses of and the intentionality of social capital. Lee and Croninger (1999) revealed that social capital was not all school-based and directed toward the students' academic development. The study suggested that social capital can have both academic and personal uses. Reservations, however, emerged among the teachers at the parochial school regarding the level of personal interest that they should have. In the inner-city school, the study revealed that teachers found it difficult to develop personal relationships with the students while maintaining high academic standards. These students often took advantage of such relationships that, in effect, created tensions between the teachers and students. Irrespective of the relationship between the teachers and the students, the teachers served as a form of social capital. The difference primarily existed in the degree of and type of interest shown toward their students.

Internal Networks of Social Capital

McNeal (1999) examined the degree to which parental involvement determines behavioral patterns and the degree to which these effects are positive for disadvantaged groups. This research conceptualizes parental involvement as a form of social capital and its impact upon cognitive outcomes (i.e., science achievement) and behavioral outcomes (i.e., truancy, dropping out, etc.). The study further examines the role of race, socioeconomic status, and household structure within this discussion. The study considers social capital to consist of three elements: form, norms of obligation and reciprocity, and resources. Forms consist of the structural aspects of social networks and relations (i.e., breadth of the network, depth or intensity, existence of structural hole, and the nature of the relations, etc.). The norms of obligation and reciprocity are based on the level of investments and returns stemming from obligations, trusts, and so on. Resources are part of the external linkages that exist between the members occupying status in a social hierarchy as well as those who do not necessarily have financially-rewarding or status-based positions.

This quantitative study consisted of a sample of eight and tenth graders from the National Educational Longitudinal Study (NELS: 88). A sample of 17,049 cases was used for analyses, examining academic achievement and truancy as well as the impact of parental involvement's effects upon dropping out. The research study denoted that parental involvement as social capital entailed the components of parent–child discussion, PTO involvement, monitoring, and educational support strategies. The study revealed that social capital is associated with increased academic achievement and decreased patterns of deviant conduct. Social capital has greater effects on behavioral than on cognitive behavior. McNeal (1999) asserts the following:

> The only dimension of parent involvement that is remotely consistent in terms of improving achievement and reducing problematic behavior is parent-child discussion. Nonetheless, even discussion does not consistently prove beneficial to all three outcomes, showing a nonsignificant relationship to dropping out. However, consistent with the hypothesis set forth earlier, parent involvement in general significantly reduces incidents of problematic behavior while showing inconsistent effects on achievement. (p. 129)

These findings clearly state that while social capital is important to the overall schooling processes, social capital does not forge higher academic outcomes. The study also reveals that white students from non-single-headed households who participate in parent–child discussions experience increased science achievement and decreased likelihood of truancy and dropping out. These same students whose parents are involved with PTO experience decreased science achievement and the likelihood of truancy and dropping out.

For minority students in single-headed households, the level of parent–child discussions and educational support strategies negatively impacts their behavioral outcomes. Surprisingly, the study further reveals that these negative behavioral outcomes are also associated with increased level of science achievement. McNeal (1999) has no explanation for this phenomenon. In addition, the study revealed that the estimated effect pertaining to the educational support strategies for students in single-headed households is statistically different from those students in non-single-headed households. Therefore, the implications of educational support strategies upon academic achievement assume seemingly greater importance within single-headed households.

Furthermore, parental involvement is more effective for those students from higher socioeconomic backgrounds. The argument suggests that while social capital (i.e., parent–child discussion, PTO involvement, monitoring, etc.) decreases the likelihood of truancy and dropping out and occasionally increases levels of science achievement, members from lower socioeconomic backgrounds are less likely to experience the same effects from similar involvements. The impact of parent–child discussion and PTO involvement on dropping out are inconsequential. There is no impact. While PTO involvement and monitoring negatively influences science achievement for middle-SES students, these same components increase the outcomes of science achievement for students from upper class backgrounds. McNeal (1999) clearly states that "parent involvement's positive effect of raising achievement and reducing problematic behavior tends to be a valid presumption predominately for members of middle and upper socioeconomic standing" (p. 134). In effect, the findings demonstrate that given comparable levels of involvement, single headed households and parents from minority and lower socioeconomic status backgrounds, receive less benefits for their active participation and involvement in their child's education.

Parcel and Dufur (2001) conducted a study on the effects of family and school capital (i.e., social, human, and financial) on student math and reading achievement. The quantitative study used the National Longitudinal Survey of Youth (NLSY 1992), which contains data about individuals between the ages of 14 and 21 and their elementary and secondary schools. The study also included data from the Child–Mother Data (1994) about maternal background and occupational conditions, family conditions, child attributes, and child cognitive outcomes. The study consisted of samples of 2,034 for math achievement and 2,203 for reading recognition. The study primarily used these samples to understand the role of different forms of school capital upon educational outcomes. For the purpose of this literature review, the implications of social capital only will be extracted.

The study defines social capital as resources that are contained in relationships between and among individuals. Social capital includes the time and attention that parents give to their children. This interactive or quality time is considered useful in promoting child socialization. The argument infers that two-parent families provide benefits in child rearing that other family forms do not present. Two-parent families are presumed to have more social capital to offer their children that become useful for their educational performance. Parcel and Dufar (2001) also suggest that two-parent families are able to forge bonds with their children. These bonds contribute to the decreased levels of misbehavorial conduct in schools. Parcel and Dufar (2001) assert the following:

> Children's home environments reflect parental investment in child well-being. These environments are a function of material resources, but after a certain level of basic expenditure, home environments reflect parental orientation to providing the types of interpersonal resources that favor child development. Parental investments in age-appropriate cognitive stimulation, an affectively warm style of interacting with children, and in general cleanliness and safety of the home environment combine to promote positive child outcomes. (p. 882)

The undergirding idea of this perspective on social capital remains that parental stability provides children with a variety of resources that are necessary for stimulating their cognitive and affective skills. These families are also able to connect with other like families and form social connections.

The social connections entail certain benefits and assets that their children are privileged to enjoy.

Parcel and Dufar (2001) find that better home environments increase the outcomes of math achievement. The notion of better home environments is based on two-parent families where the mother does not work. The finding is consistent with the hypothesis that suggests that the mother is better able to nurture children in such ways that foster intellectual development. The study also reveals that the amount of social capital acquired from both home and school environments significantly determines the level of math achievement. This finding suggests a close linkage between home and school environments that contribute to the maximized benefits of social capital. The study further states that the while social capital influences educational outcomes, the context of the school has a greater impact. This finding clearly infers that the school environment compensates in those areas where the home environment lacks in providing social capital.

Bianchi and Robinson (1997) examined how the length of time parents spend with children influences their level of cognitive and social development. Their article, "What Did You Do Today? Children's Use of Time, Family Composition, and the Acquisition of Social Capital," used four different activities to determine this influence: reading or being read to, watching TV, studying, and doing household chores. The study further extracted how time varied according to these four family characteristics: parental education, maternal employment, number of parents in the household, and family size. The undergirding perspective for this study linked social capital to the length and quality of time that parents spent with their children that, in effect, impacted educational outcomes. In light of this perspective, the study sought to answer the following questions:

1. Do children of mothers who are at home full-time spend more time in cognitive enhancing activities, such as reading, than children of mothers who are in the paid labor force? Are there differences in the amount of time children spend doing housework, watching TV, or studying by the labor force status of their mother?
2. Do children in two-parent households spend more time reading, doing household chores, and studying, and less time watching TV than children in one-parent households?
3. Do children in smaller families spend more time in these four activities than children in larger families?
4. How does parental education relate to these activities? Do children of better-educated parents spend more time studying and reading and less time watching TV than children of less well-educated parents? (Bianchi & Robinson, 1997, p. 333).

The study used data from the Survey Research Center (SRL) at the University of California at Berkeley (UC–Berkeley) and the California Children's Activity Pattern Survey (CCAPS). Data from SRL at UC–Berkeley focused on the proportion of time spent in specific indoor and outdoor locations (i.e., living room, workplace) and in specific activities (i.e., active sports, hobbies, etc.) by children in California aged 11 years or younger according to demographic subgroups. The CCAPS specifically extracted the quality and quantity of time that adults spent with their children in the UC–Berkeley survey.

An initial pilot study was conducted with 38 households that consisted of children aged 11 or younger. Based on the results from the pilot study, both interviews and survey methods were employed in a probability sample of California children ranging from the ages of 3–11. Interviews occurred from April 1989 to March 1990 in order to forge a better understanding of the seasonal variations in activity and location patterns. A total of 1,200 respondents were interviewed. The survey questionnaire was divided into three parts: an adult section, a children's section, and a daily time diary. Three hundred sixteen (316) surveys were randomly distributed, and the survey return rate was 78%.

Bianchi and Robinson (1997) revealed that among the tested demographic characteristics (i.e., age, race, gender) of the child, age was more significant. The study suggested that as age increased, the likelihood of studying, doing household chores, and watching TV increases. No major differences existed between minority and non-minority children as it related to TV watching and their likelihood of studying. However, white, non-Hispanic children spent more time doing household chores. As it pertains to gender, the study revealed that males spent more time watching TV and less time doing household chores than girls. In addition, Bianchi and Robinson (1997) suggested that the size of the family did not detract from the length of study time or the likelihood of being read to or reading, although the study reveals that as the number of children in the household increases, the number of minutes doing household chores also increases. More specifically, the study examined the role of parental education upon social capital. The findings from the study include the following: 25% of the sampled children lived with a parent who had a college education or more; 29% of the children lived with a parent who attended college but did not graduate; 33% of the children lived with a parent who was a high school graduate with no other schooling; 11% of the children lived with a parent who dropped out before completing high school.

Bianchi and Robinson (1997) reveal that children's time spent reading or being read to is significantly higher in those households where parents are college educated. The number of minutes that are spent reading per day to children who live with a college educated parent is not different from children who live with a parent who has attended graduate school or completed postgraduate education. Children whose parents have attended but have not completed college, who are high school graduates, or who did not complete high school spend less time reading to their children than those children who have college-educated parents. Higher income parents spend more time reading to their children than parents from lower income backgrounds. Bianchi and Robinson (1997), however, contend that a child who resides with only one parent is not any more likely to read or study less and watch TV more than a child from a two-parent family. This finding suggests that the family structure does not delimit the cognitive development of the child. The study further argues that contrary to expectations, children of mothers who are employed part-time watch significantly less TV than children of mothers at home full-time. Therefore, the notion that stay-at-home mothers spend more time engaging in intellectually stimulating activities than working moms gets challenged. The study, nonetheless, does support their original thesis that parental education is a major predictor of the kind of social capital that children acquire.

Parcel and Menaghan (1994) examined the impact of parental working conditions on the cognitive ability and social development of children. The quantitative study used data from the National Longitudinal Survey of Youth (NLSY) that investigated the effects of early maternal employment on child outcomes. The study extracted two different samples of mothers whose children ranged from three-to-six years old in 1986. The first sample consisted of 768 mothers who were employed at this time in order to examine the impact of early influences upon cognitive ability. A second sample consisted of 526 employed mothers whose children ranged from four-to-six years to measure social outcomes. The sample did not include three-year olds because their assessment instrument of maternal perceptions of children's behavior is not designed for children younger than four years old.

Parcel and Menaghan (1994), unlike Bianchi and Robinson (1997), reveal that part-time working mothers as opposed to stay-at-home mothers are better able to influence the cognitive ability of their children. Likewise, this study also finds that children benefited more significantly in their verbal capacities when the mothers' current profession reinforces her cognitive skills, whereas the mother who engages in routine or repetitive forms of work are less able to promote verbal capacities. These particular findings imply a relationship between the type of work that the mother engages and her ability to influence adequately the cognitive development of her child. The cognitive stimulation of children does not require the constant attention of a parent. Bianchi and Robinson (1997) assert the following:

> [W]e find minimally negative effects of early maternal employment on child outcomes. The data suggest that mothers who do not work during the child's

> first three years may, if their occupational prospects are poor, facilitate verbal fluency in their children; however, this effect is reversed for mothers whose later occupations are high in complexity.

The argument rejects the notion that stay-at-home mothers during the early years are more likely to enhance their child's learning and intellectual abilities. Therefore, the idea that working mothers negatively impact the acquisition of social capital does not receive support from this study. In fact, the study suggests that the employment conditions of the mothers' work serve to compliment their capacity to assist with cognitive enhancement strategies in parenting that, in effect, increase social capital.

The study further challenges the notion that the more time parents spend with their children the more likely they are to develop stronger cognitive skills. The study finds that limited work hours, particularly engaged by the mother, do not necessarily lead to increased intellectual abilities. The length of time that parents spend with their child is not a guarantor of educational success. To argue that the level of parental involvement is an indicator of higher educational outcomes remains predicated upon a limited set of factors that influence academic performance. While this study does not negate the importance of parental involvement, the findings demand that the ways in which social capital gets associated with the perceptions of traditional nuclear families should be expanded. The acquisition of social capital is not solely limited to the scope of family resources.

Arriaza (2001) explored the social context that comprises the educational environment where social capital is generated and/or denied. More specifically, this action ethnographic research examines the social dynamics behind the discipline statistics as determined referrals. The study is part of a larger research project that considers the ways in which social conflict facilitates the socialization of children of color in an urban middle school setting in San Francisco, California. The author defines social capital as the capacity of individuals and groups to negotiate social borders and institutional barriers. This capacity is one that is developed via social networks and the intervention of protective agents. The following question thereby is used to guide the study: In what ways do conflict between teachers and students relationships in terms of social capital?

The study was conducted at Huerta Academy, a middle school of 6th–8th grade students. The school is located in an upper middle class neighborhood. The racial demographics include 42% Latino, 26% African-American, 12% White, and 10% Other Nonwhite; the remaining groups are Filipino and Chinese. Data were collected via in-depth interviews, focus groups, document analyses, observations, and field notes. There were 14 participants in this research study.

Arriaza (2001) found that African Americans are disproportionately referred to the office, primarily due to "defiance" and "repeated disruption." Latino children follow, although not at the same rate. This disproportionate phenomenon is linked to cultural, racial, and linguistic issues, given that seven out of nine teachers were white. Particularly as it relates to African-American children, the author identifies detention as one form of repercussion to deal with behavioral misconduct. The use of detention usually stems from a mishap between the teacher and the student. Detention suggests that the student remains in the classroom or a particular place in the school, which, in effect, prohibits students from socializing with their peers. Detention does not provide the most conducive means to build social capital among minority students. Arriaza (2001) asserts the following:

> Discipline rules and regulations provide the context for socializing children to cultural norms that might deny or build social capital. Some teachers operate their classroom as a place where 'no-no' regulates every more. No hats, no food, no chewing, no talking, no standing up, no answering the intercom. Few activities are left to chance. When 'no' rules are used as a management strategy, students will inevitably try to break each of them. (p. 30)

This argument clearly suggests that discipline serves as a control mechanism that leads to resistance and dissonance among African-American students. The culture in which social capital is fostered is very strict and rigid. This type of school environment inherently limits the range of options to African-American students to negotiate their position within such instances.

In order to address this type of "no-win" situation, the author states that school administrators and teachers should develop better skills on conflict mediation. Students should not be separated from their peers because this creates negative feelings. This perspective suggests that teachers and administrators need to assume a collective role in building social capital in more positive ways. Acknowledging the implications of cultural, racial, and linguistic differences provide one means to understand the norms that frames the socialization experience. Administrators can then draw from those reference points to forge social capital among African-American students in predominately white settings.

SUMMARIZING VIEWPOINTS OF ECONOMIC, HUMAN, CULTURAL AND SOCIAL CAPITAL

Dynamics of economic, human, cultural, and social capital have distinct roles as consumer, producer, and regulator for schools and the larger society. Consumer-based characteristics of economic capital suggest that financial assets yield power and influence. Wealth, possession, or financial capital dictates the kind of people who sit on elementary, secondary, and/or higher educational boards to enact policies and affect practices. The amount of economic capital regulates the accessibility of material and/or nonmaterial resources. Economic capital, as a concept primarily based upon monetary possessions, however, evokes challenges for educational settings. Highly desirable individual qualifications from schooling are easily acquired by the highest bidder and those who can literally purchase their education. From buying into the right neighborhoods to enrolling in prestigious colleges and universities via legacy admission, the disproportionate allocation of economic capital broadens the gap between the "haves" and the "have nots." The integrity of the academic process becomes subject to the influence of the controlling, invisible hand of money.

Education as a consumer of human capital presupposes a level playing field. Inequalities are considered naturally part of the academic and social matriculation processes. Levels of opportunities are primarily determined by individual meritocracy. Education as a producer of capital resonates as a type of "change agent." In this capacity, educational credentials serve as legitimate means to enhance the quality of lifelong options made available. Undergirding ideas of human capital as producer and consumer are fundamentally linked to education as regulating the potential for upward economic and social status for individuals. From an institutional perspective, however, human capital denies or even negates the existence of educational inequalities. Past remnants of segregation, present realities of tracking, and future occurrences of white flight continue to directly impact academic outcomes and opportunities, particularly for children of color. From an individual perspective, educational achievements are not solely based upon the conjoined efforts of intelligent capacity and hard work. The quality of educational achievements is inextricably tied to a system of educational inequalities. Those who are able to navigate this system are those who are able to acquire the more desirable kinds of human capital.

Consumer effects of cultural capital resonates within families that individuals are born. Internal "teachings" or "learnings" that occur within family socialization influence the kinds of literal and/or nonliteral expressions, behavioral patterns, knowledge base, and other communicative gestures. Often, such external depictions of cultural capital may or may not adequately reflect cognitive, intellectual abilities or potentials. Education, as a producer of cultural capital, generates exposure to the forms of knowledge and know-how considered legitimate in schools and society. From participation in arts-related activities to enrollment in significant numbers of AP courses, the quality of educational outcomes and opportunities are impacted by the symbolic nature of culturally identifiable forms of capital. The current system of education and schooling serves to regulate the implications of having various forms of cultural capital. Given that the concept of cultural capital changes according to racial and/or socioeconomic status, any participation in cultural activities that are not based upon the Eurocentric traditions of the upper class is considered "'low culture." It is important to note that what constitutes "low culture" in schools and society does not necessarily lead to lower educational achievement. The challenges, however, resonate in the ability to know both forms of cultural capital and to understand their transferal processes in respective contexts.

Social capital is gained through affiliation with influential networks. Sufficient levels of trust and cooperative efforts are maintained through these informal relationships. The notion of education as a producer of social capital suggests that the quality of interactions is linked to the types of opportunities made available. The right kinds of information are transferable into the right kinds of jobs. As a consumer of social capital, education operates in a hierarchically stratified manner. Only those individuals belonging to certain networks or having particular credentials and other forms of pedigrees gain access into reputable colleges and universities. Like human and economic capital, education as consumer of social capital prioritizes resources that deliver financial and/or material gains. In effect, the selective nature of this process shifts education into functioning as a regulator of social capital. The possession of educational degrees or privileged association serves as a "weeding out" mechanism for who acquires social mobility and economic stability.

Educational policies and practices are linked to the diverse tenets of economic, human, cultural, and social capital. The fluid nature of capital determines the kind of practical experience and nonpractical knowledge for individuals to succeed within given contexts. Particularly, various forms of and different interactions of capital are needed to effectively matriculate through the academic pipeline. The level of resource availability and accessibility upon educational performance is significantly impacted by capital as consumer, producer, and regulator. Consequently, K–12 environments and higher education institutions must continuously negotiate the resulting policy effects of the "capital haves" and the "capital have nots" in public settings.

REFERENCES

Allensworth, E. & Rosenkranz, T. (2000). *Access to magnet schools in Chicago.* (Report No. UD 033799). Chicago, IL: Joyce Foundation. (ERIC Documentation Reproduction Service No. ED 446 171).

Anderson, R. (1995). *Social capital, cultural capital, and parent involvement: Analyzing educational outcomes.* Doctoral dissertation, University of Nebraska. Dissertation Abstracts International, 57-01.

Anheier, H. K., Gerhards, J., & Romo, F. P. (1995). Forms of capital and social structure in cultural fields: Examining Bourdieu's social topography. *The American Journal of Sociology, 11*, 859–903.

Arai, K. (1998). *The economics of education: An analysis of college-going behavior.* Tokyo: Springer-Verlag.

Archbald, D. (2000). School choice and school stratification: Shortcomings of the stratification critique and recommendations for theory and research. *Educational Policy, 14*, 214–240.

Arnold, K. (2002). Getting to the top—What role do elite colleges play? *About Campus, 7*, 4–12.

Arriaza, G. (2001, April). *Crime and punishment: Social capital and children of color.* Paper presented at the Annual Meeting of the American Educational Research Association, Seattle, WA.

Atkinson, A. B. (1983). *The economics of inequality* (2nd ed.). Oxford: Oxford University Press.

Babbie, E. (1998). *The practice of social research* (8th ed.). Belmont, CA: Wadsworth Publishing.

Baptiste, I. (2001). Educating lone wolves: Pedagogical implications of human capital theory. *Adult Education Quarterly, 51*, 184–201.

Baron, S., Field, J., & Shuller, T. (Eds.). (2000). *Social capital: Critical perspectives.* Oxford: Oxford University Press.

Becker, G. S. (1964). *Human capital: A theoretical and empirical analysis, with special reference to education.* New York: National Bureau of Economic Research.

Becker, G. S. (1993). *Human capital: A theoretical and empirical analysis, with special reference to education* (3rd ed.). Chicago: University of Chicago Press.

Becker, G. S. & Tomes, N. (1986). The family and the distribution of economic rewards. *Journal of Labor Economics, 4*, 1–39.

Bell, D. (Ed.). (1980). *Shades of brown: New perspectives on school desegregation.* New York: Teachers College.

Bell, D. (1995). Brown v. Board of Education and the interest convergence dilemma. In K. Crenshaw, N. Goanda, G. Peller, & K. Thomas (Eds.), *Critical race theory: The key writing that formed the movement.* New York: New Press.

Bellah, R. N. (Ed.). (1973). *On morality and society: Selected writings.* Chicago: University of Chicago Press.

Berg, I. (1971). *Education and jobs: The great train robbery.* Boston: Beacon Press.

Beteille, A. (1996). The mismatch between class and status. *The British Journal of Sociology, 47*, 513–525.

Blaug, M. (1972). The correlation between education and earnings: What does it signify? *Higher Education, 1*, 53–76.

Blumer, H. (1969). *Symbolic interactionism: Perspective and method.* Berkeley: University of California Press.

Board of education of the city of Chicago. (1982, January 22). *Comprehensive student assignment plan.* Chicago: Author.

Bourdieu, P. (1977). *Outline of theory and practice* (Richard Nice, Trans.). Cambridge: Cambridge University Press.

Bourdieu, P. (1984). *Distinction: A social critique of the judgment of taste.* Cambridge, MA: Harvard University Press.

Bourdieu, P. (1986). The forms of capital. In J. G. Richardson (Ed.), *Handbook of theory and research for the sociology of education,*(pp. 241–258). New York: Greenwood Press.

Bourdieu, P. (1989). Social space and symbolic power. *Sociological Theory, 7,* 14–25.

Bourdieu, P. & deSaint Martin, M. (1974). Scholastic excellence and the values of the educational system. In J. Eggleton (Ed.), *Contemporary research in the sociology of education* (pp. 338–371). London: Methuen.

Bourdieu, P. & J. C. Passeron. (1979). *The inheritors: French students and their relations to culture* (Richard Nice, Trans.). Chicago: University of Chicago.

Bourdieu, P., Wacquant, L., & Farage, S. (1994). Rethinking the state: Genesis and structure of the bureaucratic field. *Sociological Theory, 12,* 1–18.

Bowles, S. (1972). Schooling and inequality from generation to generation. *The Journal of Political Economy, 80,* 219–251.

Bowman, M. J. (1966). The human investment revolution in economic thought. *Sociology of Education, 39,* 111–137.

Bradburd, R. & Mann, D. (1993). Wealth in higher education institutions. *Journal of Higher Education, 64,* 472–493.

Braddock, J. H. II & Dawkins, M. P. (1984). Long-term effects of school desegregation on southern Blacks. *Sociological Spectrum, 4,* 365–381.

Braddock, J. H., II & McParland, J. (1989). Social-psychological processes that perpetuate racial segregation: The relationship between school and employment desegregation. *Journal of Black Studies, 19,* 267–289.

Braddock, J. H., II, Dawkins, M. P., & Trent, W. (1994). Why desegregate? The effect of school desegregation on adult occupational desegregation of African Americans, Whites, and Hispanics. *International Journal of Contemporary Sociology, 31,* 109–119.

Braddock, J. H., II, & McPartland, J., & Trent, W. (1984). *Desegregated schools and desegregated work environments.* Paper presented at the Annual Meeting of the American Educational Research Association, New Orleans, LA.

Brown v. Board of Education. (1954). 347 U.S. 483, 74 S.Ct. 686, 98 L.Ed 873.

Brownell, B. (1946). The college and the community. *Journal of Higher Education, 17,* 294–300.

Brubaker, R. (1985). Rethinking classical theory. *Theory and Society, 14,* 745–775.

Carter, R. (1996). The unending struggle for equal educational opportunity. In E. Lagemann & L. Miller (Eds.), *Brown v. Board of Education: The challenge for today's schools* (pp. 19–26). New York: Teachers College.

Castle, E. (2002). Social capital: An interdisciplinary concept. *Rural Sociology, 67,* 334–349.

Chandler, A. D., Hagstrom, P., & Solvell, O. (1998). *The dynamic firm: The role of technology, strategy, organization and regions.* Oxford: Oxford University Press.

Chicago Public Schools. (2003, April 2). Retrieved from http://research.cps.k12.il.us/resweb/ReportServlet

Clark, H. F. (1930). Economic effects of education. *Journal of Higher Education, 1,* 141–148.

Cohen, D. & Prusak, L. (2001). *In good company: How social capital makes organizations work.* Boston: Harvard Business School Press.

Cohn, E. (1972). *The economics of education.* Lexington, MA: Heath Lexington Books.

Coleman, J. S. (1968). *Equality of educational opportunity.* Washington, DC: U.S. Department of Education.

Coleman, J. S. (1986). *Public and private high schools: The impact of communities.* New York: Basic Books.

Coleman, J. S. (1988). Social capital in the creation of human capital. *American Journal of Sociology, 94,* 95–120.

Coleman, J. S. (1990). *Foundations of social theory.* Cambridge: Harvard University Press.

Collins, R. (1987). A micro-macro theory of intellectual creativity: The case of German idealist philosophy. *Sociological Theory, 5,* 47–69.

Cookson, P. W. & Persell, C. H. (1985). English and American residential secondary schools: A comparative study of the reproduction of social elites. *Comparative Education Review, 29,* 283–298.

Couch, K. & Dunn, T. A. (1997). Intergenerational correlations in labor market status. *The Journal of Human Resources, 32,* 210–232.

Crain, R. (1984). *The quality of American high school graduates: What personnel officers say and do about it.* Report No. 354. Baltimore, MD: The Johns Hopkins University.

Crain, R. & Mahard, R. (1981). Minority achievement: Policy implications of research. In W. Hawley (Ed.), *Effective school desegregation* (pp. 55–84). Thousand Oaks, CA: Sage Publications.

Crenshaw, K., Gotanda, N., Peller, G., & Thomas, K. (Eds.). (1995). *Critical race theory: The key writings that formed the movement.* New York: The New Press.

Crump, D. (1999). *Road to school reform: The Chicago model.* (ERIC Documentation Reproduction Service No. ED 447 606).

Dawkins, M. P. (1983). Black students' occupational expectations: A national study of the impact of school desegregation. *Urban Education, 18,* 98–113.

Dawkins, M. P. (1989). The persistence of plans for professional careers among Blacks in early adulthood. *Journal of Negro Education, 58,* 220–231.

Dawkins, M. P. & Braddock, J. H., II. (1994). The continuing significance of desegregation: School racial composition and African-American inclusion in American society. *Journal of Negro Education, 63,* 394–405.

DeGraaf, N. D., DeGraaf, P. M., & Kraaykamp, G. (2000). Parental cultural capital and educational attainment in the Netherlands: A refinement of the cultural capital perspective. *Sociology of Education, 73,* 92–111.

deMarrais, K. B. & LeCompte, M. D. (1999). *The way schools work: A sociological analysis of education* (3rd ed.). New York: Longman.

Dekker, P. & Uslaner, E. (Eds.). (2001). *Social capital and participation in everyday life.* London: Routledge.

Denzin, N. & Lincoln, Y. S. (Eds.). (1994). *Handbook of qualitative research.* Thousand Oaks, CA: Sage.

Dewey, J. (1938). *Experience and education.* New York: Macmillan Company.

DiMaggio, P. (1976). Social class and arts consumption: The origins and consequences of class differences in exposure to the arts in America. *Theory and Society, 5,* 141–161.

DiMaggio, P. (1982). Cultural capital and school success: The impact of status culture participation on the grades of U.S. high school students. *American Sociological Review, 47*, 189–201.

DiMaggio, P. (1992). *Race, ethnicity, and participation in the arts: Patterns of participation by Hispanics, Whites, and African Americans in selected activities from the 1982 and 1985 surveys of public participation in the arts.* Washington, DC: Seven Locks Press.

DiMaggio, P. & Mohr, J. (1985). Cultural capital, educational attainment, and marital selection. *American Journal of Sociology, 90*, 1231–1261.

DiMaggio, P. & Ostrower, F. (1990). Participation in the arts by black and white Americans. *Social Forces, 68*, 753–778.

DiMaggio, P. & Useem, M. (1978). Cultural democracy in a period of cultural expansion: The social composition of arts audiences in the United State. *Social Problems, 26*, 179–197.

DuBois, W.E.B. (1903). *The souls of black folk.* Chicago: McClurg.

Eckaus, R. (1973). *Estimating the returns to education: A disaggregated approach.* New York: McGraw Hill.

Engel, M. (1984). Ideology and the politics of higher education. *The Journal of Higher Education, 55*, 19–34.

Fagerlind, I. (1975). *Formal education and adult earnings: A longitudinal study on the economic benefits of education.* Stockholm: Almqvist & Wiksell International.

Farkas, G. (1990). Cultural resources and school success: Gender, ethnicity, and poverty groups within an urban school district. *American Sociological Review, 55*, 127–142.

Farkas, G. (1996). *Human capital or cultural capital? Ethnicity and poverty groups in an urban school district.* New York: Aldine De Gruyter.

Franklin, V. P. & Savage, C. J. (2004). *Cultural capital and Black education: African American communities and the funding of black schooling.* Charlotte, NC: Information Age.

Frazier, E. F. (1957). *Black bourgeoisie: The book that brought the shock of self-revelation to middle-class blacks in America.* New York: Free Press.

Freeman, A. (1995). Legitimizing racial discrimination through antidiscrimination law: A critical review of Supreme Court doctrine. In K. Crenshaw, N. Gotanda, G. Peller, & K. Thomas (Eds.), *Critical race theory: The key writings that formed the movement* (pp. 29–46). New York: The New Press.

Freeman, K. (1997). Increasing African Americans' participation in higher education: African American high-school students' perspectives. *The Journal of Higher Education, 68*, 523–550.

Garnier, M. A. & Robinson, R. V. (1985). Class reproduction among men and women in France: Reproduction theory on its home ground. *American Journal of Sociology, 91*, 250–280.

Gaudiani, C. (2000). *The greater good: How philanthropy drives the American economy and can save capitalism.* New York: Times Books.

Gerth, H. H. & Mills, C. W. (1946). *From Max Weber: Essays in sociology.* New York: Oxford University Press.

Giroux, H. (1981). *Ideology, culture, and the process of schooling.* Philadelphia: Temple University.

Glass, G. V. & Hopkins, K. D. (1995). *Statistical methods in education and psychology*, (3rd ed.). Boston: Allyn & Bacon.

Goldhaber, D. (2000). School choice: An examination of the empirical evidence on achievement, parental decision making, and equity. *Educational Researcher, 28*, 16–25.

Goldin, C. (2001). The human capital century and American leadership: Virtues of the past. *Journal of Economic History, 61*, 263–292.

Gonzalez, N. (2002). *School kids/street kids: Identity development in Latino students.* New York: Teachers College.

Gordon, E. W. (1996). The promise of accountability and standards in the achievement of equal educational opportunity. In E. Lagemann & L. Miller (Eds.), *Brown v. Board of Education: The challenge for today's schools* (pp. 151–156). New York: Teachers College.

Gordon, E. W. (2001). Affirmative development of academic abilities. *Pedagogical Inquiry and Praxis, 2*, 1–8.

Gorseline, (1932). *The effects of schooling upon income.* Bloomington: Indiana University Press.

Gouldner, A. (1979). *The future of intellectuals and the rise of the new class.* New York: Seabury Press.

Grootaert, C. & Bastelaer, T. V. (Eds.). (2002). *The role of social capital in development: An empirical assessment.* New York: Cambridge University Press.

Grosskopf, S. & Moutray, C. (2001). Evaluating performance in Chicago public high schools in the wake of decentralization. *Economics of Education Review, 20*, 1–14.

Guba, E. G. & Lincoln, Y. S. (Eds.). (1994). Competing paradigms in qualitative research. In N. Denzin & Y. S. Lincoln (Eds.), *Handbook of qualitative research* (pp. 105–117). Thousand Oaks, CA: Sage.

Habermas, J. (1971). *Knowledge and human interest.* Boston: Beacon Press.

Haddad, W. D. (1981). The World Bank's education sector policy paper: A summary. *Comparative Education, 17*, 127–139.

Hagedorn, L., & Tierney, W. (2002). Cultural capital and the struggle for educational equity. In W. Tierney & L. Hagedorn (Eds.), *Increasing access to college: Extending possibilities for all students* (pp. 1–8). Albany: State University of New York Press.

Haller, A. (1970). Changes in the structure of status systems. *Rural Sociology, 35*, 469–487.

Haller, A. O. & A. Portes. (1973). Status attainment processes. *Sociology of Education, 46*, 51–91.

Hartog, J., & Oosterbeek, H. (1998). Health, wealth, and happiness: Why pursue a higher education. *Economics of Education Review, 17*, 245–256.

Hauser, R., & Daymont, T. (1971). Schooling, ability, and earnings: Cross-sectional findings 8 to 14 years after high school graduation. *Sociology of Education, 50*, 182–206.

Hayes, W. L. (1994). *Statistics* (5th ed.). Fort Worth, TX: Harcourt Brace College Publishers.

Helms, J. (Ed.) (1990). *Black and white racial identity: Theory, research, and practice.* New York: Greenwood Press.

Hess, G. (1999). Understanding achievement and other changes under Chicago school reform. *Educational Evaluation & Policy Analysis, 21,* 67–83.

Heubert, J. P. & Hauser, R. M. (Eds.). (1999). *High stakes: Testing for tracking, promotion, and graduation.* Washington, DC: National Academy Press.

Holme, J. (2002). Buying homes, buying schools: School choice and the social construction of school quality. *Harvard Educational Review, 72,* 177–205.

Hornbeck, D. & Salamon, L. (Eds.). (1991). *Human capital and America's future: An economic strategy for the '90s.* Baltimore: Johns Hopkins University Press.

Hurn, C. (1993). *The limits and possibilities of schooling: An introduction to the sociology of education* (3rd ed.). Boston: Allyn and Bacon.

Institute for Higher Education Policy. (1998). *Reaping the benefits: Defining the public and private value of going to college.* Washington, DC: Author.

Irvine, J. (1990). *Black students and school failure: Policies, practices, and prescriptions.* Westport, Connecticut: Greenwood Press.

Isserles, R., & Dalmage, H. (2000). Cultural capital as rules and resistance: Bringing it home in the introductory classroom. *Teaching Sociology,* 28, 160–165.

Jacobs, J. (1996). Segregation, desegregation, and resegregation. In Lomotey, K. & Teddlie, C. (Eds.), *Forty years after the Brown decision: Implications of school desegregation for U.S. education* (Vol. 13). New York: AMS Press.

Kalmijn, M. & Kraaykamp, G. (1996). Race, cultural capital, and schooling: An analysis of trends in the United States. *Sociology of Education, 69,* 22–34.

Karen, D. (1990). Toward a political-organizational model of gatekeeping: The Case of elite colleges. *Sociology of Education,* 63, 227–240.

Katsillis, J. & Rubinson, R. (1990). Cultural capital, student achievement, and educational reproduction: The case of Greece. *American Sociological Review,* 55, 270–279.

Katz, M. (1992). Chicago school reform as history. *Teachers College Record, 94,* 56–72.

Katz, M., Fine, M., & Simon, E. (1997). Poking around: Outsiders view Chicago school reform. *Teachers College Record,* 99, 117–157.

Keller, R. T. (2001). Cross-functional project groups in research and new product development: Diversity, communications, job stress, and outcomes. *The Academy of Management Journal, 44,* 547–555.

Key, S. (1996). Economics or education: The establishment of American land grant universities. *The Journal of Higher Education, 67,* 196–220.

Kozol, J. (1991). *Savage inequalities.* New York: Harper Perennial.

Labaree, D. (1986). *Proletarianizing the high school teacher.* Washington, DC: National Institute of Education.

Ladson-Billings, G. (1995). Toward a theory of culturally-relevant pedagogy. *American Educational Research Journal,* 32, 465–491.

Lagemann, E. & Miller, L. (Eds.). (1996). *Brown v. Board of Education: The challenge for today's schools.* New York: Teachers College.

Lamont, M. & Lareau, A. (1988). Cultural capital: allusions, gaps, and glissandos in recent theoretical developments. *Sociological Theory, 6,* 153–168.

Landry, B. (1987). *The new black middle class.* Berkeley: University of California Press.

Lareau, A. (1987). Social class differences in family-school relationships: The importance of cultural capital. *Sociology of Education, 60,* 73–85.

Lareau, A. & Horvat, E. (1999). Moments of social inclusion and exclusion: Race, class, and cultural capital in family-school relationships. *Sociology of Education, 72,* 37–53.

Lauglo, J. (2000). Social capital trumping class and cultural capital: Engagement with school among immigrant youth. In S. Baron, J. Field, & T. Schuller (Eds.), *Social capital: Critical perspectives* (pp. 142–167). Oxford: Oxford University Press.

Lawrence, C. (1980). One more river to cross—Recognizing the real injury in Brown: A Prerequisite to shaping new remedies. In D. Bell (Ed.), *Shades of brown: New perspectives on school desegregation* (pp. 48–69). New York: Teachers College.

Lee, V. E. & Croninger, R. G. (1999). *Elements of social capital in the context of six high schools.* (Report No. EA 031052). Washington, DC: Office of Educational Research and Improvement. (ERIC Document Reproduction Service No. ED 454 582).

Lenski, G. (1967). Status inconsistency and the vote: A four nation test. *American Sociological Review, 32,* 298–301.

Lenski, G. (1966). *Power and privilege.* New York: McGraw-Hill.

Levin, H. (1979). *Education and earnings of blacks and the* Brown *decision.* Stanford, CA: Institute for Research on Educational Finance and Governance.

Limits of choice: School choice reform and state constitutional guarantees of educational equality. *Harvard Law Review, 109,* 2002–2019.

Lipman, P. (2002). Making global city, making inequality: The political economy and cultural politics of Chicago school policy. *American Educational Research Journal, 39,* 379–419.

Litten, L. (1980). Marketing higher education: Benefits and risks for the American academic system. *The Journal of Higher Education, 51,* 40–59.

Lomotey, K. & Teddlie, C. (Eds.). (1997). *Forty years after the Brown decision: Social and cultural effects of school desegregation.* New York: AMS Press.

Lord, G. (1977). A dynamic theory of racial differences. In P. A. Wallace & A. LaMond (Eds.), *Women, minorities, and employment discrimination* (pp. 153–186). Lexington, MA: Lexington Books.

Martin, B., & Szeleny, I. (1987). Beyond cultural capital: Toward a theory of symbolic domination. In R. Eyerman & T. Soderquist (Ed.), *Intellectuals, universities, and the state.* Berkley: University of California.

Marx, K. (1996). *Later political writings* (Terrell Carver, Trans. and Ed.). Cambridge: Cambridge University Press. (Original work published 1867)

Matthijs, F. & Parker, L. (1999). Choice: The route to community control. *Theory Into Practice, 38,* 203–208.

McCoy, M. P. (1999). *Black picket fences: Privilege and peril among the black middle class.* Chicago: University of Chicago.

McDonough, P. (1994). Buying and selling higher education: The social construction of the college applicant. *Journal of Higher Education, 65,* 427–446.

McDonough, P. (1997). *Choosing colleges: How social class and schools structure opportunity.* Albany: State University of New York Press.

McNeal, R. (1999). Parental involvement as social capital: Differential effectiveness on science achievement, truancy, and dropping out. *Social Forces, 78,* 117–144.

McNeil, L. M. (2000). *Contradictions of school reform: Educational costs of standardized testing.* New York: Routledge.

Mead, G. (1934). *Mind, self, & society: From the standpoint of a social behaviorist.* Chicago: University of Chicago Press.

Mennell, S., & Goudsblom, J. (1998). (Eds). *Nobert Elias: On civilization, power, and knowledge.* Chicago: University of Chicago Press.

Meyers, J. W. (1971). Forms of status inconsistency. *Social Forces, 50,* 91–101.

Metz, M. (1986). *Different by design.* New York: Routledge.

Mohr, J. & DiMaggio, P. (1995). The intergenerational transmission of cultural capital. *Research in Social Stratification and Mobility, 14,* 167–199.

Morgan v. Kerrigan, (1976). 530 F.2d 401.

Morrow, R. A. & Torres, C. A. (1995) *Social theory and education: A critique of theories of social and cultural reproduction.* New York: State University of New York Press.

Nettles, M. T., Perna, L. W., & Freeman, K. E. (1996). *Two decades of progress: African Americans moving forward in higher education.* Fairfax, VA: Frederick D. Patterson Research Institute of the United Negro College Fund.

Nieto, S. (1996). *Affirming diversity: The sociopolitical context of multicultural education* (2nded.). New York: Longman Publishers.

Oakes, J. (1985). *Keeping track: How schools structure inequality.* New Haven: Yale University.

Ogbu, J. (1986). Black students' school success: Coping with the "burden of 'acting White'". *Urban Review, 18,* 176–206.

Ogbu, J. (1995). Cultural problems in minority education: Their interpretations and consequences—Part one: Theoretical background. *Urban Review, 27,* 189–205.

Olneck, M. (2000). Can multicultural education change what counts as cultural capital? *American Educational Research Journal, 37,* 317–348.

Parcel, T. & Dufur, M. (2001). Capital at home and at school: Effects on student achievement. *Social Forces, 79,* 881–911.

Parcel, T. & Menaghan, E. (1994). Early parental work, family social capital, and early childhood outcomes. *American Journal of Sociology, 99,* 972–1009.

Pascerella, E. & Terenzini, P. (1991). Twenty years of research on college students: Lessons for future research. *Research in Higher Education, 32,* 83–92.

Patterson, J. T. (2001). *Brown v. Board of Education: A civil rights milestone and its troubled legacy.* Oxford: Oxford University Press.

Peller, G. (1997). Cultural imperialism, white anxiety, and the ideological realignment of *Brown.* In A. Sarat (Ed.), *Race, law, and culture: Reflections on Brown v. Board of Education.* New York: Oxford University Press.

Pels, D. (1995). Knowledge politics and anti-politics: Toward a critical appraisal of Bourdieu's concept of intellectual autonomy. *Theory and Society, 24,* 79–104.

Persell, C., & Cookson, P. (1987). Microcomputers and elite boarding schools: Educational innovation and social reproduction. *Sociology of Education, 60,* 123–134.

Pope, W. (1998). Emile Durkheim. In R. Stones (Ed.), *Key sociological thinkers* (pp. 46–58). New York: New York Universities Press.

Porath, Y. (1980). The f-connections: Families, friends, and firms and the organization of exchange. *Population and Development Review, 6,* 1–30.

Portes, A. (1998). Social capital: Its origins and applications in modern sociology. *Annual Review of Sociology, 24,* 1–24.

Putnam, R. D. (1995). *Making democracy work: Civic traditions in modern Italy.* Princeton, NJ: Princeton University Press.

Putnam, R. D. (1997). The prosperous community: Social capital and public life. In F. Ackerman et al. (Eds.), *Human well-beings and economic goals.* Washington, DC: Island Press.

Putnam, R. D. (2000). *Bowling alone: The collapse and revival of American community.* New York: Simon & Schuster.

Ravitch, D. (1980). Desegregation: Varieties of meaning. In D. Bell (Ed.), *Shades of Brown: New perspectives on school desegregation* (pp. 30–47). New York: Teachers College.

Richardson, J. G. (Ed.). (1986). *Handbook of theory and research for the sociology of education.* New York: Greenwood Press.

Riordan, C. (1994). The value of attending a women's college: Education, occupation, and income benefits. *The Journal of Higher Education, 65,* 486–510.

Robinson, R., & Garnier, M. (1985). Class reproduction among mena dn women in France: Reproduction Theory on its home ground. *American Journal of Sociology, 91,* 250–280.

Roscigno, G. J. & Ainsworth-Darnell, J. W. (1999). Race, cultural capital, and educational resources: Persistent inequalities and achievement returns. *Sociology of Education, 72,* 158–178.

Rossell, C. H. (1987). Does school desegregation policy stimulate residential integration?: A critique of the research. *Urban Education,* 21, 403–420.

Rutledge, D. (Ed.). (1995). *Research in race and ethnic relations,* 8th ed. Greenwich, CT: JAI Press.

Sander, W. (2001). Chicago public schools and student achievement. *Urban Education, 36,* 27–38.

Schuller, T., Baron, S., & Field, J. (2000). Social capital: A review and critique. In S. Baron, J. Field, & T. Schuller (Eds), *Social capital: Critical perspectives* (pp. 1–38). New York: Oxford University Press.

Sedlackek, W. & Brooks, G. (1976). *Racism in American education: A model for change.* Chicago: Nelson Hall.

Schultz, T. (1960). Capital formation by education. *Journal of Political Economy, 68,* 571–583.

Schultz, T. (Ed.). (1961). *Investment in human beings.* Papers presented at a conference called by the Universities-National Bureau Committee for Economic Research, New York, NY.

Sheenhan, J. (1973). *The economics of education.* London: George Allen & Unwin.

Smrekar, C. & Goldring, E. (1999). *School choice in urban America: Magnet schools and the pursuit of equity.* New York: Teachers College.

Smith, A. (1953/1776). *An inquiry into the nature and causes of the wealth of nations.* Chicago: H. Regnery.

Smith, M. K. (2001). 'Social capital', *the encyclopedia of informal education.* www.infed.org/biblio/social_capital.htm

Spencer M. B. (1984). Black children's race awareness, racial attitudes and self concept: A reinterpretation. *Journal of Child Psychology and Psychiatry, 25,* 433–441.

Stetar, J. M. (1985). In search of a direction: Southern higher education after the Civil War. *History of Education Quarterly, 29,* 341–367.

Student desegregation plan for the Chicago Public Schools: Recommendations on educational components.

Szelenyi, I. & Martin, B. (1988). The three waves of new class theories. *Theory and Society, 17,* 645–667.

Tatum, B. D. (1997). *Why are all the black kids sitting together in the cafeteria?* New York: Basic Books.

Taylor, W. (1997). The role of social science in school desegregation efforts. *Journal of Negro Education, 66,* 196–202.

Teachman, J. D. (1987). Family background, educational resources, and educational attainment. *American Sociological Review,* 52, 548–557.

Thomson, P. (1952). Ends and means in the finance of higher education. *Journal of Higher Education, 23,* 429–433, 457.

Throsby, D. (2001). *Economics and culture.* Cambridge: Cambridge University Press.

Thurow, L. (1999). *Building wealth: The new rules for individuals, companies, and nations in a knowledge-based economy.* New York: HarperCollins.

Tierney, W. & Hagedorn, S. (Eds.). (2002). *Increasing access to college: Extending possibilities for all students.* Albany: State University of New York Press.

Trent, W. (1997). Outcomes of school desegregation: Findings from longitudinal research. *Journal of Negro Education, 66,* 255–257.

Veblen, T. (1994/1899). *The theory of the leisure class.* New York: Penguin.

Velez, W. (1989). High school attrition among Hispanic and non-Hispanic white youths. *Sociology of Education,* 62, 119–133

Viadero, D. (2000, March 22). Lags in minority achievement defy traditional explanations. *Education Week,* pp. 1–8.

Waldrip, D. R., Marks, W., & Estes, N. (Eds.). (1993). *Magnet school policy studies and evaluations.* Austin, TX: Morgan Printing.

Walsh, J. R. (1935). Capital concept applied to man. *Quarterly Journal of Economics, 49,* 255–285.

Webb, L. (1982). Race, education, and the new economics. *The Journal of Negro Education, 51,* 372–391.

Wells, A. S. (1993). *Time to choose: America at the crossroaads of school choice policy.* New York: Hill and Wang.

West, K. C. (1994). A desegregation tool that backfired: Magnet schools and classroom segregation. *The Yale Law Journal, 103,* 2567–2592.

Westlake School Admission Battle Tuesday. (1975, April 7). *Chicago Sun Times,* p. 3A.

Willie, C. V. (1988). The intended and unintended benefits of school desegregation. *Urban League Review, 11,* 127–135.

Willie, C. V. (2001). The contextual effects of socioeconomic status on student achievement test scores by race. *Urban Education, 36,* 461–478.

Wolcott, H. F. (2001). *Writing up qualitative research* (2nd ed.). Thousand Oaks, CA: Sage Publications.

Woolcock, M. (1998). Social capital and economic development: Toward a theoretical synthesis and policy framework. *Theory and Society, 27,* 151–208.

World Bank. (1990). *World Development Report 1990.* Washington, DC: World Bank.

Yu, C. M. & Taylor, W. L. (Eds.). (1997). *Difficult choices: Do magnet school serve children in need? Report of the Citizens Commission on Civil Rights.* Washington, DC: Rock Creek Publishing.

Zhou, M. & Logan, J. R. (1989). Returns on human capital in ethic enclaves: New York City's Chinatown. *American Sociological Review, 54,* 809–820.

Zweigenhaft, R. L. (1993). Prep school and public school graduates of Harvard: A longitudinal study of the accumulation of social and cultural capital. *Journal of Higher Education, 64,* 211–225.

PART I

EDUCATIONAL CONTEXT AND THE CONSUMER ASPECTS OF CAPITAL

CHAPTER 2

LEGAL INFORMATION AS A SOURCE OF SOCIAL CAPITAL

The Need for Broad and Sustained Engagement in School Policy Affairs

Mario S. Torres
Texas A & M University

INTRODUCTION

Public awareness of law and policy is greater than ever before. Presumably, much of the growing interest may be explained by expansion and development in deliverable and accessible information through various media forms. With respect to schooling, media such as the television and the Internet have not only accelerated traditional functions such as grade delivery and parent–teacher communication, but this has also resulted in greater transparency in how schools govern and operate. On the other hand, less is known about to what degree parents and students critique policy and legal information pertaining to schooling. While socioeconomic factors may predict levels of student/community engagement and action, little research has looked into this engagement in legal affairs. All the while, studies sug-

Contemporary Perspectives on Capital in Educational Contexts, pages 61–78

gest differences in the manner in which students are educationally served or legally treated, most notably by race and class.

This chapter uses the concept of social capital to propose levels and types of student, parental, and community engagement in school governance that may be needed to monitor student freedoms and protections. While other forms of capital (e.g., cultural, human, intellectual) are equally important, social capital is an especially relevant concept to rights and privileges of individuals, especially minors. Legal information can serve as a powerful source of social capital, according to Coleman (1988), as it "[provides] a basis for action" (p. 104). Along with information, norms and trust prove to be equally powerful types of social capital but are of less concern to the present chapter. As such, this chapter examines the complex interface between social capital and law using desegregation and student privacy as exemplars and further argues that schools and communities must routinely scrutinize the laws under which schools are governed to evaluate their desirable and undesirable social effects. Implications for leadership, practice, and policy are discussed in conclusion.

SOCIAL CAPITAL AND THE LAW—INDIVIDUALS AND COMMUNITIES AS AGENCIES OF SOCIAL CAPITAL

Interest in social capital continues to endure. Its broad utility and application to social issues attracts scholars and practitioners alike (Portes, 2000a). The concept originated mostly through the work of James Coleman and Pierre Bourdieu, both suggesting that people benefitted from social interactions and relationships. For Coleman, community interaction and involvement yielded benefits to the individual primarily but also imparted benefits to the community (Portes, 2000a). Coleman (1988) recognized the collective benefits of capital in his work on purposive action where the "actions of the individual in particular contexts" were tantamount to the "development of the organization" (p. 96). That social capital could be transacted solely for community rather than individual benefits was however not a claim advanced by Coleman. Rather, Coleman (1988) insisted on social capital serving a "function" consisting of "social structures" and "actors." To Coleman (1988), "social capital is productive, making possible the achievement of certain ends that in its absence would not be possible" (p. 98). Putman and others (Portes, 2000a) would later morph the individual-based theory to one encompassing benefits to groups such as communities, cities, states, and so on. While pursuing individual and collective benefits may be socially desirable, they may occasionally work at cross purposes. For instance, social interactions for purely selfish political reasons may do little to serve the public good.

In contrast to Coleman, Bourdieu looked at social capital as a more transactional act, meaning the relationships that individuals form through their own capital may be used to generate other forms of capital (e.g., economic). Simply put, Bourdieu (Portes, 2000a) believed capital in whatever form was "fungible" whereby assets or goods of one could be exchanged for assets or goods of another (Portes, 2000a). Less clear for Bourdieu were the dynamics involved in the exchange. While exchanges from an economic standpoint seem straightforward, the narrative preceding the exchange is far less clear. As Portes (2000b) depicts Bourdieu's approach to social capital, it is "characterized by less transparency and more uncertainty" (p. 45). Portes (2000b) notes further that "transactions involving social capital tends to be characterized by unspecified obligations, uncertain time horizons, and the possible violation of reciprocity expectations" (p. 45). Bourdieu's interpretation of social capital also included the concept of social reproduction. That is, relationships were instrumental in reinforcing status and class, which tacitly or overtly maintained social stratification.

Despite differences, Coleman and Bourdieu appear to agree that *agency* or the means by which problems are acted or not acted upon may be partly due to the intensity and quality of relationships and interactions at personal and collective levels. Law as *agency* for action can serve as a powerful form of social capital. Agency has been clearly demonstrated by routine judicial involvement in numerous social issues such as abortion, desegregation and speech. For law to serve as a valid source of social capital, its content must be available not only to legal professionals but to the general citizenry (Wise & Schauer, 2007). As Wise and Schauer note, "When governments—federal, state, and local—provide easy access to legal information, they are helping citizens not only learn about the law, but also further their common goals and strategies" (p. 268).

Wise and Schauer (2007) further suggest two ways law can evolve into forms of social capital. First, law naturally forms collectivities based on a common legal problem. Groups divided ideologically (e.g., atheists and religious fundamentalists) may display an equally zealous interest in defending student speech protection under the Equal Access Act, despite core differences in beliefs. Law effectively becomes the common denominator for groups despite their incompatibility, which by effect generates social capital. Second and most relevant to this chapter, legal information in its purest form can serve as a source of social capital. For this reason, one form of capital especially relevant to a discussion of law and policy is consumer capital (Schultz, 1961). Under the purview of consumer capital, human productivity is not reflected solely by gains in economic wealth but rather the extent to which the consumption of education improves life outcomes or, as Schultz (1961) notes, the "quality of consumption of students throughout the rest of their lives" (p. 13). As such, education as a desired good is reflected through the totality of consumable inputs, both material and social, and its impact on life outcomes. These inputs come in a variety of forms—quality teachers, instructional resources, and facilities being the most familiar and prominent. One study suggests that student relationships with teachers can serve as a powerful form of consumer capital for students, especially for at-risk students (Croninger & Lee, 2001).

The consumption of education capital remains largely enigmatic, however, primarily because factors such as culture and wealth mediate the consumption. Consequently, well-intentioned law and policy are often thwarted because of unforeseen costs or a lack of individual or group capacity to sustain their proper application. For instance, it has been suggested that programs aimed at assisting the disadvantaged will demand the "labor, investments, and involvement" of the consumers themselves (Cahn, 1997, p. 64). While substantial attention has been placed on addressing unequal access to educational quality, the goal of developing critical consumers of legal capital in schools and communities has generated far less interest. This is not to suggest that communities are not conscious and active in and around legal issues. In point of fact, legal information is commonly grappled over. Most common are groups, many times latent, that coalesce around state tax increases, bond elections, textbook adoptions, and the selection of science curricula. Less common are groups—particularly those involving students and historically marginalized and powerless populations—that contest the legal and ethical posture of school policy. Many of these policies, state and local, have a direct bearing on access to educational quality, such as school funding. Yet, while more engagement is crucial, the prevailing standard of student and parent involvement in school affairs may actually be working counter to the acquisition of social capital for some students and families. As Carvalho (2001) notes, traditional notions of involvement and participation often mirror values ascribed to the middle to upper class and as such capture little of the complexity of community, culture, and family. Thus, as Carvalho (2001) hypothesizes, these involvement efforts project the image that education is the sole province of the school rather than a shared and valued enterprise. All in all, these issues seemingly call for a new form of civic action and engagement in legal matters that is nurtured rather than stifled by the school.

LEGAL INFORMATION AS A SOURCE OF SOCIAL CAPITAL

Why is critique of legal information necessary? In law, there are no assurances or guarantees. While law appears supra-rational, self-evident, and resistant to human desire, politics, and local influence (Clark, 1985), history has shown context is a pivotal factor (Rebell & Block, 1982). To further argue the need for *agency*, scholars suggest that people and organizations are impacted by law in unique ways, which may lead to inconsistent implementation and outcomes. For instance, the scope and breadth of the legal issue (Johnson 1967; Wasby, 1973) or social policy (Johnson & Canon, 1984) may influence the degree to which individuals or groups comply to the language and spirit of the ruling. Other factors worthy of note include political and value cultures (Dolbeare, 1973; Peltason, 1961; Wasby, 1973), the population to which the ruling is intended (Johnson & Canon, 1984; Wasby, 1973), resources and commitment (Johnson & Canon, 1984), the unanimity of the court ruling (Marshall, 1989), and the clarity and manner in which the ruling was communicated (Levine & Becker, 1973; Wasby, 1973).

Our current understanding of judicial impact comes largely at the hands of the *Brown v. Board of Education* (1954) ruling. Supreme Court decisions seldom implement themselves (Johnson & Canon, 1984). After the monumental 1954 decision of *Brown v. Board of Education*, much of the maligned treatment of minority student populations persisted unabated as Southern states, in protest to desegregation orders, instituted creative measures to block the ruling in *Brown* from achieving its intent. Blaustein and Ferguson (1973), in their analysis of the aftermath of *Brown*, found that some states, in an effort to frustrate federal government orders to integrate, imposed the pre-Civil War doctrine of interposition (i.e., the notion that states maintain constitutional authority over Federal government acts) in an attempt to nullify the sovereignty of the court over state affairs. Other states created a morass of regulation and policy aimed at making recourse or access to litigation extremely difficult if not impossible for black plaintiffs. In certain states, school systems determined enrollment eligibility and classification upon results of an aptitude test (e.g., the ability to maintain proper health and morals), which in effect maintained separate schools, but not explicitly by race.

Perhaps the best-known illustration of judicial defiance occurred at Central High School in Little Rock, Arkansas (Reutter, 1982). Governor Faubus, in opposition to a school board desegregation plan approved by a district court, deployed the state national guard to prevent the enrollment of nine black students. An injunction filed by the U.S. Attorney General and affirmed by the Eighth Circuit Court of Appeals ordered the Governor to vacate all troops and proceed with the student integration plan with which the Governor complied. Efforts by the local authorities to preserve order among the protestors were problematic, however, forcing President Eisenhower to dispatch federal troops to facilitate the integration.

By accounts of the Little Rock school board, problems of various magnitude ensued for the school district in providing adequate safety and protection to the nine students. The school board issued a request to the district court for a two-and-a-half-year delay in implementing the plan, which the district court approved. By the district court's assessment, compliance to the integration order was unattainable at the time in light of a school environment engulfed in pandemonium; social unrest among parents, students, and staff; violence targeted against black students; and a considerable financial burden of maintaining order incurred by the district (Reutter, 1982). The Eighth Circuit Court of Appeals disagreed, reversing the district court ruling and thereby ordering the plan to be implemented at once. Although the Supreme Court issued *Brown II* (1955) to clarify and validate the demands set forth by the initial *Brown* (1954) ruling in addition to ordering its enforcement, acts of resistance and avoidance persisted.

Southern school systems were dismayed with the U.S. Supreme Court's psychological rationale for desegregation, which many southern politicians argued was anchored in illegitimate, "pseudo-scientific" evidence (Mitau, 1967, p. 61). In South Carolina, school districts were penalized and stripped of state aid if they chose to comply with a pupil transfer policy. A Louisiana constitutional amendment divided schools for whites and blacks and denied state funding to those schools that chose to comply with the *Brown* ruling. Alabama, Arkansas, Florida, Georgia, and Mississippi repealed compulsory education statutes and issued state tuition grants for whites to invest in private school education (Mitau, 1967).

The aftermath of *Brown* illustrates the import and necessity of social debate and discussion of legal information at all levels. Efforts at generating social capital for the underprivileged have routinely met resistance in direct and indirect ways. The school board's insistence on an implementation delay due to logistical and social considerations that would ease the transition fell short of meeting the spirit of *Brown* according to the U.S. Eighth Circuit and furthermore signified an attempt to deny social capital. The reasons that impel states and school systems to undermine law are complex. While social capital was gained in principle, in reality, the capital eluded its intended beneficiaries through deceitful acts and practices. Clearly in this instance, masked "dynamics" of race, culture, and power prevented lawful exchanges of capital. Perhaps of equal concern was the implicit message conveyed in *Brown* that a Eurocentric education was superior to all other forms. The perverse implication seemed to suggest white curriculum and white teachers represented advancement in educational quality and that other schools were inferior. A social movement led by the Reverend Martin Luther King would soon follow, dismantling more social constructions of inequality. In the 1960s, people were generally more exposed to the indignities brought upon blacks and other groups of color through various forms of media. Information became a powerful and indispensible vehicle to generating social capital for the underprivileged. Today, controversial policy areas such as immigration, national defense, and healthcare can be accessed through numerous forms of media and critiqued by unprecedented numbers. Case in point, the state of Arizona's legislative attempt to endorse aggressive measures (e.g., harassment) to control immigration implicates a host of legal questions such as whether immigration policy is the sole province of the federal government (http://www.nytimes.com/2010/07/29/us/29arizona.html?scp=2&sq=arizona&st=cse). By what has unfolded by way of rallies and demonstrations for and against the measure, legal information served as a crucial wellspring of capital for civic engagement. Without question, the same level of community activism is needed as far as school policy goes.

Persistent struggles to desegregate and mounting threats to student privacy illustrate the importance of legal information as a critical source of social capital. The *Keyes* case, while a symbol for unmet expectations from the civil rights crusade, serves as a cautionary tale for acquisition of social capital from a legal context.

Avoidance: The Case of Keyes

In *Keyes v. School District* (1973), parents of children attending the Denver public system accused the school district of engaging in system-wide *de jure* segregation practices by gerrymandering attendance zones, adding mobile classroom units, and issuing staff decisions based on race to create a dual education system. Both the Colorado federal district court and the Tenth Circuit Court of Appeals disagreed with the plaintiffs' argument on grounds that *de jure* segregation practices were confined to one particular area and not others and that one could categorize blacks and Hispanics together as a Fourteenth Amendment category. The Supreme Court, refuting the lower court findings, ruled Hispanics and blacks were categorically identical with respect to Fourteenth Amendment classification and that "intentional segregation as to a portion of a school system is not devoid of probative value in assessing the school authorities' intent with respect to other parts of the same school systems" (*Keyes*, p. 207). Vacating the lower court rulings, the court remanded the case to the federal district court for further deliberation of evidence and facts to confirm whether the school board's actions were indeed deliberate and intentional.

However, the pursuit of racial enrollment equity for the Denver district would result in years of legal and political chaos (Fishman & Strauss, 1990). The district was ordered to address the marked racial discrepancies in racial distribution and devise a plan of action to prevent future segregation enrollment patterns for the entire district. The initial plan offered by the school board in 1974 and adopted by the federal district court included the establishment of a busing system, rezoning attendance lines, reassigning students, and specific requirements for racial percentages.

Other aspects of the plan, which included dual campus placements, policy exemptions afforded to schools serving high percentages of Hispanic and bilingual children, and efforts at school consolidation, were rejected by the U.S. Court of Appeals because of their potential adverse effect on establishing racial balances.

Citing effects of the present plan on outward migration of the Anglo population, the federal district court in 1976 approved a school board request to issue a moratorium on student reassignment to allow time to make appropriate modifications to the existing plan. Board politics, procrastination, and philosophical turf battles would continue, until finally the Consensus Plan, which called for the continued busing of children, more walk-in schools, and the creation of two magnet campuses, was agreed upon by the board and district court in 1982—thirteen years after the filing of the *Keyes* suit.

Although the plan had finally met acceptance, the aftermath of this decade-long struggle was merely an overture for further battles and resistance. For example, the Denver school district's racial landscape had changed dramatically since the *Keyes* ruling, which, in effect, weakened the substance and purpose of the new plan. The school board became more politically divisive, and bureaucratic politics sabotaged efforts to support implementation. School staffs were ill prepared to follow and abide by the plan's goals and mission. Classrooms became the microcosm of segregation as Anglo students routinely enjoyed more academic advantages. The episodic legal challenges would persist for the district for years to come. As this case aptly illustrates, the implementation of court orders are seldom self-executing.

Other school systems devised duplicitous strategies (i.e., *defacto* segregation) to evade or avoid the spirit of the *Brown* ruling, which routinely required federal court intervention. Although school systems complied procedurally with "racially neutral student assignment policies," (Reutter, p. 76) it was entirely possible to resist the intent and substance of those orders. Accordingly, state and local systems employed several such strategies including instituting transfer policies, gerrymandering, altering feeder patterns, and shutting down school systems to elude orders (Gordon, 1989; Mitau, 1967; Reutter, 1982).

While capital in the form of equality was sought and gained incrementally over the course of more than a decade, judicial acts were unable to stall the outward migration of families away from the cities. Judicial decisions in other civil liberty realms would encounter similar resistance and policy manipulation. Despite the legalization of abortion and constitutional protection given to women in *Roe v. Wade* (1973), numerous efforts by federal and state legislatures were made to dissolve the ruling. Laws and statutes routinely circumvented *Roe* by attaching more restrictive provisions including the requirement of spousal approval, proof of residency, and stripping economic assistance to poor women who sought the procedure (Bond & Johnson, 1982). Many hospitals overtly refused to offer such services (Johnson & Canon, 1984).

As to student privacy, growing concerns persist over safety as well as the expectations of privacy for students. This balance is difficult to strike. Recent evidence may indicate schools' preferences to forsake student privacy rights to secure public confidence concerning safety and order. This more recent legal phenomenon too deserves more scrutiny.

Student Privacy and the Perils of Discretion

In *Tinker v. Des Moines,* Justice Fortas wrote that a balance be struck between the duty of the school to maintain discipline and order and the school's obligation to secure Constitutional protections for all its students. Recent events like Columbine, however, have greatly impacted the complexion of student entitlements with respect to privacy and discipline. National exposure (Beger, 2002; Stefkovich & Guba, 1998; Stefkovich & Miller, 1999; Stefkovich & O'Brien, 1997) to incidents of violence in schools has prompted school systems to institute regular searches of students and state legislatures to enact more punitive statutes aimed at curbing crime and violence (e.g., metal detectors, security guards). While schools turn to policy and practices that seemingly serve the good of the organization, the concern becomes to what extent students sacrifice legitimate expectations of privacy.

The contours of student privacy have been largely shaped by four U.S. Supreme Court opinions. Although the three most recent cases resolved disputes around drug testing (*Vernonia v. Acton, Board of Education v. Earls*) and strip searches (*Safford v. Redding*), it was the seminal case of *New Jersey v. T.L.O.* (1985) that established the legal doctrine for student searches and privacy. In truth, it was commonly believed prior to *T.L.O.* that schools could act *in loco parentis* or in the place of the parent even if searches needed to be administered. The court in T.L.O. disagreed. The court held that students are entitled to a legitimate expectation of privacy and consequently searches should be administered under a standard of reasonableness.

The court in *T.L.O.* concluded searches must be justified at their inception and reasonable in scope in light of the age, maturity, and gender of the student. To be justified, according to the court, there is reasonable belief to suspect "the search will turn up evidence that the student has violated or is violating either the law or the rules of the school" (*T.L.O.*, p. 342). As for the scope of the search, the court ruled a search is "permissible in scope when the measures adopted are reasonably related to the objectives of the search and not excessively intrusive in light of the age and sex of the student and the nature of the infraction" (*T.L.O.*, p. 342). While the language appears clear and direct, it is by no means interpreted the same. Prior studies on the student privacy have noted disparities in the manner students are searched (Stefkovich, 1994; Stefkovich & Miller, 1999; Stefkovich & O'Brien, 1997; Stefkovich & Torres, 2003).

A search policy in Champaign, Illinois illustrates how policy and practical responses to a law can vary and at times deviate from the law's seemingly obvious intentions. The following district policy derives from a statute established by the Illinois General Assembly giving school officials the power to

> inspect and search places and areas such as lockers, desks, parking lots, and other school property and equipment owned or controlled by the school, as well as personal effects left in those places and areas by students, without notice to or the consent of the student, and without a search warrant. (McIntyre, 2000, p. 1034)

The school district's posted parking policy read: "The person driving any vehicle is deemed to consent to a complete search of the vehicle for any reason" (p. 1026). McIntyre (2000) suggests such policies serve to discourage offensive behavior and provide notice. While it was reported that hyper-aggressive searching seldom occurred and the policy was meant only to promote safety, the message seems to convey that students' rights may be expendable if the situation warrants.

Research on student privacy demonstrates a critical need for individuals and groups to be discerning about how students' privacy rights are treated. A prior study by the author (Torres & Callahan, 2008) of 230 search-and-seizure cases revealed discrepancies in the manner searches were conducted and decided in schools with contrasting ethnic profiles. The study compared case features and outcomes between cases that occurred between schools with student populations 84% or greater of students of color and those having 4% or less students of color. Differences were found in factors related to the enrollment of children of color within the school where the search occurred, the reliability of the information used to initiate the search on the student, and whether the search would later result in criminal prosecution. The analysis revealed that students in the high minority school settings lost more in court, their searches were motivated more by less reliable information (anonymous tips, hunches), and in substantially more (42%) of the cases, criminal prosecution was sought.

As these findings suggest, context may be important consideration. Nevertheless, the sensitivity of the courts and the general public to students' rights still hinges largely on social circumstances and values. Consider the ruling in *Tinker v. Des Moines* (1969). That a ruling upholding students' passive protest of the Vietnam War as constitutionally protected behavior in the late 1960s could occur in the same period of American history marked by widespread social change seems more than a mere coincidence. While social policy and law may be impacted by broader social movements, local agencies are entrusted to apply the law appropriately.

Yet, as the aftermath of numerous desegregation rulings reveals, compliance seldom occurs in a rational fashion. The inconsistency in implementation may be due largely to the functional limits of the judicial system. Courts generally resist urges to make policy and opt rather to map out a legal framework. Its logic is oftentimes incremental, cautious, and indeterminate (Salomone, 1986). Some suggest the Supreme Court operates in a methodical way to maintain public approval (Barclay & Birkland, 1998; Jacob, 1972; Johnson & Canon, 1984; Salomone, 1986). More often, the Court tends to move cautiously on certain issues that are too important but not unimportant (Goldman & Jahnige, 1985). Hence, the responsibility falls largely on policymakers, practitioners, and the general public to design the policy and monitor compliance. This can spell problems if rulings are misunderstood and misapplied.

Justice Stevens, in the dissenting opinion in *T.L.O.*, warned of an overly permissive standard, which he argued would validate searches for the most "trivial" of school infractions (*T.L.O.*, p. 377). Similarly, Sanchez (1992) argued the narrow *T.L.O.* standard could potentially provoke administrators to react to a false sense of student guilt if the student refused to oblige the suspicion. Although greater discretionary latitude (e.g., the involvement of police, intrusive searches) may be needed in some circumstances, it would seem too that its misuse slowly chips away at fundamental rights. Groups such as the American Civil Liberties Union (ACLU) have expressed concern over the effects of an ambiguous ruling that failed to establish clear limits to schools' power to search students. The ACLU expressed concern over the undifferentiated powers of police and school officials with respect to standards of suspicion that are used to initiate a search and use of evidence recovered (Sims, Karpatkin, & Goodman, 1983).

Because the issue of use of evidence was not addressed in *T.L.O.*, it has given lower courts and local schools considerable discretion in determining how evidence should be managed. As Dolbeare (1973), Wasby (1973), and Peltason (1972) theorized, when discretion and authority are distributed in uncertain terms, the manner in which a critical decision or choice is made is subject to a wide array of influence. In the case of large school settings and schools in predominantly minority communities, local and state political and value cultures exert considerable influence on the magnitude of certain legal issues.

For instance, a question may arise as to whether student infractions should be channeled through school disciplinary policy or state criminal statutes. School administrators in large urban environments may feel more compelled by community politics and the risk of poor publicity to use whatever measures are necessary to sanction the student. Conversely, administrators in smaller school systems may confront less external pressure to involve the criminal justice system and instead resort to school disciplinary policies. To this point, a report by the NAACP Legal Defense and Education Fund (http://naacpldf.org/files/case_issue/Dismantling_the_School_to_Prison_Pipeline.pdf) suggests that conditions within certain types of schools lead to undesirable social outcomes especially for children of color. The study suggests that long-term negative social outcomes (i.e., incarceration) stem largely from harsh disciplinary treatment of children, particularly children of African-American descent, and inadequate school resources. All the while, the cases clearly suggest that the manner by which law and policy is administered is largely particularistic.

FOSTERING ENGAGEMENT IN STUDENTS' RIGHTS: IMPLICATIONS FOR SOCIAL CAPITAL

In view of the high level of uncertainty surrounding students' rights, policymakers, leaders, practitioners, and communities should be more discerning to the limitations and unintended consequences of law. The outcomes of desegregation and privacy rulings plainly illustrate the contextualized nature of legal interpretation and implementation. Without a comprehensive and open assessment of the actions, behavior, and/or capacities expected from local schools and agencies, laws and policies may never realize their intentions.

While social capital provides a framing through which the pursuit of social benefits seems reasonable and attainable, it may not account fully for the effect of powerful extraneous factors (i.e., education, age, sex). Prior research clearly illustrates how even negative behaviors may manifest from "bonding capital" as groups of people with similar values and characteristics exert power and control over basic rights and privileges (Putnam, 2000). Be that as it may, schools serve the public good and in principle are obliged to maintain systems that grant reasonable public access and control. From the standpoint of consumer capital, families and communities must own a larger stake in the educational enterprise if students are to maximize the inputs offered by formal schooling. Largely absent are opportunities for students and parents to serve as authentic co-producers of education (Cahn, 1997). Yudof, Kirp, Levin, and Moran (2002) argue in a similar way that "expertise and professionalism have their place, but ultimately there should be an ongoing process of consultation and consent that renders the exercise of expertise and professionalism acceptable" (p. 855).

Moreover, law can bridge individuals and groups together who otherwise share little in common. As Wise and Schauer (2007) note, "the bonds that are created by shared legal status can be understood as a form of social capital, the mechanism of cooperation and coordination by which communities perform tasks that could not be performed, or could not be performed as well, by unconnected individuals acting atomistically" (p. 268). Thus, bonding and bridging opportunities through civil engagement in school legal matters can potentially break new ground in forming social capital.

During the course of designing school policy, much consideration will need to be given to culture, values, and perhaps people's moral proclivities to comply with the law. As one study suggests (Bilz & Nadler, 2009), it may be the more preferred or even desired path for collectivities to recognize the moral imperative to change prior to governments exercising force and compulsion through policy. The political and financial prospects are far more enticing when the passage of a law only reinforces existing moral shifts in attitude and behavior. Yet, with minimal exactness in measuring moral shifting, laws and codes must do more than function symbolically—they must regulate and in the context of this discussion protect and safeguard fundamental rights. Furthermore, mandates oblige people and groups to critique "pre-existing" mandates of what is "believed to matter" rather than "what matters" (Welner, 2001, p. 234). Contrary to pressing diversity as a *common* resource or privacy as a *common* democratic ideal, schools are prone rather to resort to normative behaviors and routines that reinforce the status quo. Legal information may, as Wise and Schauer (2007) suggest, "provide a platform for discussion and debate that makes it clear to all of those who are discussing and debating that they are involved in a common enterprise" (p. 271).

Steady engagement in school legal affairs will demand a unique form of civic activism nurtured by the school and community—one that must involve those who have been historically excluded from the political process. Mobilizing social collaboration will not happen easily. Research on political participation suggests that the cultivation of social capital occurs in complex ways among individuals and groups of people (Ling, 2006; Liu, Wright-Austin, & D'Andra-Orey, 2009). One study found that church attendance as a construct for social capital largely explained African American political participation using voting as a proxy (Liu et al., 2009). The authors suspect, however, that the lack of a modern "social movement" to "mobilize the political capital of African Americans" may be minimizing the potential for social activism. In contrast, a study by Ling (2006) suggests the monolithic descriptions of the African-American church largely fail to capture the immense social and ideological diversity within the African-American religious community. Moreover, while the pursuit of broader political involvement is praiseworthy, dependence on and faith in general metaphors like bonding or bridging may actually "gloss over" the inequalities and conflicts that manifest in modern social conditions (Lewandowski & Streich, 2007, p. 592). The aftermath of the *Brown, Keyes,* and *T.L.O.* rulings seem to more closely reflect this stance. Many school systems, especially following the major desegregation decisions, resorted to forms of manipulation. In each of the rulings, context consistently impacted the application of the law. Because context has consistently been a factor, it would seem that sustained civic engagement in school legal affairs would be essential.

To be sure, the explanations for why and when citizens coalesce for civic engagement are varied. Notions such as "social capacity" and "loose connections" do, however, add promising perspectives toward reconsidering civic involvement in school legal affairs. Under social capacity, public relationships are facilitated to accomplish civic goals with little governmental direction and control (Lichterman, 2009). It assumes that people act collectively and take responsibility, in the absence of governmental compulsion, to address pressing social concerns. As for "loose connections" (Wuthnow, 1998), people's engagement in the civic process is described as very efficient, individualistic, and interest-specific vis-à-vis the broad issue spectrum of major political parties (e.g., the Democratic and Republican parties), and clubs (e.g., Lions Club). The concept of "loose connections" suggests people today prefer short-term, flexible commitments to engaging in social problems (e.g., occasional tax referendums, board member elections) as opposed to sustained and open-ended personal investments (Lichterman, 2009).

Although its efforts are ongoing, grassroots organizations like the Texas Civil Rights Project (TCRP) demonstrate the promise and potential of social capacity to address legal problems for the underserved. The TCRP started as a community-based, non-profit group in 1990. Situated now in Texas' Rio Grande Valley, it is committed to primarily serving the legal needs of historically marginalized groups. Because of the region's many social challenges, it has largely focused its efforts in legal areas such as "voting rights, police and border patrol misconduct, sex discrimination, employment bias, privacy, disability rights, grand jury discrimination, and traditional civil liberties," to name a few (http://www.texascivilrightsproject.org/?cat=37). Among the accomplishments it lists as "achievements we are most proud of," it includes no-cost legal services available to the poor and persons who are victims of discrimination, numerous human rights reports, extensive amount of newspaper editorials, and training of 22,000 lawyers and community members on civil liberty topics (http://www.texascivilrightsproject.org/?cat=41).

While efforts like the TCRP are highly desirable, they are difficult to replicate given scarce resources including facilities, personnel, time, and money. Short-term, issue-based coalitions may, on the other hand, work more effectively than sustained efforts like the TCRP in certain settings and situations. Regardless of the approach, civic engagement into students' rights will need to occur with greater intensity and frequency. Policymakers must recognize the organizational complexities inherent in policy and law. First, because authority and practice tend to be "loosely coupled," school officials possess more discretion in their duties, which, in the case of searches, may infringe inappropriately upon student civil liberties. Second, in view of the effect of values and politics on the choices of school officials, most notably in desegregation rulings, greater external oversight and community engagement is needed on how various policies are interpreted and implemented across diverse school contexts. Third, school administrator and teacher certification policies should adopt more rigorous standards with respect to knowledge of education law. Many problems linked to inappropriate discretion or misinterpretation of law result directly from deficits in legal knowledge.

For schools and families, the implications for policy engagement are far reaching given today's social conditions. First, much needed is internal and external scrutiny of present practices relating to student and parental involvement in legal affairs. The ever-present mindset in schools is that conflict is damaging and runs contrary to the mission of the school. Conflict can lead to very positive outcomes. Schools must welcome and embrace critique of law and policy and perhaps take a significant role in facilitating civic engagement in different ways. One possibility is establishing community forums to discuss critical legal matters in an open, candid, and meaningful way or offer colloquia around legal matters such as student privacy, special education, sex education, and accountability. Schools can further open lines of communication by setting up listservs and websites that relay legal information and permit open discussion on legal matters. Within such a model, the school serves as one key enabler but certainly not the only enabler in setting conditions that not only support maximum utilization of school inputs but create and sustain norms of trust between schools and communities. As addressed early on (Cahn, 1997), these ambitious and necessary initiatives will demand the varied talents and gifts of teachers, parents, community members, and students to ensure their success. In reality, however, time and energy are precious resources for both schools and families so such initiatives need be planned thoughtfully. Second, teachers should seize upon the law as an instructional asset and, in doing so, encourage authentic student democratic engagement. Conditions should be established that enlist students to academically explore the social benefits of law and challenge its ethical posture by looking through alternative lenses such as justice, critique, and caring. Ideally, from the analysis, students discover tacit dimensions such as power and privilege and realize that not all needs and values are addressed on equal terms. Moreover, such activities will hopefully motivate students to speak out and engage in civic discussions around legal matters. Hence, students are better prepared to be consumers of law.

As for attending to justice, all stakeholders must pay closer attention to patterns or trends that reveal disproportionate rulings by demographic profile. Although states have taken more aggressive steps to regulate school powers, especially in the area of search and seizure in schools, greater civic engagement may serve as a meaningful hedge against differential treatment. In the area of policy development, school district leaders and policymakers should also be mindful to the limitations of law. Although political pressures may in some ways dictate a policy agenda, school boards and district administrators are obligated to comply with state and federal law. The decisions and actions of practitioners will largely determine whether rules and policy are unfairly tipped against students. In reality, school administrators and teachers are typically the final legal arbiters. However, as this chapter suggests, a more concerted community-wide effort to closely scrutinize legal information pertaining to educational and disciplinary practices may engage more citizens in the political process, thereby creating rich opportunities for social capital acquisition.

REFERENCES

Archibold, R.C. (2010, July 28). Judge blocks Arizona's immigration law. *The New York Times*. Retrieved from http://www.nytimes.com/2010/07/29/us/29arizona.html?scp=2&sq=arizona&st=cse

Barclay, S. & Birkland, T. (1998). Law, policymaking, and the policy process: Closing the gaps. *Policy Studies Journal, 26*(2), 227–243.

Beger, R. R. (2002). Expansion of police power in public schools and the vanishing rights of students. *Social Justice, 29*(1/2), 119–130.

Bilz, K & Nadler, J. (2009). Law, psychology, and morality. *Psychology of Learning and Motivation, 50,* 101–131.

Blaustein, A. P. & Ferguson Jr., C. C. (1973). Avoidance evasion and delay. In T. L. Becker & M. M. Feeley (Eds.), *The impact of Supreme Court decisions* (pp. 100–109). New York: Oxford.

Board of Education v. Earls, 536 U.S. 822 (2002).

Bond, J. R. & Johnson, C. A. (1982). Implementing a permissive policy: Abortion services after *Roe v. Wade. American Journal of Political Science, 26*(1), 11–24.

Brown v. Board of Education, 347 U.S. 483 (1954).

Brown v. Board of Education II, 349 U.S. 294 (1955).

Cahn, E.S. (1997). The co-production imperative. *Social Policy, 27,* 62–67.

Carvalho, M.E. (2001). *Rethinking family–school relations: A critique of parental involvement in schooling.* Mahwah, NJ: Erlbaum.

Clark, G. L. (1985). *Judges and the cities: Interpreting local autonomy.* Chicago: University of Chicago Press.

Coleman, J.S. (1988). Social capital in the creation of human capital. *The American Journal of Sociology, 94,* 95–120.

Croninger, R.G. & Lee, V.E. (2001). Social capital and dropping out of high school: Benefits to at-risk students of teachers' support and guidance. *Teachers College Record, 103*(4), 548–581.

Dolbeare, K. (1973). The Supreme Court and the states: From abstract doctrine to local behavioral conformity. In T. L. Becker & M. M. Feeley (Eds.), *The impact of Supreme Court decisions* (2nd ed., pp. 202–210). New York: Oxford University Press.

Fishman, J. J. & Strauss, L. (1990). Endless journey: Integration and the provision of equal educational opportunity in Denver's public schools: A study of *Keyes v. School District No. 1*. In B. Flicker (Ed.), *Justice and school systems: The role of the courts in education litigation* (pp. 185–232). Philadelphia: Temple University.

Goldman, S. & Jahnige, T. P. (1985). *The federal courts as a political system* (2nd ed.). Philadelphia: Harper & Row.

Gordon, W. M. (1989). School desegregation: A look at the 70s and 80s. *Journal of Law & Education,18*(2), 189–214.

Jacob, H. (1972). Policy making and norm enforcement. In J. B. Grossman & R. S. Wells (Eds.), *Constitutional law and judicial policy making* (pp. 26–30). Hoboken, NJ: Wiley.

Johnson, C. A. & Canon, B. C. (1984). *Judicial process: Implementation and impact.* Washington, DC: Congressional Quarterly.

Johnson, R. M. (1967). *The dynamics of compliance: Supreme Court decision-making from a new perspective.* Evanston, IL: Northwestern University Press.

Keyes v. School District No. 1. (1973). 413 U.S. 189.

Levine, J. P. & Becker, T. L. (1973). Toward and beyond a theory of Supreme Court impact. In T. L. Becker & M. M. Feeley (Eds.), *The Impact of Supreme Court Decisions* (2nd ed., pp. 230–244). New York: Oxford University Press.

Lewandowski, J. & Streich, G. (2007). Democratizing social capital: Liberal egalitarianism. *Journal of Social Philosophy, 38*(4), 588–604.

Lichterman, P. (2009). Social capacity and the styles of group life: Some inconvenient wellsprings of democracy. *American Behavioral Scientist, 52*(6), 846–866.

Ling, P. (2006). Social capital, resource mobilization and origins of the civil rights movement. *Journal of Historical Sociology, 19*(2), 202–214.

Liu, B., Wright-Austin, S.D., & D'Andra-Orey, B. (2009). Church attendance, social capital, and black voting participation. *Social Science Quarterly, 90*(3), 576–592.

Marshall, T. R. (1989). Policy-making and the modern court—When do Supreme-Court rulings prevail? *Western Political Quarterly, 42*(4), 493–507.

McIntyre, J. B. (2000). Empowering schools to search: The effect of growing drug and violence concerns on American schools. *University of Illinois Law Review* (3), 1025–1052.

Mitau, G. T. (1967). *Decade of decision: The Supreme Court and the constitutional revolution, 1954–1964.* New York: Scribners.

NAACP Legal Defense and Education Fund (2010, n.d.). *Dismantling the school to prison pipeline.* Retrieved from http://naacpldf.org/files/case_issue/Dismantling_the_School_to_Prison_Pipeline.pdf

New Jersey v. T.L.O. (1985). 469 U.S. 325.

Peltason, J. W. (1961). *Fifty-eight lonely men.* New York: Harcourt Brace.

Peltason, J. W. (1972). A political science of public law. In J. B. Grossman & R. S. Wells (Eds.), *Constitutional law and judicial policy making* (pp. 8–9). Hoboken, NJ: Wiley.

Portes, A. (2000a). The two meanings of social capital. *Sociological Forum, 15*(1), 1–12.

Portes, A. (2000b). Social capital: Its origins and applications in modern sociology. In E. Lesser (Ed.), *Knowledge and social capital: Foundations and applications* (p. 43–67). Boston: Butterworth-Heinemann.

Putnam, R.D. (2000). *Bowling alone.* New York: Simon & Schuster.

Rebell, M. A. & Block, A. R. (1982). *Educational policy making and the courts.* Chicago: University of Chicago.

Reutter, E. E. (1982). *The Supreme Court's impact on public education*: Phi Delta Kappa & National Organization on Legal Problems in Education.

Roe v. Wade, 410 U.S. 113 (1973).

Safford v. Redding, 557 U.S. __ (2009).

Salomone, R. C. (1986). *Equal education under the law.* New York: St. Martin's Press.

Sanchez, J. M. (1992). Expelling the Fourth Amendment from American schools: Students' rights six years after T.L.O. *Journal of Law & Education, 21*(3), 381–413.

Schultz, T.W. (1961). Investment in human capital. *The American Economic Review, 51*(1), 117.

Sims, C. S., Karpatkin, D. H., & Goodman, B. S. (1983). *Amicus curiae brief for New Jersey v. T.L.O.* (83712): The American Civil Liberties Union.

Stefkovich, J. A. (1994). Strip searching after Williams: Reactions to the concern for school safety? *West's Educational Law Reporter, 93,* 1107–1123.

Stefkovich, J. A. & Guba, G. J. (1998). School violence, school reform, and the Fourth Amendment in public schools. *International journal of educational reform, 7*(3), 217–225.

Stefkovich, J. A. & Miller, J. A. (1999). Law enforcement officers in public schools: Student citizens in safe havens? *Brigham Young University Education and Law Journal,* Winter, 24–69.

Stefkovich, J. A. & O'Brien, G. M. (1997). Students' Fourth Amendment rights and school safety—An urban perspective. *Education and Urban Society, 29*(2), 149–161.

Stefkovich, J. A. & Torres, M. T. (2003). The demographics of justice: Student searches, student rights, and administrator practices. *Educational Administration Quarterly, 39*(2), 259–282.

Texas Civil Rights Project. (n.d.). *Homepage for Texas Civil Rights Project.* Retrieved from http://www.texascivilrightsproject.org/

Tinker v. Des Moines, 393 U.S. 503 (1969).

Torres, M.S. & Callahan, J.L. (2008). Investigating fourth amendment judicial outcomes across contrasting minority school settings. *Education and Urban Society, 40*(3), 377–405.

Vernonia v. Acton, 515 U.S. 646 (1995).

Wasby, S. L. (1973). Toward impact theory: An inventory of hypotheses. In T. L. Becker & M. M. Feeley (Eds.), *The impact of Supreme Court Decisions* (2nd ed., pp. 214–217). New York: Oxford University Press.

Welner, K.G. (2001). *Legal rights, local wrongs.* SUNY Press: Albany.

Wise, V.J. & Schauer, F. (2007). Legal information as social capital. *Law Library Journal, 99*(2), 267–284.

Wuthnow, R. (1998). *Loose connections: Joining together in America's fragmented communities.* Cambridge, MA: Harvard University Press.

Yudof, M.G., Kirp, D., Levin, B., & Moran R. (2002). *Educational policy and the law.* Belmont, CA: West: Thompson Learning.

CHAPTER 3

A PEDAGOGY OF SELF-DEVELOPMENT

Making Room for Alternative Forms of Capital

Carlos R. McCray
Fordham University

Floyd D. Beachum
Lehigh University

The skill sets needed to become successful (i.e., maintaining a decent standard of living and the enhancement of posterity) in today's society have changed drastically over the last fifty years. The world has become increasingly smaller in the sense of the plexus of communication, networking, and commerce that is taking place throughout the world. The corollary of such a plexus of interaction among nation-states has been the increasing demand for human capital regardless of geopolitical demarcations to supply the ever-growing need for those who can perform certain requirements and tasks of the 21st century (Bartee & Brown, 2007; Brooks, 2010; Fried-

Contemporary Perspectives on Capital in Educational Contexts, pages 79–100

man, 2005). Regardless of whether one feels that countries are headed in the right direction with regard to trade policies, national goals, etc., the fact remains that human capital is going to be required to satisfy the demands of technological advances that lead to prosperity and posterity of not only nation-states but also individual families (Brooks, 2010; Hornbeck & Salamon, 1991). The great recession that started in 2008 was ominous with regard to those who could be adversely impacted by unstable economic conditions. In reference to this recent economic crisis, Herbert (2010) opined, "The people suffering the most drastic employment reversals in this recession have been those who were in the lower-income groups to begin with—the young, less well-educated workers, especially black and Hispanic high school dropouts, and certain categories of service workers, such as food preparers and building cleaners" (p. 1).

Alas, for those individuals who were not afforded the opportunity to cultivate skill sets suited for the jobs and careers of the 21st century, the future can seem extremely bleak. Many African American students and students of color from low-wealth communities are now being disregarded and ostracized due to the lack of cultural, social, and economic capital they have accumulated in their lifetime, and it is placing them at a disadvantage in the learning process with the corollary being a life of unemployment and underemployment (Bartee & Brown, 2007; Beachum & McCray, in press; Dantley, 2009; Ferguson, 2001; Herbert, 2010; Wilson, 2009).

As we initiate this analysis, it is important to clarify our definitions related to capital (i.e., economic, human, and cultural). Economic capital has to do with finances and wealth. "Individual possessions determine the amount of exchange and assets, both material and non-material, that are involved" (Bartee & Brown, 2007, p. 1). Human capital can be defined as the "acquired skills, knowledge, and ability of human beings" (Hornbeck & Salamon, 1991, p. 3). Our use of cultural capital here relates to "certain kinds of acquired knowledge, value systems, language patters, and/or visible dispositions" (Bartee & Brown, 2007, p. 1). The comprehension of these notions is critical to understanding the frameworks and ideas noted in the following discussion.

In order for African American students and students of color from low wealth backgrounds to have a fighting chance to succeed in this increasingly global economy where the acquisition of the aforementioned capital is crucial, there has to be an earnest interrogation into how educators and school leaders are engaging these student populations. This earnest critique and interrogation must lead to the dismantling of approaches that have intentionally or unintentionally promoted unilateral diktats leading to social injustices (Bartee & Brown, 2007). Dantley (2003) provides a compelling rationale as to why the unpacking of hegemonic practice has to take place. According to Dantley (2003),

> The classical model of education has dismissed most students in the urban core. They have been deemed to be atonal, incorrigible, educable mentally retarded, at risk, or some other code description for being the other. The traditional cadence and harmonic structure of schools have been alien and somewhat uncomfortable to many of the students who reside in America's urban centers. Their everyday lives are marked by dissonance and syncopation, and therefore the traditional strategy of schools, played in a steady rhythm with pleasant harmonic progressions, leaves many voiceless and left behind in the educational process. (p. 278)

Dantley (2009) went on to lament that the "ultimate goal" for educational leaders must be an "institutional reconstruction" that is undergirded by egalitarian principles (p. 45).

Bartee and Brown also echo Dantley's sentiment response to the conditions facing many low wealth black and brown students in the educational system. The return on investment (ROI) that seems to be the barometer for whether the gains in educational attainment (both for the individual and society) are worth the actual expenditures by the government and tax payers is somewhat nebulous when put into practice. According to Bartee and Brown (2007), "A number of scholars have found positive correlations between educational attainment and increased earnings" (p. 9). Not only is there a positive correlation between a person's level of educational attainment and their wealth, but there is also a positive correlation with their health and their level of schooling (Bartee & Brown, 2007). An important inquiry in this chapter is how serious are educators and administrators taking the notion of ROI with regard to their understanding and acknowledgement of the importance of ensuring that black and brown students from low wealth urban areas are given the resources to enhance their chances in life via increased educational opportunities.

For the purposes of this chapter, we intend to use W. E. B. Du Bois' notion of second sight and double consciousness (Gooding-Williams, 2009) along with Feagin and Feagin's (1978) principles of organizational discrimination to explain how many African American students and students of color from low-wealth communities are severely limited in the amount of capital they have access to within the educative process. Further, we intend to illuminate how educators and school leaders' perception of the *lack of capital* students of color have is detrimentally impacting this student population. Thus, we purport here that in order for Du Bois' notion of second sight and double consciousness to dissipate among students of color, school leaders should commit themselves to eradicating discrimination. We offer here culturally relevant leadership and a commitment to a pedagogy of self-development undergirded by Yosso's (2005) six alternative forms of capital as a framework for the amelioration of racial and class hostility.

THE (UN)INTENDED DISSEMINATION OF CAPITAL WITHIN THE EDUCATIVE PROCESS

In the late 19th century, the venerable African-American scholar W. E. B. Du Bois, came up with the concepts of second sight and double consciousness, in an attempt to explain how racist policies and perceptions can have negative impacts on African Americans' sense of self-efficacy (Gooding-Williams, 2009). According to Gooding-Williams, Du Bois was adamant about his concerns with regard to how second sight and double consciousness affect African Americans' ability to enjoy what the Declaration of Independence affirms to every individual—their God-given right to "life, liberty, and the pursuit of happiness." Du Bois hypothesized how second sight gave African Americans the unique ability to comprehend the world as those who promulgate racist edicts see the world, and it also allowed African Americans to see themselves as others who held those racist feelings perceived them (Gooding-Williams, 2009). Gooding-Williams went on to explain Du Bois's notion of double consciousness. Du Bois saw double consciousness as the corollary of second sight—the often false self-conscious development of a social group (i.e., African Americans) as a result of their deployment of second sight (Gooding-Williams, 2009). Gooding-Williams promulgated his interpretation of Du Bois's pronouncement of double consciousness:

1. The sensation of seeing oneself through the revelation of the other world
2. The sensation of always looking at oneself through the eyes of others
3. The sensation of measuring one's soul by the tape of a world that looks on in amused contempt and pity

These sensations that Du Bois outlined with regard to how African Americans were able to view the world inevitably impacted the cultural, social, and economic capital they perceived themselves to have as well as the capital they ultimately projected to others. In other words, the very racism and prejudice that African Americans encountered led to the notion of second sight which ultimately produced a Double Consciousness. The difficulty of African Americans attaining cultural, social, and economic capital (i.e., privileged status) due to the visceral level of racism that they encountered from outside entities was heightened as they internalized the perceptions that were projected upon them (Gooding-Williams, 2009).

We believe that Du Bois's notions of second sight and double consciousness also have a role in the educative process and can impact African-American students and students of color from low-wealth communities just as much as they have impacted and continue to impact African Americans in general. Much research has been conducted and explicated on the deficit theory concept within the educative process. The conflation of deficit thinking with Feagin and Feagin's (1978) principles of organizational discrimination is an amalgamation of second sight and double consciousness to prevail among the most vulnerable of students.

Deficit thinking and its impact on the educative process of African-American students and students from low-wealth communities have been espoused by educational scholars (Lightfoot, 2009; McKenzie, 2001; Rodriguez, 2004; Valencia, 1997; Valencia & Solorzano, 1997; Yosso, 2005) throughout the years. Rodriguez and Fabionar (2010) stated that the deficit model and thinking are usually "explanatory models that locate the phenomenon of educational 'disadvantage' within the students' cultural backgrounds or communities... rather than framing the problem as a lack of institutional responsiveness to students' diverse educational needs" (p. 57). Deficit thinking among educators and school leaders who serve students of color and students from low-wealth communities is problematic on two levels. First, it allows those who are entrusted with educating to capitulate to the prevailing thought that there is only so much they can do with regard to educating poor students with insufficient economic means as well as students of color. It provides educators a way to contravene such axioms as "all students can learn" and embrace the notion of mediocrity while oxymoronically espousing the notion of meritocracy. Second, it gives educators and school leaders the perception that their educational charge is to provide unequivocal amelioration to students as a result of their "parents, home lives, their communities, and even their genetics" (McKenzie, 2001, p. 265). This type of thinking dehumanizes students of color and students from low-wealth communities and potentially eliminates capital they are bringing with them to school. Thus, it explicitly places cultural pluralism on the sideline and makes readily known that the "master identity" in the internal school structure is "European American, upper-middle class, English speaking, and male" (Nieto, 2000, p. 35).

Thus, deficit thinking within the internal structure of the school is undergirded by what Feagin and Feagin (1978) have coined as discriminatory behavior. According to Feagin and Feagin, there are four types of discrimination that can exist within an organization, and unfortunately, our schools are not exempt from these types of discriminatory behaviors. Feagin and Feagin (1978) proffered that the four types of discriminatory behaviors are (1) isolated discrimination, (2) small groups discrimination, (3) direct institutionalized discrimination, and (4) indirect institutionalized discrimination. As was indicated, deficit thinking, along with overt and covert racist assumptions, undergirds each of these four types of discriminations—thereby severely diminishing capital students have at their disposal. Isolated discrimination occurs within the organization when an individual has gone rogue from the "on the book" mission of the school. The educator has implicitly or explicitly brought her or his biases into the educative process. In this instance, isolated discrimination can lead to uneven, arbitrary, and subjective disciplinary referrals by the educator towards students whom the educator perceives to be already at a deficit (Ferguson, 2001; McCray & Beachum, 2006). This type of discrimination can lead to the placing of students of color into lower tracks as well as preventing them from entering gifted and talented programs (Jackson, 2008). Such decisions are originally acknowledged at the classroom level. Obiakor, Obiakor, Garza-Nelson, and Randall (2005) have found that when the teacher operates off the deficit model as well as the concept of isolated discrimination, it can lead to misidentification, miscategorization, misplacement, and misinstruction/misintervention.

The next form of discrimination Feagin and Feagin (1978) identified was small group discrimination. At this level, the hegemony that is found within the educator is projected by a concentric group who all share the same beliefs, attitudes, and dispositions that are undergirded by racist and classist perspectives that further reinforce the isolation of students from low-wealth communities and students of color who have not acquiesced to the aforementioned *master identity*. The small group discrimination practice within the educative process helps to authenticate the perfunctory deficit decision making that has been made by the individual educator. Even though small group discrimination practices can have a cogent effect on African-American students and students of color, such practices are still at risk of being anemic without the codified sanction of direct institutionalized discrimination. The codified sanction of direct institutionalized discrimination in the educative process is operationalized in many facets. According to Dantley (2009), "the bureaucratization of discriminatory behavior, as evidenced in public schools... results in public spaces that have become places of internal colonialism. The schools become the sites where the propagation of a racist agenda is realized but cloaked in a language of excellence, accountability, and proficiency" (p. 41).

Such discriminatory behavior is operationlized via the discrepancy in the funding of schools with regard to those schools found in the brown and Black communities juxtaposed to those schools found in the suburbs serving a predominately upper-class community. It is also operationlized as a result of an implicit admission of defeat by large districts to "teaching to the test"—a pseudo "assembly line" or "cookie cutter" educational approach where democratic citizenry education (Dantley, 2009) is dismissed as a waste of time. Direct institutionalized discrimination is also operationlized with the disproportionate number of students of color who are suspended and expelled due to subjective infractions without regard to the apparent pipeline to nowhere. Beachum and McCray (in press) suggest,

> In the pipeline of young Black boys' education, it seems as if it goes something like this—from the classroom to the principal's office, and then on to suspension and expulsion, from suspension and expulsion, on to becoming a high school dropout, and then on to prison. At the very best, it seems the special education placement of young Black boys represent a half-way house where they do their time waiting for what seems to be their prophetic and inevitable educational journey.

In essence, it would be a dereliction of duty, given the United States' history and the level of institutionalized discrimination found within this country, to not critique and interrogate whether our schools are adequately serving predominately brown and black students as well as the students from low-wealth communities.

The final form of Feagin and Feagin's (1978) discrimination that occurs within an organization is indirect institutionalized discrimination. This form of discrimination takes place when seemingly innocent practices and procedures produce a school atmosphere that is undergirded by racism and bigotry. According to Dantley (2009), "The rituals and forms that emanate from this... type of discrimination... appear to be harmless.... Yet, without being critically interrogated, they often secure racist policies and inequitable treatment of people of color in institutions unknowingly" (p. 42). This statement by Dantley definitely highlights how racism and bigotry can become pervasive within schools and have a negative impact on those who have not conformed to what is perceived by educators and school leaders to be an "effective and equitable system" (Yosso, 2005, p. 75). However, the statement by Dantley also underscores the need to constantly interrogate school policies and procedures as well as individual and groups' assumptions and dispositions to prevent the marginalization of students of color and students from low-wealth communities. But this type of interrogation and critique of schools due to its contradictory nature is problematic, as pointed out by Yosso (2005): "schools most often oppress and marginalize while they maintain the potential to emancipate and empower" (p. 74). In order for the emancipation and empowering of students, especially students of color and those from low-wealth communities to come to realization, educators and school officials must become more cognizant in how the perceived *lack of capital* by students of color can drastically impact their educational achievement.

RECOGNIZING ALTERNATIVE FORMS OF CAPITAL IN THE MIST OF RACIAL AND CLASS-BASED HOSTILITY

As was intimated earlier, when sociology scholar W.E. B. Du Bois came up with the concepts of second sight and Double Consciousness, he was explicating how racism and bigotry had a tremendous toll on African Americans' efforts in finding their place in a society that was undergirded by such pathological ideology (Gooding-Williams, 2009). Du Bois believed that the Black and White communities were two disparate communities with the distinct possibility of aggregation taking hold only if undergirded by a sense of what multiculturalist refer to as cultural pluralism (McCray, Alston, & Beachum, 2006). This is evident in Du Bois' Fisk Commencement address entitled, "Of Our Spiritual Striving", in 1898. This speech was also a commemoration of Du Bois graduating from Fisk University a decade earlier (Gooding-Williams, 2009). In this speech, Du Bois lectured on the need for Blacks to learn from White American society as well as in the spirit of reciprocity America learning from Black Americans. Du Bois conveyed to his audience,

> He [the Black American] would not Africanize America, for America has too much to teach the world and Africa. He would not bleach his Negro soul in a flood of white Americanism, for he knows that Negro blood has a message for the world. He simply wishes to make it possible for a man to be both Negro and an American, without being cursed and spit upon by his fellows, without having the doors of Opportunity closed roughly in his face. (As cited in Gooding-Williams, 2009, p. 83)

This passage by Du Bois from his Fisk University commencement address illuminates what he felt is the need for cultural pluralism to undergird American society, where two disparate groups are recognized has having capital.

Unfortunately, in many of our schools serving the black and brown as well as students of low wealth, this form of capital pluralism ceases to exist. Instead, educators and school officials have capitulated to the pedagogical practices undergirded by a correspondence theory comparable to Paulo Freire's (1973) Banking Model (where teachers "deposit" knowledge into students' minds as opposed to co-creating learning spaces and opportunities) combined with racist undertones as well as overtones. This, in essence, has led educators and school officials to assume the position of untrained missionary aesthetes—all but ignoring capital students of color bring with them to the educative process. Even though Du Bois in his conceptualization of the "Talented Tenth" viewed favorably the notion of *men* who were "missionaries of culture," he firmly believed that such dissemination had to be undergirded by a strong sense of mutual understanding between those who were doing the dissemination and those who were on the receiving end. Here, we submit that those educators and school officials who come to the table with a bias against students of color and students from low-wealth communities are like untrained missionary aesthetes (Feagin & Feagin, 1978). Thus, the critical query is how can African-American students as well as students of color enhance their own sense of self-efficacy in light of the notions of second sight and double consciousness? Part of the answer entails educators and school leaders recognizing that students of color have forms of capital even if they are not readily recognizable and valued by the organization (Franklin, 2002; Yosso, 2005).

Scholars (Beachum, Obiakor, & McCray, 2007; Foster, 2009; Franklin, 2002; Perry, Steele, & Hilliard, 2003; Tillman, 2009; Venkatesh, 2006; Wilson, 2009; Yosso, 2005) have maintained that cultural and social capital does exist among students of color as well as within their communities. As we have intimated, when educators and school officials choose to ignore or look down upon the cultural and social capital that students of color and their communities manifest, second sight and double consciousness have the potential to not only effect their academic achievement but their behavior as well. Yosso (2005) points out that "various forms of capital nurtured through cultural wealth include *aspirational, navigational, social, linguistic, familial, and resistant capital*" (p. 69). Yosso goes on to say that "these forms of capital draw on the knowledge students of color bring with them from their home communities into the classroom" (p. 69).

The *aspirational* form of capital Yosso (2005) has referred to deals with students of color's notion that there is a better tomorrow, and the expectation that the educative process will nurture the ambition and goals they have within them. Many African American students who are faced with daily despair still maintain high hopes for a better tomorrow through the means of education (Foster, 2009; Wimberly, 2002). According to Foster (2009),

> whereas the substantial numbers of African American students in K–12 schools held high expectations for attending college and other postsecondary institutions, only slightly more than half (56 percent) of them were progressing toward their goals, as compared to 89 percent of White students who had the same or similar aspirations. (p. 161)

Yosso's (2005) second form of capital is *linguistic* capital. Yosso indicated that this form of capital includes "multiple language and communication skills" (p. 78). According to Yosso,

> In addition, these children most often have been engaged participants in a storytelling tradition, that include listening to and recounting oral histories, parables, stories . . . and proverbs . . . . This repertoire of storytelling skills may include memorization, attention to detail, dramatic pauses, comedic timing, facial affect, vocal tone, volume, rhythm and rhyme. (pp. 78–79)

Unfortunately, this form of capital can actually work against students of color as well as those from low-wealth communities (Ovando, 2001). This type of capital can easily be parlayed into increased academic achievement but is instead looked upon as a deficit needing to be ameliorated. The use of linguistic capital as a gatekeeper to other forms of capital and perhaps as a barrier to goals and aspirations was made evident when Senator Harry Reid Spoke of then candidate Obama as being attractive to voters because he was "light skinned and had no 'Negro dialect.'" The "Negro Dialect" or Black English Vernacular (Hymes, 1981; Ogbu, 1999; Ovando, 2001; Perry & Delpit, 1998) that Senator Reid was speaking of might be sufficient grounds to keep a person out of the White House as far as voters are concerned. However, it is a mistake for educators and school leaders to juxtapose the "Negro dialect" or Black English with Standard English as a barometer for intellect and a gatekeeper for academic achievement (Delpit, 2002; Hilliard, 2002). Ovando (2001) has found that languages and dialects are cultivated within cultures and communities because they meet the needs of groups with regard to their customs and backgrounds. Thus, it is pedagogical malpractice for educators to treat students who have not mastered Standard English as educationally anemic and not capable of high achievement (Ovando, 2001).

The two other forms of capital that Yosso (2005) conveyed that students of color bring with them to the educational organization are *familial* capital and *social capital*. These two forms of capital intersect with one another. Yosso (2005) explained that *familial* capital "engages a commitment to community well being and expands the concept of family to include a more broad understanding of kinship" (p. 79). Thus, *social capital* likewise solidifies the "commitment to the community" through well-established "networks of people and community resources" (p. 79). *Familial* and *social capital* have also been viewed as essential by African-American scholars (Beachum, Obiakor, & McCray, 2007; Du Bois, 1903/1989; Foster, 2009; Karenga, 1989; McCray, 2008; Shelby, 2005) with the hopes of allowing those within the African American community who are fortunate enough to achieve their professional and personal aspiration to reach out and form relationships of solidarity with those who are less fortunate (Gooding-Williams, 2009; McCray, 2008; Shelby, 2005). This notion is what undergirded much of Du Bois' lifelong research—the belief that prosperous African Americans would reach back and help those who have yet to make it (Gooding-Williams, 2009; McCray, 2008; Shelby, 2005). Beachum, Obiakor, and McCray (2007) identified such a model as *community uplift*. McCray (2008) recognized such an effort as an *insurgency*. Fordham (1991) recognized such activity as *fictive kinship*, and Shelby (2005) conceptualized it as *Black solidarity*. Regardless of the terminology used, it calls on schools to not only recognize the *individual efforts* of African Americans' aspiration but to also embrace the *collective efforts* (Karenga, 1989). McCray (2008) "opined that *individual values* along with the *collective principles*... are needed for the improvement of the education that many Black youth [and students of color] are experiencing" (p. 264, emphasis added).

Another form a capital identified by Yosso (2005) is *navigational capital.* This form of capital is the "ability of [students of color] to maneuver through institutions not created with Communities of Color in mind" (p. 80). The Feagin and Feagin (1978) concepts of direct and indirect institutional discrimination elucidate the need for African-American students and students of color to have navigational capital at their disposal in order to achieve academically. Scholars (Allen & Solorzano, 2001; Alva, 1991; Perry et al., 2003) have found that students of color, despite "racial hostility" (Alva, 1991, p. 19), have continuously found ways to circumvent the unaccommodating school environment and achieve at high levels. Nevertheless, it would be a dereliction on our part to suggest that all African-American students have mastered the art of navigating the racial hostility found in many schools.

In essence, many African-American youth, especially those within the inner city have yielded to the structural impediments (Wilson, 2009) outlined by Feagin and Feagin (1978) with the corollary being an increased level of resignation (i.e., dropouts, underachievement, acting out, etc.) (Gregory & Mosely, 2004; Thomas & Stevenson, 2009). The navigational capital that African-American students and students of color bring with them to the educative process is contingent upon a level of cultural pluralism that allows students to build upon their self-efficacy that has long been established within their communities (Foster, 2009). According to Hersey, Blanchard, and Johnson (1996), "Resignation or apathy occurs after prolonged frustration, when people lose hope of accomplishing their goal(s) in a particular situation and withdraw from reality and the source of their frustration" (p. 31). Unfortunately, there has been a plethora of resignation among African-American students from the within the inner city (Day-Vines & Day-Hairston, 2005; Ferguson, 2001; Skiba & Peterson, 1999). In many of our urban schools, the dropout rate is increasing exponentially among these student populations. In fact, according to Chaddha, Wilson, Venkatesh (2008), "the urban graduation rate is only 34.6 percent compared to a suburban graduation rate of 81.5 percent... a gap of 47 percentage points" (p. 83). This ushering out of students is especially high among black males, with the dropout rate approaching fifty percent in many urban schools (Cosby & Poussaint, 2007).

The final form of capital Yosso (2005) identified pertaining to African American students and students of color was *resistant capital.* Yosso elucidated that resistant capital "refers to those knowledges and skills fostered through oppositional behavior that challenges inequality" (p. 80). The problem with resistant capital displayed by African American students is educators and school leaders often mistake such capital as deviant behavior in need of immediate correction. For most educators, it is a cognitive dissonance to conceive resistant conduct as an affront to the racial inequality and biases that might exist within the school climate and culture. Referring back to Du Bois' notion of second sight, African-American students and students of color not only have a firm understanding of themselves, but can recognize when educators and school leaders view such understanding as a deficit in need of drastic modification. The resistant capital has been part of the African-American community from the inception of the United States via resistance to slavery, inferior mental capacity, inadequate aesthetic appeal, inadequate educational facilities, and unequal rights (Bell, 2004; Carruthers, 1999; Collins, 2005; Feagin, 2001; Foster, 2009; Quarles, 1987). With regard to the continued manifestation of racial biases within schools, Foster (2009) says, "Unlike the physical assault that characterized the journey of earlier African Americans seeking access and admission to public education, large numbers of African American students in public schools today are targets for psychic assaults that demean their intellectual ability and competence and make them vulnerable to educational malpractice" (p. 157).

Thus, it would be a mistake for educators and school officials to presume that African American students and students of color from the poorest communities will suddenly relinquish any form of resistance in light of racial and class biases they are experiencing at school. Instead, educators need to work diligently to reduce the prejudicial judgments and biased behaviors that give rise to such resistance. Yosso (2005) has found that when such efforts are made by educators and school officials, *resistance capital* can be parlayed into a transformative resource that motivates students to perform academically as well as socially.

CULTURALLY RELEVANT LEADERSHIP FOR THE ENHANCEMENT OF CAPITAL

As we have indicated in the beginning of the chapter, students of color are acutely aware of how they are perceived by educators and school officials. We have referred to this awareness as the concept of second sight. In this chapter, we have also used Du Bois' concept of double consciousness to illustrate how these students internalize the perceptions educators and school leaders have of them. Indeed, a precept of Du Bois' double consciousness is the sensation of looking at oneself through the eyes of others. The inevitable corollary of looking at oneself through the eyes of others is the measurement of oneself based on such perceptions (Williams-Gooding, 2009). The amalgamation of Du Bois' second sight and double consciousness along with Feagin and Feagin's (1978) principles of organizational discrimination makes the educative process for African-American students and students of color problematic and all but disregards alternative forms of capital they bring with them. Feagin and Feagin's (1978) principles of organizational discrimination makes it clear that racial and class biases exist at multiple levels throughout an organization. At each level of Feagin and Feagin's (1978) types of discrimination, there are embedded assumptions that cultural, social, and economic capital at the macro level are the only relevant forms of capital (Yosso, 2005). In other words, if African-American students and students of color have not managed to attain what is tantamount to middle-class whites' education, dialect, and lexicon (cultural capital) as well as the "right" connections and networks (social capital), they are quickly labeled as being at a disadvantage (i.e., deficit thinking) (Bourdieu & Passeron, 1977; Lightfoot, 2009; McKenzie, 2001). It is also quite evident that there is an educational benefit to students who have considerable wealth and material possessions (economic capital) at their disposal (Bourdieu & Passeron, 1977; Nesbitt, 2009).

School leadership for the 21st century requires additional innovative knowledge, skills, and dispositions than in previous years. It is apparent that the demographic changes that are taking place in U.S. schools will continue to increase, encompassing more ethnic, racial, and economic diversity (Villegas & Lucas, 2002). These trends should alter the way in which schools serve diverse student populations in order to achieve educational excellence as well as equity (Obiakor & Beachum, 2005). Unfortunately, inadequate attention to the increasing ethnic and racial diversity can lead to a culture where African-American students and students of color are implicitly as well as explicitly devalued. School leaders must have the passion as well as the will to ensure that the school culture and climate promotes high expectations while valuing the ethnic and racial diversity found within their schools. Lindsey, Roberts, and Campbell-Jones (2005) indicated the following with regard to school leaders unearthing the bigotry found within their schools:

> Educational leaders who pursue the goals of pluralistic and democratic schooling act intentionally with the belief that all children and youth not only have the capacity to learn but also are learning something about themselves and others at every moment. Although these democratic educators would acknowledge that most U.S. schools are very successful in the work of educating the students for whom they were designed, they recognize that this designated group is a narrow, unicluster of students who represent the mainstream European American individualistic values that dominate public education in the United States. (p. xix)

The duty of all school leaders is to efficiently and effectively serve all students who enter their doors. We offer a framework called culturally relevant leadership as a way for school leaders to conceptualize and carry out the task of addressing the needs of all learners.

Culturally relevant leadership is a conceptual approach for educators, especially in leadership positions, to serve all students in a manner that maximizes educational excellence and equity. It borrows from earlier notions of culturally relevant pedagogy (Ladson-Billings, 1994) and culturally responsive pedagogy (Gay, 2000). However, culturally relevant leadership focuses on those with greater leadership responsibility in schools. The three basic elements of culturally relevant leadership include (1) liberatory consciousness, (2) pluralistic insight, and (3) reflexive practice.

These three tenants of culturally relevant leadership work together, assisting the leader in learning new information, processing that information, applying it to specific situations, reflecting based on experience, and engaging in practice informed by theory and vice versa. Liberatory consciousness is akin to critical consciousness and seeks to raise awareness levels and increase knowledge with regard to diversity and social justice. Dantley and Tillman (2010) have indicated that "leadership for social justice investigates and poses solutions for issues that generate and reproduce societal inequalities" (p. 20). Educational leaders thereby seek out opportunities to expand their horizons theoretically, philosophically, and intellectually. Pluralistic insight has to do with educators' attitudes towards students. It leans toward an affirming and positive notion of students (especially students of color) that acknowledges the uniqueness of their experiences and their rich diversity and the alternative forms of capital they bring (Yosso, 2005). Tatum (2007) asserts,

> Regardless of our own racial or ethnic backgrounds, we have all been exposed to racial stereotypes and flawed educational psychology, and unless we are consciously working to counter their influence on our behavior, it is likely that they will shape (subtly perhaps) our interactions with those who have been so stereotyped. (p. 52)

Reflexive practice views educators (teachers and administrators) as change agents who engage in ongoing praxis (reflection and action) for increased student success.

Thus, the work of these school leaders is dynamic and evolutionary, so what they do on a daily basis with students (especially students of color), becomes moments of meaning or opportunities of unique learning that inform future diversity-related actions (see Beachum and McCray model, Figure 3.1). Culturally relevant leadership, then, entails the means to address the aforementioned issues of double consciousness and second sight.

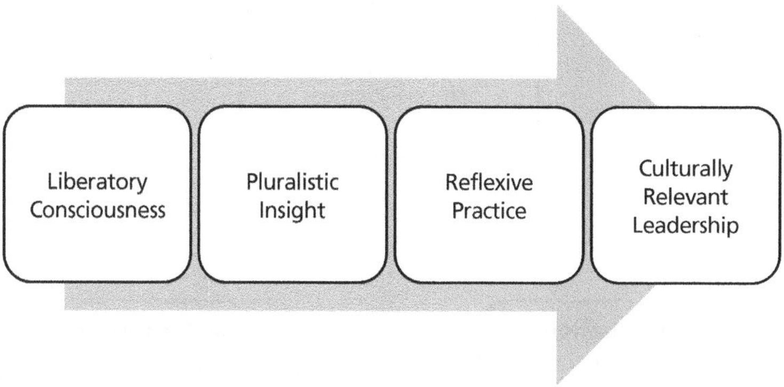

Figure 3.1 Culturally relevant leadership as a process.

TOWARDS A PEDAGOGY OF SELF-DEVELOPMENT

School leaders should focus heavily on reducing any racial or class-based hostility that might exist within the school climate or culture. Such efforts in the amelioration of racial and class bigotry or the eradication of deficit thinking fit well within the framework of culturally relevant leadership. It is disingenuous for educators and school leaders to make the faulty assumption that African-American students and students of color from low-wealth communities are going to miraculously conform to their cultural ethos. We believe such thinking is what undergirds *educational malpractice.* This type thinking by educators and school leaders leave students feeling a sense of powerlessness as well as frustration. Leaders can impact the culture of an organization and reduce such feelings among Black and Brown students (McCray, Alston, & Beachum, 2006) by providing culturally relevant leadership. Such leadership addresses negative cultural issues within schools while also subscribing to cultural pluralism that allows for alternative forms of capital to be cultivated as well as valued.

We proffer that the acceptance of alternative forms of capital students have access to will lead to a *pedagogy of self-development.* Such a pedagogy is undergirded by notions of self-realization as well as self-assertion among those students who have been disenfranchised due to their lack of social, cultural, and economic capital on the macro level. Self-realization is the way in which people feel about themselves, the world around them, and the ability to make their goals and dreams a reality. Self-assertion deals with the way in which people make themselves readily available for opportunities. The former involves believing, and the latter involves achieving. Educators play a critical role in this equation because they can assist or deter these

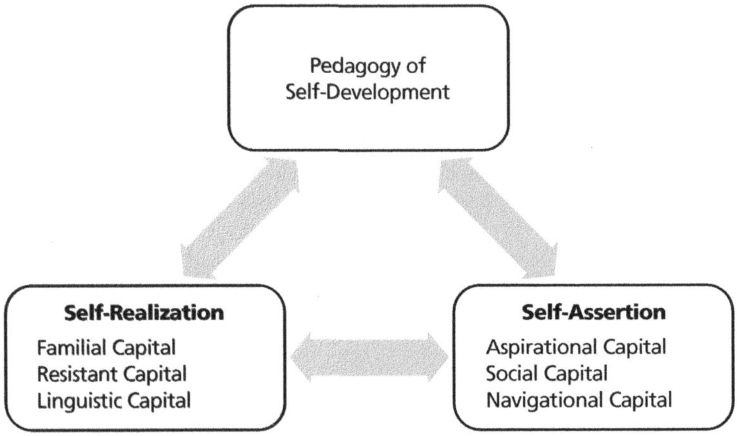

Figure 3.2 *Pedagogy of self-development and alternative forms of capital.*

efforts. Taken together, they form a *pedagogy of self-development.* Goodman (2008) defined pedagogy as "the practice of teaching, including methods and content. A pedagogy is based on a particular philosophy of education, which included the set of beliefs that form the basis upon which the teacher makes instructional decisions" (p. 264). A pedagogy of self-development has to do with teaching, because the educators and school leaders involved must be very purposeful with regard to ensuring that self-assertion and self-realization are both being addressed within the classroom. The pedagogy of self-development has particular promise when conflated with the alternative forms of capital as suggested by Yosso (2005) (see McCray and Beachum, Figure 3.2).

Self-realization contains the elements of familial, resistant, and linguistic capital. These three forms of capital are helpful as students formulate goals, careers, and dreams for the future. Self-assertion encompasses aspirational, social, and navigational capital. These forms of capital address how students cope with others, operate in society, and develop resiliency. This framework has insightful implications for teachers and school leaders.

IMPLICATIONS FOR TEACHERS AND SCHOOL LEADERS

The pedagogy of self-development provided in this work has at least three important implications for classroom teachers and school leaders who work directly with students. First, it situates the experiences and lived realities of students of color in the center of the learning process and not at the tangential realm. This means that the students are not always being compared to the norms, cultures, and capital markers of their white peers. The culturally relevant school leader who enhances his or her own liberatory consciousness can recognize when bias is occurring and not allow injustice to prevail in a conspiracy of silence (Perry, 2003). Second, it gives teachers the task of educating students not only for academic preparation, but for life preparation in a society that does not always equally value them.

> In the pre-Civil Rights era, African American children and youth lived in communities, attended schools and churches, and were members of organizations that, in response to the larger society's explicit ideology about African Americans' intellectual competence, communicated a counternarrative, about their intellectual capacity. Today, few individuals, organizations and institutions acknowledge or pay attention to the reproduction of the ideology of Black inferiority and its potential impact on African American students. (Perry, 2003, p. 96)

Although the aforementioned quote specified African-American learners, the fact of the matter is that students of color, in general, can fall prey to prescriptive pedagogy or negative perceptions. The pedagogy of self-development can provide a much-needed counternarrative to the dominant implicit messages of inferiority that are still prevalent. Culturally relevant leadership supports pluralistic insight that encourages a positive attitude towards students. For school leaders, they must make sure that this attitude permeates the entire organization and ensures that the culture supports students through encouraging self-realization and giving students opportunities for self-realization and self-assertion. The last implication focuses on the issue of enhanced accountability for teachers and school leaders. Individual teachers must hold themselves accountable to high standards. At the same time, they must realize that the students in front of them are deserving of a quality education no matter where they come from and despite the amount of perceived economic, cultural, or social capital they may bring with them to the school. For school leaders engaging in reflexive practice, this means that they too must hold themselves accountable along with all teachers. They must also support a pedagogy of self-development on a daily basis by providing resources, structured time for lesson discussion and planning, and ensuring a safe and orderly work environment (Beachum & Obiakor, 2005). The ideas proposed here are no doubt difficult, but the task of educating all students is not an easy task.

CONCLUSION

In sum, we unequivocally assert, "capital matters." Although the longstanding markers of capital (economic, human, and cultural/social) seem foremost in the minds of many educators, there should be room made for alternative forms of capital that emanate from communities of color (Yosso, 2005). In this chapter we have detailed how students of color may utilize double consciousness and second sight to view themselves through the eyes of others (usually in a deficit view). This view is usually couched in a belief that these students lack economic, human, and/or cultural/social capital. We proposed that students of color need a pedagogy of self-development, which is comprised of self-realization and self-assertion (Gooding-Williams, 2009). Additionally, we defined culturally relevant leadership and described how it could be utilized to support and sustain a pedagogy of self-development. Our work here, although solution-oriented, is also embedded in critique. It is in opposition to the status quo culture of many schools, the devaluing of communities of color, and the under-serving of far too many students of color and students from low-wealth communities throughout the United States. At the same time, our efforts are in the spirit of DuBois, who insightfully asserted, "Honest and earnest criticism from those whose interest are most nearly touched,—criticism of writers by readers, of government by governed, of leaders by those led,—this is the soul of democracy and the safeguard of modern society" (W.E.B. Du Bois, As cited by Gooding-Williams, 2009, p. 54).

REFERENCES

Allen, W. & Solorzano, D. (2001). Affirmative action, educational equity, and campus racial climate: A case study of the university of Michigan law school. *Berkeley La Raza Law Journal, 12*(2), 237–363.

Alva, S. (1991). Academic invulnerability among Mexican American students: The importance of protective resources and appraisal. *Hispanic Journal of Behavioral Sciences, 13*(1), 18–34.

Bartee, R. D. & Brown, M. C. (2007). *School matters: Why African American students need multiple forms of capital.* New York: Peter Lang.

Beachum, F. D. & McCray, C. R. (2011). *Cultural collision and collusion: Reflections on hip-hop culture, values, and schools.* New York: Peter Lang.

Beachum, F. D. & Obiakor, F. E. (2005). Educational leadership in urban schools. In F. E. Obiakor & F. D. Beachum (Eds.), *Urban education for the 21st century: Research, issues, and perspectives* (pp. 83–99). Springfield, IL: Charles C. Thomas.

Beachum, F. D., Obiakor, F., & McCray, C. R. (2007). Community uplift theory for positive change of African Americans in urban schools. In M. C. Brown & R. D. Bartee (Eds.), *Still not equal: Expanding educational opportunities in society* (pp. 269–278). New York: Peter Lang.

Bell, D. (2004). *Silent covenants: Brown v. Board of Education and the unfilled hopes for racial reform.* Oxford: Oxford University Press.

Bourdieu, P., & Passeron, J. (1977). *Reproduction in education, society and culture.* London: Sage.

Brooks, D. (2010, February 15). The lean years. *The New York Times.* Available: http://www.nytimes.com/2010/02/09/opinion/09herbert.html

Carruthers, J. H. (1999). *Intellectual warfare.* Chicago: Third World Press.

Chaddha, A., Wilson, W. J., & Venkatesh, S. (2008, Summer). In defense of the 'Wire'. *Dissent,* 83–86.

Collins, P. H. (2005). *Black sexual politics: African Americans, gender, and the new racism.* New York: Routledge.

Cosby B., & Poussaint, A. F. (2007). *Come on people: On the path from victims to victors.* Nashville: Thomas Nelson.

Dantley, M. E. (2003). Purpose driven leadership: The spiritual imperative to guiding schools beyond high-stakes testing and minimum proficiency. *Education and urban society, 35*(3), 273–291.

Dantley, M. E. (2009). African American educational leadership: Critical, purposive, and spiritual. In L. F Foster & L. C. Tillman (Eds.), *African American perspectives on leadership in schools: Building a culture of empowerment* (pp. 39–56). Lanham, MD: Rowman & Littlefield Education.

Dantley, M. E. & Tillman, L. C. (2010). Social justice and moral transformative leadership. In C. Marshall & M. Oliva (Eds.), *Leadership for social justice* (2nd ed., pp. 16–30). Boston: Pearson.

Day-Vines, N. L. & Day-Hairston, B. O. (2005). Culturally congruent strategies for addressing the behavioral needs of urban, African American male adolescents. *Professional School Counseling, 8*(1), 236–243.

Delpit, L. (2002). No kinda sense. In L. Delpit & J. K. Dowdy (Eds). *The skin that we Speak: Thoughts on language and culture in the classroom* (pp. 31–48). New York: The New Press.

Du Bois, W. E. B. (1989). *The soul of black folks.* New York: Bantam. (Originally published in 1903).

Feagin, J. R. (2001). *Racist America: Roots, current realities, and future reparation.* New York: Routledge.

Feagin, J. R. & Feagin, C. B. (1978). *Discrimination American style: Instructional racism and sexism.* Malabar, FL: Krieger.

Ferguson, A. A. (2001). *Bad boys: Public schools in the making of black masculinity.* Ann Arbor: The University of Michigan Press.

Fordham, S. (1991). Racelessness in private schools: Should we deconstruct the racial and cultural identity of African American adolescents? *Teachers College Record, 92,* 471–484.

Foster, L. (2009). Leadership in K–12 schools for promoting educational aspirations: A mental model for school advancement. In L. Foster & L. C. Tillman (Eds.), *African American perspectives on leadership in schools: Building a culture of empowerment* (pp. 157–170). Lanham, MD: Rowman & Littlefield Education.

Franklin, V. P. (2002). Introduction: Cultural capital and African American education. The *Journal of African American History, 87,* 175–181.

Freire, P. (1973). *Pedagogy of the oppressed.* New York: The Seabury Press.

Friedman, T. (2005). *The world is flat: A brief history of the twenty-first century.* New York: Farrar, Straus, and Giroux.

Gay, G. (2000). *Culturally responsive teaching: Theory, research, and practice.* New York: Teachers College Press.

Gooding-Williams, R. (2009). *In the shadow of Du Bois: Afro-modern political though in America.* Cambridge, MA: Harvard University Press.

Goodman, G. (Ed.). (2008). *Educational psychology: An application of critical constructivism.* New York: Peter Lang Publishing.

Gregory, A., & Mosely, P. M. (2004). The discipline gap: Teachers' views on the over-representation of African American students in the discipline system. *Equity and Excellence in Education, 37,* 18–30.

Herbert, B. (2010, February 8). The worst of the pain. *The New York Times.* Retrieved from http://www.nytimes.com/2010/02/09/opinion/09herbert.html

Hersey, P., Blanchard, K. H., & Johnson, D. E. (1996). *Management of organizational behavior: Utilizing human resources.* Upper Saddle River, NJ: Prentice Hall.

Hilliard III, A. G. (2002). Language, culture, and the assessment of African American children. In L. Delpit & J. K. Dowdy (Eds.), *The skin that we speak: Thoughts on language and culture in the classroom* (pp. 87–105). New York: The New Press.

Hornbeck, D. & Salamon, L. (Eds.). (1991). *High stakes: Testing for tracking, promotion, and graduation.* Washington, DC: National Academy Press.

Hymes, D. H. (1981). Foreword. In C. A. Ferguson and S. B. Heath (Eds.), *Language in the USA* (pp. v–ix). New York: Cambridge University Press.

Jackson, J. H. (2008). *Given half a chance: The Schott 50-state report on public education and African American males.* Cambridge, MA: Schott Foundation for Public Education.

Karenga, M. (1989). *The African-American holiday of Kwanzaa: A celebration of family, community, and culture.* Los Angeles: University of Sankore.

Ladson-Billings, G. (1994). *The dreamkeepers: Successful teachers of African-American students.* San Francisco: Jossey-Bass.

Lightfoot, J. (2009). Toward a praxis of antiracist school leadership preparation. In L. F. Foster & L. C. Tillman (Eds.), *African American perspectives on leadership in schools: Building a culture of empowerment* (pp. 211–236). Lanham, MD: Rowman & Littlefield Education.

Lindsey, R. B., Roberts, L. M., & Campbell-Jones, F. (2005). *The culturally proficient school: An implementation guide for school leaders.* Thousand Oaks, CA: Corwin Press.

McCray, C. R. (2008). Constructing a positive intrasection of race and class for the 21st century. *Journal of School Leadership, 18*(2), 249–267.

McCray, C. R., Alston, J. A., & Beachum, F. D. (2006). Principals' perceptions of multicultural education and school climate. *Multicultural Learning and Teaching, 1*(1), 12–22. Available: http://www.mltonline.org/current-articles/beachum2.pdf

McCray, C. R. & Beachum, F. D. (2006). A critique of zero tolerance policies: An issue of justice and caring. *Values and Ethics in Educational Administration, 5*(1), 1–8. Available: http://www.ed.psu.edu/UCEACSLE/VEEA/VEEA_Vol5Num1.pdf

McKenzie, K. B. (2001). *White teachers' perceptions about their students of color and themselves as white educators.* Unpublished doctoral dissertation, University of Texas at Austin.

Nesbitt, R. E. (2009). *Intelligence and how to get it: Why schools and cultures count.* New York: W. W. Norton & Company.

Nieto, S. (2000). *Affirming diversity: The sociopolitical context of multicultural.* New York: Longman.

Obiakor, F. E. & Beachum, F. D. (2005). Urban education: The quest for democracy, equity, and excellence. In F. E. Obiakor & F. D. Beachum (Eds.), *Urban education for the 21st century: Research, issues, and perspectives* (pp. 3–19). Springfield, IL: Charles C. Thomas.

Obiakor, F. E., Obiakor, P. H., Garza-Nelson, C., & Randall, P. (2005). Educating urban learners with and without special needs: Life after the *Brown* case. In F. E. Obiakor & F. D. Beachum (Eds.), *Urban education for the 21st century: Research, issues, and perspectives* (pp. 20–33). Springfield, IL: Charles C. Thomas.

Ogbu, J. U. (1999). Beyond language: Ebonics, Proper English, and identity in a Black-American speech community. *American Educational Research Journal, 36*(2), 147–184.

Ovando, C. J. (2001). Language diversity and education. In J. A. Banks & C. A .McGee Banks (Eds.), *Multicultural Education: Issues and perspectives* (4th Edition), (pp. 268–291). New York: John Wiley & Sons, Inc.

Perry, T. (2003). Up from the parched earth: Toward a theory of African American achievement. In T, Perry, C. Steele, & A. G. Hilliard (Eds.), *Young gifted and Black: Promoting high achieving among African-American students* (pp. 1–108). Boston: Beacon Press.

Perry, T. & Delpit, L. (1998). *The real Ebonics debate.* Boston: Beacon Press.

Perry, T., Steele, C., & Hilliard, A. (2003). *Young, gifted, and black: Promoting high achievement among African-American students.* Boston: Beacon Press.

Quarles, B. (1987). *The Negro in the making of America.* London: Collier Macmillan Publishers.

Rodriguez, G. M. (2004). Vertical equity in school finance and the potential for increasing school responsiveness to student and staff needs. *Peabody Journal of Education, 79*(3), 7–30.

Rodriguez, G. M. & Fabionar, J. O. (2010). The impact of students and schools: Exploring the social Justice Leadership implications. In C. Marshall & M. Oliva (Eds.), *Leadership for social justice: Making revolutions in education* (pp. 55–73). New York: Allyn & Bacon.

Shelby, T. (2005). *We who are dark: The philosophical foundations of Black solidarity.* Cambridge, MA: Harvard University Press.

Skiba, R. J., & Peterson, R. L. (1999). The dark side of zero tolerance: Can punishment lead to safe schools? *Phi Delta Kappan, 80*(5), 372–376.

Tatum, B. D. (2007). *Can we talk about race? And other conversations in an era of school resegregation.* Boston: Beacon Press.

Thomas, D. E., & Stevenson, H. (2009). Gender risks and education: The particular classroom challenges for urban low-income African American boys. *Review of Research in Education, 33,* 160–180.

Tillman, L. C. (2009). Facilitating African American parental involvement in urban schools: Opportunities for school leadership. In L. Foster & L. C. Tillman (Eds.), *African American perspectives on leadership in schools: Building a culture of empowerment* (pp. 75–94). Lanham, MD: Rowman & Littlefield Education.

Valencia, R. R. (1997). *The evolution of deficit thinking: Educational thought and practice. Stanford Series on Education and Public Policy.* London: Falmer Press.

Valencia, R. R., & Solorzano, D. G. (1997). Cultural deficit model thinking. In R. R. Valencia (Ed.), *The evolution of deficit thinking: Educational thought and practice* (pp. 160–210). Stanford Series on Education and Public Policy. London: Falmer Press.

Venkatesh, S. A. (2006). *Off the books: The underground economy of the urban poor.* Cambridge, MA: Harvard University Press.

Villegas, A. M. & Lucas, T. (2002). *Educating culturally responsive teachers: A coherent approach.* Albany, NY: State University of New York Press.

Wilson, W. J. (2009). *More than just race: Being black and poor in the inner city.* New York: W. W. Norton & Company.

Wimberly, G. L. (2002). *School relationships foster success for African American students.* Iowa City, IA: ACT.

Yosso, T. J. (2005). Whose culture has capital? A critical race theory discussion of community cultural wealth. *Race, Ethnicity, and Education, 8*(1), 69–91.

CHAPTER 4

SEGMENTATION, CAPITAL, AND COMMUNITY COLLEGE TRANSFER STUDENTS

Exploring Community Colleges as Agents of Currency

Eboni M. Zamani-Gallaher
Eastern Michigan University

Stanley Bazile
St. John's University

Tamara N. Stevenson
Eastern Michigan University

INTRODUCTION

Forty years ago, it was commonplace for individuals to leave secondary education centers for the world of work. In contrast, the contemporary labor force of the millennium is marked with an increasing demand for

Contemporary Perspectives on Capital in Educational Contexts, pages 101–132

high-skilled laborers. Little economic or occupational mobility exists for those who have not acquired some training beyond high school (Carnevale, Strohl, & Smith, 2009). Consequently, the call for more education is seen as quintessential to individual social capital, further developing America's human capital, and fueling economic growth.

Postsecondary educational access has not always been readily attainable for the masses. Many underrepresented, disenfranchised groups remain at the margins of full participation. One notable threshold for marginalized populations to gain entry into higher learning has been in the doorsills of community colleges. The present chapter seeks to examine the segmentation of community college students in higher education and in what ways their previous two-year institutions equip them with capital necessary to transition to senior-level colleges and universities. More specifically, this chapter will explore whether community college transfer students look upon themselves as a capital good relative to their self-efficacy for navigating their pursuit of the baccalaureate. It is important to note that the manner in which a consumer engages with the marketplace of the American community college is complex and inconsistent based on the individual's capital. Due to the fluidity of the term *capital,* this chapter in many ways seeks to contribute to the discourse on community colleges as agents of capital. More specifically, we contend that the transfer function of community colleges is an untapped currency area that deserves greater attention as a means for optimizing capital in the form of currency for the student consumer. Forms of capital under examination in this chapter include social, educational, human, and knowledge capital. In sum, this chapter endeavors to explore how those distinctions directly affect community college students, particularly how successfully managing transfer begets a form of capital (e.g., currency to spend at a senior level institution) that may impact the consumer's currency.

Not since the explosion of community college expansion in the 1950s and 1960s has the community college sector been a more important agent of currency. Given the impact of globalization on the education and society, obtaining currency (i.e., the various forms of capital) is critical in succeeding in the knowledge-based, world market. This conversation is especially timely due to the increase attention of community college's as a result of (1) the rising cost of higher education at four-year institutions, (2) the open access and flexibility of community colleges, and (3) the call to action set forth by President Barack Obama to use community colleges as the infrastructure to rebuild the depressed economy and enhance the workforce with high-skill/high-demand laborers.

REVIEW OF LITERATURE

Origin and Evolution of Community Colleges

Since their origination over 100 years ago, community colleges have served as a crucial pathway for individuals seeking postsecondary education. From the early 1900s, the development of community colleges exemplified innovative educational delivery, providing access to postsecondary education to segments that had previously been overlooked due to a myriad of factors (such as race/ethnicity, gender, income, disability, and geography) (Aragon & Zamani, 2002). With the establishment of the first community college (Joliet Junior College in 1901), a paradigm shift took root, from education for the elite to the massification of postsecondary opportunities (Cohen & Brawer, 2008).

At the beginning of the 1930s, there were 450 community colleges in 45 states (Brick, 1994). There were approximately 575 community colleges by the end of the decade. The average enrollment in these schools was 400 students (Cohen & Brawer, 1996). The roles of these colleges would likely have remained the same if not for World War II.

During the 1940s, the United States made considerable changes to its higher education system. The changes had a great effect on what is now known as the U.S. community college system. At the beginning of the 1940s, approximately 160,000 students graduated from college each year. By 1946, students were returning to college by the hundreds of thousands. In 1947, 49% of those enrolled in U.S. colleges were veteran students. In 1950, approximately 500,000 were graduating (Wyatt, 1992). This boost in student enrollment placed significant strain on the nation's higher education system.

In 1947, President Harry S. Truman responded to the growing educational needs of the country. President Truman established the Commission on Higher Education for American Democracy. The commission was assigned the broad task of exploring possible original initiatives in which the United States higher education system could respond to the new educational climate of the nation. In their report, the commission felt that a college education should not only be available to those who could afford it. Commonly referred to as *The Truman Report*, the recommendation was set that all citizens were entitled to an education and that community colleges be used to achieve this task (Gabert, 1991; Vaughan, 1997).

College enrollment among first-generation students was more attainable during the postwar era, with President Truman calling for a broader network of postsecondary partners as he considered the community college sector key in creating a more democratic society (Ayers, 2010). President

Truman's commissioned report fueled the growth of the modern community college movement. Accordingly, the 1950s to 1970s denote a period of unprecedented expansion of two-year institutions charged with offering an alternate route to higher education.

The roles of two-year institutions have changed over the years since the inception of Joliet Junior College (Gabert, 1991). The early profile of these U.S. colleges was very simple. Their primary focus was to provide individuals with access to the first two years of lower-division college course work. Upon completion, students were able to have their courses transferred to four-year colleges and universities (Brint & Karabel, 1989a, 1989b; Wechsler, 1989). However, the community college mission evolved to include the transfer function, in addition to general education, continuing education, vocational/occupational education, and developmental education.

Community colleges have long played a role in assisting students who seek transfer in closing academic skill gaps. A number of those enrolled during the early period of the community college era were those students who were academically underprepared and required remediation, particularly in the areas of writing and mathematics. Additionally, the first community colleges provided some other advantages to those enrolling such as proximity to home, allowing students to pursue their education without the expense of leaving home and the ability to continue working (Gabert, 1991).

Shifting Gears in Community College Education

In the early 1980s, enrollment at community colleges was roughly four million students. This was an impressive increase from two million students in 1970 (National Center for Education Statistics, 2001). The increased enrollment prompted Astin (1985) to predict a continuation of this trend. At the turn of the 20th century, statistics indicated that nearly 5.5 million students were attending community colleges (Cohen & Brawer, 2008). Hunter (2007) reported that number had grown to be approximately 6.6 million.

To help with this new direction, many states established an open-access admissions policy for community colleges. Some argue that this open-access course of action began a cycle of poor success of transfer students (Bandyopadhyay, 2008; Brint & Karabel, 1989a, 1989b; Christie & Hutchinson, 2003; Clark, 1960; Cohen & Brawer, 2008; Dougherty, 1987, 1994). With much more emphasis being placed on specific areas of education such as technical, occupational, vocational, and community education, transfer success became less of a priority (Bandyopadhyay, 2008; Cohen & Brawer, 2008). The reputation of community colleges as institutions that delivered less rigorous courses than four-year institutions escalated. Many argue that the new era of community colleges provided fewer advantages than access. In addition, some contend that matriculating at community college increased the likelihood of a student not completing his or her baccalaureate degree (Brint & Karabel, 1989a, 1989b; Dougherty, 1987, 1994; Pascarella &Terenzini, 2005; Pincus & Archer, 1989).

The Transfer Function: Catalyst or Impediment to Baccalaureate Attainment

In the decades that followed the extension of postsecondary access, community colleges saw a steady decline in successful transfer from community colleges to four-year institutions (Zamani, 2001). Students who start their postsecondary career at community colleges are frequently viewed as academically deficient, and their two-year institutions are looked upon as an extension of high school (Cain, 1999). Community college students are described as unmotivated and seen as "second class citizens" (Ling, 2006, p. 3). This stigma is magnified by the lack of success experienced by many transfer students (Berger & Malaney, 2003). Consequently, four-year institutions—particularly selective, predominantly white institutions (PWI)—have been cautious to admit students who began their postsecondary careers at community colleges. Case in point, the transfer rate from community colleges to four-year institutions in 1972 was 29%. By 1980, that number had decreased to 20% (Grubb, 1991). This decline brought increased scrutiny to community colleges that continues at present.

According to Berger and Malaney (2003), 80% of first-year college students at community colleges express an interest in transferring to a four-year institution. Unfortunately, only 40% of those students end up on a transfer track. Of even greater concern, of that 40%, a mere 10% eventually transfer to a four-year institution. Existing data indicate that the difficult process continues once these students matriculate at four-year institutions. According to Kerr (2006), the National Center for Education Statistics reported that approximately 80% of the students who begin their postsecondary career at a community college and then transfer to a four-year institution have not obtained their bachelor's degree six years later.

The underwhelming performance of transfer students has been a concern for the community colleges as well as for the four-year receiving schools. While a considerable number of undergraduate students in the United States attend four-year institutions, past statistics indicate there is a larger enrollment of students at community colleges than four-year institutions (Flowers, 2006; Laanan, 2004). Many students from disenfranchised groups have no other postsecondary opportunity than a two-year institution, and their rates of transfer are differential when disaggregated by race/ethnicity (Lee & Frank, 1990). Community colleges enroll over two-fifths of the nation's undergraduates, many of which are from underrepresented racially/ethnically diverse students. In fact, 42% of African American, 45% of Asian American, 52% of Hispanic and 52% of Native American students attend community colleges (Ayers, 2010).

Demand for Community College Education and the Case for Transfer

According to Cohen and Brawer (2008), over half of the students who seek some form of postsecondary education in this country matriculate at a community college. The enrollment of students at community colleges shows no sign of decreasing (Berger & Malaney, 2003; Laanan, 2004). Factors contributing to the heightened interest in community colleges include the increasingly competitive admissions requirements of four-year institutions, consistent tuition increases, a decrease in financial assistance, lack of quality teachers, and an increase in poorly funded and inadequate high schools (Cohen & Brawer, 2008; Kerr, 2006). Additionally, the population of traditional-age students has increased. In 2001, 42% of the students enrolled at a community college were under the age of 22 (Adelman, 2005). Rice (2008) supports this assessment with the following: "Traditional students (i.e., students who are coming straight from high school with baccalaureate degree aspirations) enrolling in community colleges suggests that the transfer function will become of greater importance" (p. 12). Third, colleges have been forced to provide tangible assessment procedures to receive highly competitive state and federal assistance (Bailey & Alfonzo, 2005). Fourth, the percentage of community college students interested in eventually receiving at the very minimum a bachelor's degree shows no sign of decreasing (Doyle, 2006).

To understand the struggles of transfer students one must dissect this process carefully. Rice (2008) recommends examining it through three separate stages. The first stage is pre-transfer. The second is point-of-transfer, and the last stage is post-transfer. Pre-transfer refers to the student's time at their original institution. As previously discussed, a large number of students who begin their college careers at community colleges never transfer.

PURPOSE OF THE STUDY

This exploratory study employed a dominant/less-dominant design. The dominant overarching quantitative methodological approach and a less dominant approach focused on the second stage of transferring (i.e., finding a four-year institution to transfer to, familiarity with articulation agreements, and the resources available at the community college to help facilitate the transfer process) via open-ended survey items and follow-up focus group interviews. Community college student background characteristics such as parent's highest level of education and financing of college attendance (as measures of social capital) may lend insights on transfer student perceptions of community college rigor, belief in their abilities, and transfer preparedness. The present study was initiated to delve into the degree to which there is an association between social capital, self-efficacy, community college rigor, transfer preparedness, and satisfaction with transfer advising. Additionally, this research sought to explore if differences surfaced among the above constructs by race/ethnicity. The guiding research questions were:

1. Are student background characteristics such as gender, race/ethnicity, and GPA significantly related to social capital and self-efficacy among community college transfer students?
2. Are transfer student perceptions of community college rigor related to high self-efficacy and transfer preparedness?
3. Does social capital influence community college transfer students differently by race/ethnicity?
4. Is there a difference in the level of satisfaction with community college transfer advising, transfer preparedness, or self-efficacy by race/ethnicity?
5. What are the overall experiences of transfer students relative to ease or difficulty in navigating the transfer process and transitioning from a two-year to a four-year institution?

THEORETICAL PERSPECTIVES

Psychosocial Adjustment, Transition, and Transfer Shock

Few researchers have attempted to focus their research on transfer students' psychosocial adjustment and transition through the transfer process (Ling, 2006). Those who have attempted to conduct inquiries into this area have typically referred to the popular concept of transfer shock. As a result, researchers have fallen into what Laanan (2004) considers a limited use of this concept as the only framework to guide their work.

The term *transfer shock* was first introduced in research by Hill (1965) during the late 1920s to the mid-1960s on junior college students. Originally, this term was used to explain the decline in transfer students' GPA during their first semester at a four-year institution. This was believed to be caused by increased academic rigor and lack of preparedness of the student. Laanan (2004) argued that transfer shock merely describes the cognitive outcome of the transfer student‘s process rather than the equally important emotional and psychological development of the student. Similarly, Berger and Malaney (2003) concluded the following:

> There is a wide range of academic and social interactions and outcomes that must be considered in a comprehensive view of the college adjustment process. It is important to consider how well students adjust to and fit in with the academic and social environments of a campus in order to have a more complete understanding of how well transfer students adjust to a four-year university. (p. 4)

Others also saw a similar connection between academic and social success. Townsend and Wilson (2006) argued that the psychological frustration of adjusting subsequently leads to poor academic performance. Rice (2008) added that when exploring the psychosocial component of a student's adjustment, financial concerns must be taken into account.

Schlossberg's Transition Theory

Select research has sought to characterize the psychological development of students as they seek to move from one academic community to the next (Schlossberg, 1995). According to that research, a main component of the transfer process for community college transfer students has to do with transition. Schlossberg (1995) defined transition as the occasion on which a person experiences change. It is during this experience with change that many transfer students fail or succeed. Some of the results associated with failure versus success include academic, psychological, and vocational domains. Many researchers accept Schlossberg Four S's concepts of transition as legitimate factors that affect a student's transition experience. According to Schlossberg (1995), these four factors are: (1) situation, (2) support, (3), self, and (4) strategies. For readers who may lack familiarity with these concepts, definitions of the four factors are provided below:

1. *Situation* relates to how the individual transfer student views the experience. For example, does the student believe this transition to be positive or negative, voluntary or involuntary, and expected or unexpected?
2. *Support* refers to the student's network. This network includes but is not limited to family, friends, peers, or other persons they feel they can depend on while navigating their way through the transition.
3. *Self* is based on the preexisting characteristics of the student. Ling (2006) mentioned experiences as one example of characteristics (i.e., has the student done this before?). This plays an important role

because if the student has done it before it increases the likelihood for success.

4. *Strategies* refer to the plan, tactic, and approach used by the student to deal with the transition (Ling, 2006).

Schlossberg (1995) suggested that successfully dealing with transition requires the student to assimilate into the existing culture of the institution. This helps prevent the student from remaining anxious with the experience. Transition requires the unlearning of old schemas and learning of new schemas. The more adept an individual is at dealing with the transfer process, the more likely he or she is to succeed (Ling, 2006).

The ability to learn a new system has traditionally been a problem for transfer students. Factors related to this generally include larger campuses, which result in bigger classes. Also important is the development of new friendships and learning the culture of a new location (Laanan, 2004). Some studies suggest that transfer students are more likely to feel isolated and unvalued in college. This lack of belonging is consistent with other literature on transfer students (Jackson & Healy, 1996; Kerr, 2006).

Segmentation Theories

The sociology of higher education primarily focuses on the psychosocial affects of college on students as well as the inequities and stratification of postsecondary educational opportunities (Clark, 1973). Generally, segmentation refers to how individuals are stratified within various occupations, particularly nonprofessional or paraprofessional jobs (Richardson & Bender, 1987). More specifically, Glazer (1991) contends that segmentation refers to "hierarchically ranked labor markets across which there is virtually no worker mobility; these markets differ from each other in wage levels and benefits, steadiness of employment, job autonomy, and other conditions of employment" (p. 352).

Segmentation theories have been utilized to explain workplace segregation and wage differentials by gender as well as labor force segmenting along racial/ethnic lines. For example, the nursing profession is heavily female. Therefore, stratification by gender is not at issue. More than 90% of nurses' aides, licensed practical nurses (LPNs) and registered nurses are women. However, there is racial/ethnic segmentation in the nursing field, as African-American and Hispanic women are disproportionately represented in middle (i.e., LPNs) and lower job grades (e.g., nurses' aides) in contrast to Asian-American and white women who have higher percentages in the upper grades (Glazer, 1991). Hence, segmentation theories serve as useful conceptual frameworks to deal with the strata of collegians within and across institutional contexts.

Human and Social Capital Theories

Many students aspiring to nursing careers reflect the stratified profession in terms of their participation in postsecondary education, given the higher percentages of first-generation, low-income, racially/ethnically diverse students enrolling in community college nursing programs. The vocational/occupational focus of education has received greater attention in recent years (Bragg, 2001). Relative to other vocational/occupational and traditional transfer-track program offerings, an estimated 11 million adults and out-of-school youth could benefit from postsecondary education and training at community colleges, as many jobs in the new knowledge economy require some postsecondary preparation (Carnevale, Stroh, & Smith, 2009).

The forecasted occupational outlook and mobility for most high school graduates (particularly, low-income/working-class students) is bleak without conferral of a college degree. The growing need for a more educated workforce in the U.S. is partly due to the impact of globalization (Romano & Dellow, 2009). Community colleges, like other American institutions have found their stakeholders affected by job migration, labor alterations, and marketization, among other things (Levin, 2002a, 2002b). One means of addressing how the U.S. has begun to lag in terms of human resources (i.e., the shortage of high-skill/high-demand laborers is evident from the stalemate triggered from the worst recession since the Great Depression) and curbing the effects of globalization to compete internationally is by investing in our human capital.

Human capital, according to Schultz (1961), encompasses "direct expenditures on education, health, and internal migration to take advantage of better job opportunities are clear examples. Earnings forgone by mature students attending school and by workers acquiring on-the-job training are equally clear examples" (p. 1). Furthermore, human capital theory holds that persons have to embody key characteristics that will enable them to produce earned income that is typically acquired through personal investment such as pursuing more training, education, and professional development (Darity, 1982). Therefore, in the absence of holding the requisite skill set (e.g., postsecondary attainment, minimally a community college credential), one is apt to have less capital in today's marketplace.

It is essential that new labor market participants possess a skill set that adds value in driving economic growth. In fact, U.S. President Barack Obama has addressed the need for investing in America's human capital to raise the skills of our citizens to keep pace with technological advances, rebuild the capacity of American businesses in an effort to create jobs, reduce deficits, and increase global competitiveness (The White House, 2009). In remarks given at Macomb Community College in Michigan, President Obama announced the American Graduation Initiative (AGI), which calls for an additional five million community college degrees and certificates by 2020. Consequently, as the largest segment of American higher education, the Obama administration does not view community colleges from a deficit model but as a viable option capable of providing affordable workforce training in high skill/high demand areas such as nursing, advanced manufacturing, and green jobs.

Human capital investments arguably can be instrumental in producing social capital. The theory of social capital highlights the necessity of social connections or relationships consistently maintained to produce mutually beneficial resources (i.e., capital) (Jovel, 2008; Putnam, 1995; Schaefer-McDaniel, 2004; Wells, 2008). The related concept of cultural capital, as initially theorized by Bourdieu, delineates the exposure to and knowledge of certain valued components of the dominant culture (e.g., standards of beliefs, traditions, and behaviors) most useful to generate social, educational, and economic success (Jovel, 2008; Schaefer-McDaniel, 2004; Wells, 2008, 2009).

Contemporary research on social capital in schooling (particularly with underrepresented diverse populations) illustrates the importance of social networks, feeling a sense of belonging/place attachment, and necessity that one's sense of agency is acknowledged (Farmer-Hinton & Adams, 2006; Pascarella, Pierson, Wolniak, & Terenzini, 2004; Schaefer-McDaniel, 2004; Stanton-Salazar, 1997; Strayhorn, 2008, 2010). As it relates to the community college context, Gonzalez, Stoner, and Jovel (2003) found that both two- and four-year Latina college students identified parents as sources (or institutional agents) of social capital in the form of encouragement and emotional support during their primary and secondary schooling experiences. However, major differences emerged between the two groups with regard to accessing social capital through school-based honors programs, teachers, counselors, college outreach, and preparation programs, and peers.

Students of color, in contrast to their white peers, are perceived to have less social capital given disparities in living conditions, limited parental exposure and experience with postsecondary education, and "spatial isolation of educational attainment" (Farmer-Hinton, 2008, p. 128), in which fewer college graduates reside in predominantly urban (black and Hispanic) communities. As such, academic counselors must be mindful of the differing messages given about college as a viable option that may be contradictory to the mindsets and circumstances of students' relatives and community members. Thus, school-based social capital is critical for students of color—particularly first-generation African-American and Hispanic students—who wish to gain access to guidance and support to prepare for college (Farmer-Hinton & Adams, 2006; Farmer-Hinton, 2008). If community college transfer students lack social capital, they are subsequently limited in terms of access to knowledge, networks, and resources to four-year postsecondary educational opportunities and/or viable career pathways (Brown & Davis, 2001; Gonzalez, Stoner, & Joval, 2003; Palmer & Gasman, 2008).

Social Capital and Community Colleges

With regard to two-year institutions of higher education, educational access to the masses, student achievement, persistence, retention, and transfer to four-year colleges, particularly by race/ethnicity and social class have been explored with the social capital concept. To explore how social (and cultural) capital affect first- to second-year persistence of students at both two- and four-year colleges, Wells (2008, 2009) drew data from the 1988–1994 National Educational Longitudinal Study, restricting data to the 1992 enrollment to result in a sample size of 1,726 college and university students. Wells (2008) speculated that higher amounts of social and cultural capital guide community college student choices that subsequently influence persistence between community college and university students. In brief, major results from the study show the utility of social and cultural capital to examine social class, the necessity to direct retention resources toward students with lower levels of social and cultural capital, and the indication that social and cultural capital affects persistence in different ways for students who start postsecondary education at two-year versus four-year colleges. The author reasoned that meritocracy may explain the differing effects of social and cultural capital across institutional context. "The notion that community colleges may be more socially equitable in this regard may lead policy makers, as well as community college personnel, to exploit this finding to the further advantage of students with less access to various types of capital" (Wells, 2008, p 41).

Theory of Optimum Currency

Overall, capital is access to social networks that allow for some means of production that can be exchanged (e.g., exchanged for access to education, training, wages, etc.). U.S. workers have to adjust to the changing dynamics of the labor market in stimulating the economy and fueling new industries. The community colleges are touted by the Obama administration to be the centerpiece in promoting college completion. However, a significant percentage of students who enter community colleges with degree completion and/or transfer to a four-year institution fall short of their educational goals. Given the low rate of transfer, can community colleges, as the "Cinderella" of the Obama administration, provide attendees with greater social capital (that is capital as currency to the student as consumer) to expend in the world market?

According to Schultz (1961), all capital is associated to income, and the purse holding the national income/resources has become increasingly empty, making a case for investment in human capital, which can foster both the public and private good of education. The theory of optimum currency[1] (Mundell, 1961) may provide a general argument for defining the community college, and more specifically the transfer function, as a currency area. While community colleges have been subject to institutional elitism within postsecondary education and among the public-at-large, it is inconclusive in the extant literature if students perceive a favorable exchange in providing capital for those who take advantage of alternate routes to the baccalaureate. In sum, postsecondary educational attainment does not represent a single currency, as there are areas of currency (e.g., community college transfer) that do not straight away impair student mobility and/or propagate segmentation in education and the workforce. Perhaps the community college may illicit strong, functional ties with the two-year context (such as bonding social capital) that may bridge and not necessarily hamper student transitions from open-admissions colleges to more selective institutions of higher learning.

Self-Efficacy Theory

As scores of community college students seek to move from two-year to four-year institutions of higher education, an important factor in their ability to matriculate and make a successful transition lies in their belief that they can meet the academic and social challenges, thereby successfully negotiating their educational/career pathways (Bong, 1997; Jimenez, 2006). Therefore, the degree to which a student is confident about his or her academic and social ability is exhibited by efficacious behaviors, shaped by personal interactions, and affected by their environment or their own behavior (Lent, Brown, & Hackett, 1994; Parajes, 2002). Correspondingly, Bandura (1977, 1997) argued that self-efficacy is not synonymous with confidence, as the latter does distinguish the strength of the belief without acknowledging any certainty regarding ability. Therefore, self-efficacy best reflects how one expects to perform in a certain domain such as academic performance, social skills, speaking in public, and so on (Smith & Betz, 2000).

The above theoretical perspectives preliminarily provide an analytic lens to explore the relationships between transfer preparedness, community college rigor, self-efficacy, and social capital. It is thought that these theoretical lens compliment the overarching conceptual underpinnings of segmentation theory and whether the transfer function bears any association to capital as optimum currency to be exchanged in a four-year institutional context.

METHOD

Setting and Participants

The study sample was comprised of students at a comprehensive public university in the Midwest. The campus is the academic home to roughly 23,000 students pursuing undergraduate, graduate, specialist, doctoral, and certificate degrees in the arts, sciences, and professions. The university offers more than 200 majors and minors in five colleges, plus the Honors College. The most popular majors are education, business, social sciences and history, science and engineering, English, and the health professions. Sixty-nine percent of undergraduates are full time, and 60% are women. The student body is 70% white, 16% African American/black, 6% undeclared, 3% international, 2.5% Asian-American, 2% Hispanic, and 0.5% Native-American.

Among the points of pride for this institution are being the most affordable four-year university and one of five institutions to earn the Carnegie Foundation's Community Engagement classification in its home state. The university places a strong emphasis on undergraduate education and is noted for having highly respected, nationally recognized programs (e.g., one of the best Midwestern colleges and one the best business schools). The institution is noted as one of the most diverse campuses by *U.S. News and World Report*.

The target population for this exploratory study included students who were identified as new entering undergraduate transfers from various community colleges, the vast majority located in state. The study reflects a nonprobability sample drawn from incoming transfer students recruited for participation in the study at the Transfer Student Orientation held during 2006 and 2007. The 141 students that completed usable surveys out of 156 returned[2] represent a convenience sample. Nonetheless, we felt there was good reason to believe that this particular convenience sample would allow for adequate exploration of the guiding research questions posed.

Instrumentation

Again, this exploratory investigation utilized a dominant/less-dominant approach by employing survey research methods as the overarching quantitative strategy with the integration of the less-dominant open-ended qualitative items specific to the context and participants. A modified version of the long form of the Laanan-Transfer Student Questionnaire (L- TSQ) was used for data gathering (Laanan, 2004), as it integrates both quantitative and qualitative research components. This 304-item instrument was augmented, and the community college experiences segment of the survey was employed for our study. Additionally, the L-TSQ was an ideal instrument as it measures non-cognitive, affective traits of community college transfer students. Transfer student beliefs, attitudes, and interests across various areas were primarily measured using Likert scales to assess levels of agreement about academic experiences, perceptions of the transfer process, among other community college activities.

RESULTS

Descriptive Statistics

The average age of community college transfer students in this study was 24.21 years. Well over two-thirds (70%) of the respondents were female. Relative to the race/ethnicity of students, 70.2% of the sample identified as white (non-Hispanic), just over one-quarter (26.3%) were students of color (i.e., African American, American Indian/Alaska Native, Asian American/Pacific Islander, and Hispanic); 3.5% reported "Other" for race/ethnicity. Among students of color, African-American students comprised the largest group, accounting for 14.2% of the sample. Hence, this subset of transfer students surveyed at Transfer Orientation closely mirrors the overall racial/ethnic characteristics of the larger student population.

Sixty-four percent of the transfer students responding to the survey attended one community college prior to transferring to this four-year university. Twenty-eight percent attended two community colleges before transferring, while 7.9% reported attending three or more community colleges prior to transferring to their new four-year home institution. Thirty-seven percent of the respondents indicated that they previously attended a four-year institution, which reflects some degree of spiraling in student transfer patterns. Relative to degree plans, 37.7% of these community college transfers aspire to the baccalaureate degree, 46.4% desire master's degrees, 6.5% wish to earn a PhD or EdD., 5.8% want a professional degree (e.g., MD, JD, DDS, MBA, etc.) and 3.6% stated "Other" degree plans. However, when asked their top reason for attending their new transfer institution, 69.7% said to obtain a BA/BS, while15.2% stated that they wanted to gain skills for new job/occupation. Just 10.6% stated that they want to prepare for pursuit of a graduate/professional degree; 3.8% wanted to satisfy a personal interest, and only .8% acknowledged their reasons for transferring to the university was for financial gain.

Research has noted parallels between mother and father's highest educational attainment as a means of social capital to their offspring that subsequently shapes their educational aspirations (Strayhorn, 2010). There was a notable difference in the educational attainment of the 141 survey respondents. For this sample, 4.3% of students reported "Don't know" for their mother's highest educational attainment while 5.8% responded "Don't know" for their father's highest educational attainment. Six percent of the participants mothers had less than a high school diploma (H.S.), while 5.8% of fathers had less than H.S. Little over one-quarter (26.4%) of mothers had less than two years of vocational education past H.S., while 21.6% of students reported this as the highest level of educational attainment for their fathers. Nineteen percent of the respondents' fathers had less than two years of college while 10.1% of fathers had two or more years of college (which includes associate's degrees). In contrast, 14.3% of mothers had less than two years of college and 18.6% had two or more years of college. It is interesting to note that 25.2% of the community college transfers in this study reported their father's highest educational attainment as the baccalaureate degree, while only 16.4% of respondents' mothers held a BA/BS. Twelve percent said their mothers had master's degrees while 6.5% of fathers of these transfer students held master's degrees. Lastly, 5.8% of the students' fathers held a PhD, EdD, JD, MD, or other professional degree, while only 1.4% of their mothers held the same credentials.

Seventy-three percent of the community college transfers reported having some type of financial aid. Over half (51.8%) reported self-support as their primary form of paying for school while 49.1% indicated parental support as their primary means of managing college costs. Although 38.9% reported working while attending the community college, 27.2% indicated that they would spend 30 or more hours per week working while enrolled at their new transfer institution and 27.9% stated they intended to work 21–30 hours weekly, 16.2% would expend 16–20 hours per week working, and 6.6% of students had 11–15 hours of weekly work. Roughly 6% of students reported that they would be working 10 hours or less, and 16.2% were unemployed.

In transitioning from two-year to four-year institutions, 40% of students transferred having conferred their associate's degree and 57.6% of respondents stated that they were familiar with the articulation agreements for transfer of general education credits. The average number of credit hours transferring was 47.1 while the mean total expected to transfer was 50.9 credit hours. The self-reported final community college grade point average was 3.30 on a four-point scale. The top five declared majors were health/human services (19.6%), education (18.8%), business (13.8%), social sciences (9.4%), and biological sciences (7.2%).

Constructs

We attempted to measure the reliability of multiple indicator variables representing various constructs of interest in this study. In order to assure that the items measure the same thing, we tested for unidimensionality using Cronbach's Alpha. Cronbach's Alpha is a common test used to measure the intercorrelation of items. If the alpha was greater than or equal to .60, then we considered the items an accurate measure of the construct of interest (i.e., social capital, self-efficacy, transfer preparedness, and satisfaction with transfer advising). Overall, what was purportedly considered to measure the following constructs were one-dimensional and subsequently operationalized well.

Social Capital

Social capital was operationalized with two items—measures of mother's and father's highest educational attainment (Strayhorn, 2010). The response choices for parents' highest level of education ranged from 1 = Don't Know, 2 = Less than high school, 3 = Less than two years of vocational, trade or business school beyond high school; 4 = Less than two years of college, 5 = Two or more years of college (including an Associate's degree); 6 = Four-year college degree, 7 = Master's degree, to 8 = Ph.D., Ed.D., J.D., M.D.. or other equivalent professional degree. The two items illustrate homogeneity and are reliable measures of social capital with a Cronbach's Alpha of .721.

Self-Efficacy

There were seven items comprising the self-efficacy construct. More specifically, self-efficacy was measured by asking community college transfers to rate themselves in terms of academic ability, leadership ability, math ability, writing ability, leadership ability, social confidence, intellectual confidence, and drive to achieve. Each was measured on a five-point Likert scale from 1 = Lowest 10%, 2 = Below average, 3 = Average, 4 = Above average, to 5 = Highest 10%. The Cronbach's Alpha reliability test yielded a .748 coefficient for the self-efficacy items.

Community College Rigor

As community colleges have been depicted in the literature and the media as less academically stringent collegiate contexts, student perceptions of curricular rigor was measured by level of agreement on a four-point Likert scale that included the following eight items:

- The community college courses developed my critical and analytical thinking.
- The community college courses demanded intensive writing assignments and projects.
- Overall, the community college courses were intellectually challenging.

- The community college courses prepared me for the academic standards at this institution.
- The community college courses prepared me for my major at this institution.
- The community college course requirements were demanding.
- The community college courses required extensive reading and writing.
- I sought academic tutoring for the classes.

The Cronbach Alpha revealed a reliability coefficient of .812

Transfer Preparedness

Variables reflecting transfer preparedness received a Cronbach's Alpha of .695 for the seven items comprising this construct indicative of student familiarity with the transfer process. The seven questions measuring transfer preparedness were anchored on four-point Likert scales that queried whether community college transfers disagreed strongly (i.e., 1 = strongly disagree to 4 = strongly agree) or agreed strongly with the following:

- I researched various aspects of four-year college or university to get a better understanding of the environment and academic expectations.
- I knew what to expect at the four-year college or university in terms of academics.
- I visited the four-year college or university campus to learn where offices and departments were located.
- I felt confident about the new challenges at the four-year university.
- I visited the admissions office at the four-year college or university.
- I spoke to former community college transfers to gain insight about their adjustment experiences.

Satisfaction with Transfer Advising

The scale for transfer advising satisfaction produced a Cronbach's Alpha reliability coefficient of .82. Seven items gauging level of agreement on a four-point Likert scale from 1 = Strongly disagree to 4 = Strongly agree with items such as the transfer center being helpful in providing valuable information about transfer, to the staff responsiveness to student needs and requests and sponsoring of information fairs and sessions for prospective students. Each of the three aforementioned items was asked with respect to satisfaction with previous community college transfer advising and satisfaction with transfer advising at the receiving institution.

Correlation Analysis

Are student background characteristics such as gender, race/ethnicity, and GPA significantly related to social capital and self-efficacy among community college transfer students? Are transfer student perceptions of community college rigor related to high self-efficacy and transfer preparedness? In addressing these questions, we conducted a correlation analysis to determine if there was a relationship between the variables representing the constructs with the designated student demographics. In testing whether a statistically significant association exists between these factors, we employed a nonparametric test, Spearman's rank correlation, as it does not assume that the variables are normally distributed. For students of color independently of whites, there were no significant correlations found at the .05 probability level, though a slightly moderate positive relationship approaching statistical significance was found between final community college GPA and transfer preparedness ($r = .326$, $p = .056$); the higher the GPA, the greater the transfer preparedness.

By comparison, for white community college transfer students, the Spearman's test yielded a statistically significant positive relationship at $p < .01$ level between gender and final community college GPA ($r = .282$, $p = .007$). For the entire sample combined, a very weak relationship was found to be statistically significant between gender and transfer preparedness ($r = 168$, $p < .05$). Additionally, positive weak relationships were found significant between race/ethnicity with final community college GPA ($r = .207$, $p < .05$) and gender was associated with final community college GPA ($r = .229$, $p < .01$). In short, though the relationships found to be significant were not particularly strong, higher GPAs were more associated with white female students.

ANOVA

A Kruskal-Wallis one-way ANOVA was conducted in addition to the usual ANOVA that test for homogeneity of means. We assumed the groups would be heterogeneous, have different means and unequal variances. Hence, this non-parametric method for comparing three or more unpaired groups of sample data was most appropriate for responding to the question, "Does social capital influence community college transfer students differently by race/ethnicity?" A one-way ANOVA indicated significant between-group differences by race/ethnicity with social capital $F(2, 135) = 5.264$, $p = .006$. However, the homogeneity of variance was violated; therefore, the Kruskal-Wallis one-way ANOVA is reported. There was a marginally significant difference among community college transfer students by race/ethnicity on social capital (Chi sq = 5.343, df = 2, $p = .069$), suggesting that the samples have slightly different levels of social capital by race/ethnicity.

Our fourth query asked, "Is there a difference in the level of satisfaction with community college transfer advising, transfer preparedness, or self-efficacy by race/ethnicity?" Again, based on the initial ANOVA, as we suspected any assumption of homogeneity of variance was broken. Therefore, we referenced the Kruskal-Wallis one-way ANOVA and found no statistically significant differences on self-efficacy, transfer preparedness, or satisfaction with transfer advising by race/ethnicity among community college transfer students.

Qualitative Component

The last question of interest in this study was, "What are the overall experiences of transfer students relative to ease or difficulty in navigating the transfer process and transitioning from a two-year to four-year institution?" The open-ended items on the L-TSQ as well as the follow-up focus group interview with transfer orientation attendees served as the less-dominant approach to respond to this query and provide qualitative data to augment the survey data. There were four open-ended items on the survey:

1. What factors assisted your adjustment to the university?
2. What factors have contributed to your successful transfer and transition?
3. What key factors made the transfer process difficult?
4. How much do you think your opinions can have an impact on the transfer process at this institution?

Building upon their participation in the survey, we sought to employ focus group research. While the use of standard survey questions is key in group interviewing, it is not standard in focus group research; hence, no structured interview protocol was used (Krueger & Casey, 2000; Morgan, 1997). The only topic explored through the exchange of this group discussion pertained to community college experiences and perceptions of the transfer process.

Initially, 15 students agreed to participate. However, two of the 15 were lateral four-year transfers who did not fall within our criteria for participation. Subsequently, four community college transfers who originally expressed interest did not return calls to confirm participation, yielding nine community college transfer students who volunteered for the focus group discussion. All participating in the focus group were traditional college-aged (20–24 years), employed (i.e., ranging from 10–35 hours per week), and enrolled full-time (i.e., 12 or more credit hours attempted). Two transfer students identified as white, five African American, one Asian American, and one Hispanic; four of the nine participants were male.

The following themes emerged from the open-ended items[3] and discussion with the nine focus group participants: (1) academic rigor and institutional culture, (2) effectiveness of academic and student services efforts, and (3) climate concerns.

Academic Rigor and Institutional Culture

Most of the participants expressed views regarding academic rigor and preparedness. The data from the open-ended items and focus group interview revealed two subcategories: (a) coursework and placement matters and (b) collegiality of campus environment.

Coursework and Placement Matters

The literature suggests there are a growing number of students who are not college ready. By and large, the students surveyed and interviewed varied with respect to their feelings surrounding the courses and levels of difficulty experienced, due in part to whether or not they had deficiencies in certain areas. A few students in the focus group expressed that remediation presented an obstacle in their quest to earn transferable college credits. One young man asserted:

> Everyone takes a developmental math class even if their high school grades were good. I think community college assessments hinder you, slow you down, and get the school more money since you're here longer, because you have take time out to redo the basics.

There was a general conviction that developmental course offerings were not effective in remediation of students who were not deemed college ready for particular areas. With regard to remedial classes, one of the students remarked:

> They will grade your papers saying you should already know this. The English 099 class I had didn't give enough thorough feedback to let you know where you went wrong. My professor told me I should have listened more in high school, so how does that help me in reaching the college-level course work I need to take? As a student of color, it seems that the white students get more technical assistance from this instructor.

Critics of the community college contend that there exists a lack of academic rigor and collegiality in the organizational culture (Dougherty, 1987; Pincus & Archer, 1989). Research suggests that community colleges have a profoundly adverse impact on student degree attainment, arguing that community college students are less likely to reach their baccalaureate degree goals (Brint & Karabel, 1989; Dougherty, 1994; Richardson & Bender, 1987). With respect to academic rigor and collegiality, some students explained:

> Some of the teachers should not be rated. Some of them let us out in 30 minutes when it is supposed to be an hour or hour and a half long class.

> The class intensity is moderate. I believe it is the open access that affects the curriculum and how intense it is. Because this community college it accepts all students and needs all of its students. Just look at the application, you don't need much to get in. This school accepts anybody and they need to accept a better bunch. As long as anybody can and will come, the standards will stay minimal. So if you get kicked out of a university, where do you go? The transfer function needs to be strengthened because the universities may perceive our two-year transfers as being not as prepared and from weaker academic standards.

The following illustrates the large number of student opinions relative to orientation and institutional culture. Overall, the students' opinions about the institutional climate and primary orientation of the community college and receiving institution were met with mixed opinions.

> My community college counselor was very, very helpful. He returned phone calls, mailed me documents, met with me and had follow-up e-mails and letters to help me transition into university.

> The community college is what I consider a big high school. That's what community colleges are; just more expensive compared to others.

> The course offerings are okay but there needs to be more transferable courses. The transfer center wasn't too specific on what the university would accept. I want to transfer to over in Sociology and minor in Criminal Justice. I did not even receive an invitation for orientation. I was aware of it and attended by tagging along with another student.

> It seemed as if there were many barriers when I tried to register for classes. Things I should have already done that I did not know about. It would have been nice to get a package with my pre-registration requirements and counseling appointments.

> The transfer orientation was too long, I thought I was going to learn something, and could have gained the same amount of knowledge from a mail packet.

Effectiveness of Academic and Student Services Efforts

The students differed on the extent to which they felt faculty, administrators, and support staff provided valuable services that fostered their ability to make a successful and seamless transition from the community college to the four-year institution of their choice. Roughly half offered that there are opportunities for self-actualization and positive goal fulfillment, such as:

> My professors were very good at teaching material. They could be found to ask questions in their office and were very hands-on. Other students were nice and I made friends easily.

> Student activities at my community college went out of their way to let you know what is going on academically in terms of the college programs promoted. They even used the social events for promoting the academic programs. I feel they go out of their way to get the information for the students, but it is up to the students to take advantage of it or not.

> I credit all of my easy adjustment to Jamie (pseudonym) at the transfer center. I have never been helped so efficiently, honestly and effectively than by her. She spoke candidly about what was truly important and with a phone call took care of anything I needed, even if I didn't know at the time I needed it.

Other respondents expressed that they were dissatisfied with student support services. Many also acknowledged the need for better communication of transfer requirements and advising.

> I would not call it successful. They [advising] never gave me a straight answer and I was transferred too many times to count and disconnected a lot. It was by accident that I was successful and with no help from the school.

> The college trains you to go to work for others, not be independent thinkers trained to be the employer, the leaders and not be led or be the employee. I won't say any names, but I told one administrator at my community college I wanted to become a lawyer and I was told I shouldn't go into law since there are so many brothers [black men] in jails. What does that mean? And how is that encouraging to me? In terms of classes taken, the advisors in the transfer center counseled me wrong. They gave me classes that I did not need and none of them transferred, so now I have to go summer school to make up the hours.

> My counselor treated me with no respect, made the transfer process very hard, causing me to delay my transfer an entire semester.

Campus Climate Concerns

Of the students interviewed, two expressed being satisfied with the amount of diversity at their previous colleges. With respect to diversity, some of the students had problems with what they perceived as a lack of diversity among the student body. Others took issue with there not being enough faculty and staff of color (i.e., a representative amount based on the percentage of the population at large in this area). What follows are remarks some of the students made regarding the institutional culture's lack of inclusion and diminutive keenness for diversity.

> If you got all of us here together [i.e., students of color] we could fit into this small room. I was the only Latino student in my class; the rest of the class was all white. I think that this lack of diversity in terms of students that attend this college is important regarding persistence because it can be a very isolating experience being the only one in your class. Now having transferred it is not different. When I was at my community college, at first I felt my voice wasn't as big since I was the only person of color in my classes. Then I began to meet other Latino students, slowly since there are so few of us. But my point is that I did not feel recognized by my peers or my teachers of Anglo descent.

> Student body diversity at my previous institution was is poor in my opinion. But I am not sure this school will have a better mix academically or socially, not as far as I can tell.

> Now that I have transferred, it is early but I haven't seen too many Latino/a or Asian students; but it appears to be quite a few black and plenty white. So on one end this college is diverse racially because there is some of just about every group, but I personally would like to a larger portion of Latino/a students enrolled here.

In addition to the concerns surrounding diversity, participants echoed that they found their collegiate experiences complicated by the fact that there was an absence of multiculturalism infused in the curriculum. Although the participants' perceptions of the severity of issues surrounding diversity varied, there was general uniformity in their expressed views regarding inclusion and multiculturalism.

> This school and any other, needs to realize the demographics are changing and they have to fill the needs of the new diversity in this community and not just focus on the needs of the majority students. There is always a need for more classes, programs, and faculty of color, not faculty that sees a minority and sees us in stereotypic ways, making judgments about the type of persons we are.

> I am sure that if there were more instructors of color, then students would do a lot better and go on to graduate.

> Like with examples given in class, people use examples from their experiences. Being white and rural, I still do not see my experience. When there is a lack of participation from students, like myself it is because I just can't relate to what is being discussed. Maybe there is not enough multiculturalism infused in the curriculum; but the needs of different types of students besides African American and Hispanic students are overlooked too.

DISCUSSION

Consistent with the literature, participants felt that barriers to transfer are in part due to not receiving appropriate advising with regard to what courses will actually transfer to four-year colleges and universities (Laanan, 2004; Townsend, 1995; Townsend, McNerny, & Arnold, 1993). Hence, in a higher education, consumer-driven market, community colleges are primed to address capital and increase student currency when responsive to student preferences. While there is a high desire for transfer among many baccalaureate aspirants, there often is a disconnect between student aspirations and the actualization of their desired degree plans. Consumer theory posits that when the price of products increase (e.g., the cost of a college education), the consumer (i.e., the student) will be cognizant of the pricing and may select a less expensive option (e.g., the community college) (Mirowski & Hands, 2006).

Because of the wide range in institutions of higher learning, it is sometimes difficult for students to ascertain what is acceptable relative to transferring credit hours earned. Concomitantly, articulation has not been established across all programs of study or two- and four-year institutions. Thus, practitioners must maintain continued systematic efforts and services to ensure seamless continuity of matriculation that will not obstruct educational progress between various segments of higher education.

Within predominately white institutions of higher education, students of color may often feel that the campus climate is not inclusive nor the environment welcoming (Zamani, 2001; Zamani-Gallaher, Green, Brown, & Stovall, 2009). Students wanted to see reflections of themselves, and to the extent that this did not occur, their interpretation of the institutional culture at their community colleges and projected feelings at the receiving institution were mixed. The students responding in this study expressed a desire for the college to actively encourage multiculturalism within the curriculum and promote a diverse campus environment. Additionally, a fair number of those participating wanted to feel that there was a greater commitment to fostering their academic and social development.

Principally, since many minority students begin their postsecondary career in community colleges, the aforementioned adjustment difficulties of transfer students are particularly important when looking at students of color who may arguably have less access to the repositories of social capital (Koenigbauer, 2006). According to Koenigbauer (2006), racial and ethnic minority students constitute approximately one-quarter of the enrollment in community colleges. The idea of college is often foreign to many students of color, chiefly since they are the first in their family to go to college (Cohen & Brawer, 2008). Once these students arrive at the institution, they may experience a hostile environment. Several institutions of higher education ignore the challenges faced by students of color (Gurin, Dey, Hurtado, & Gurin, 2002; Hurtado, 1992; Tatum, 2000; Zamani-Gallaher et al., 2009).

As previously stated, the research on transfer students is significant. Unfortunately, much of it simply focuses on the hindrances faced by transfer students. Few researchers have focused on the variables associated with transfer success. The few who have researched this area claim transfer success can be measured through academic, psychological, and career variables.

Ling (2006) cited Alpern's (2000) study in which he suggested that the retention of a transfer student at a four-year institution was related to expectations about the transfer process and career and educational goals. Davies and Casey (1999) claimed that psychological issues play a key role in retention. These psychological issues include transfer shock (Laanan & Starobin, 2004; Kodama, 2002). Based on Kodama's (2002) study, transfer students who had fewer sources of support from their institution did not perform well, which contributed to feelings of marginality. Other researchers have supported this concept. According to Davies and Casey (1999), transfer students who had less support had negative college experiences.

The role of social capital (as a form of social mobility) is important in facilitating the transfer process. Jovel (2008) studied the community college transfer process of Chicana/o students through a qualitative exploration. The findings of this exploratory study support that social capital can be tapped into through effective, accurate, and consistent interaction with faculty and student services staff in building networks, relationships, and access to resources and information necessary to navigate transferring from two-year to four-year institutions of higher learning.

Limitations

As with most studies, this study is not without shortcomings. Among the limitations was that this study was not drawn from a probability sample as there was no random selection of transfer students. Therefore, this study cannot claim to be representative of the entire transfer population as it was an opportunity sample close at hand. The sample was not robust enough for high-level quantitative analysis, and thus the sample size probably was not large enough in one or more of the groups. Although the reliability of the social capital scale used for this study was strong (i.e., Cronbach's Alpha .721), it was a limited measure of social capital as it did not include the myriad of factors that potentially inform this construct (e.g., family income). Finally, the findings yielded few statistically significant associations, and those emerging can only suggest the possible existence of causation.

CONCLUSIONS

Considering the current trends of increased growth in the two-year college sector coupled with the worst economy in the U.S. since the Great Depression, despite the mixed views of transfer students from this sample, the overall desire to navigate from open-door institutions to those with more selective admissions in pursuit of the baccalaureate remains desirable. There is little likelihood that community colleges will be in less demand given the increased need for postsecondary attainment for gainful employment. Furthermore, with the economic recovery of the U.S. unknown, consumer demand for community colleges suggests that even students who have other postsecondary options are examining their financial situations to get the most educational bang for their buck. Despite the transfer function not being seamless across two- and four-year contexts, it is perceived as carrying a utilitarian function, poised to be a catalyst for consumer optimization of educational and career plans.

In closing, a great deal of research is still needed to address the transfer student population. This is an exciting time for research on community college students. Scholars such as Laanan (2004) have called for a greater commitment by higher education institutions to addressing transfer issues. Empirical studies need to focus on the crucial needs of this population, their perceptions of transfer readiness, self-efficacy, and whether either foster capital in the form of currency to be spent upon transfer. Also important is gauging student satisfaction with their transfer institutions as well as the receiving universities in facilitating a seamless transition from two- to four-year colleges.

NOTES

1. The theory of optimum currency supposes that there is no single currency; instead there is a system of flexible exchange rates creating a common currency subsequently increasing the flow of capital over the long term (Mundell, 1961).
2. Fifteen of the returned surveys were from lateral transfers of students from other four-year institutions.
3. Responsiveness on the open-ended questions of the survey was apparent, as 140 out 141 of those completing the instrument replied to all four items.

REFERENCES

Adelman, C. (2005). *Moving into town—and moving on: The community college in the lives of traditional-age students.* Washington, DC: U.S. Department of Education.

Alpern, B.E. (2000). *Factors that influence community college transfer students' satisfaction with their baccalaureate institutions.* Retrieved from http://eric.ed.gov/PDFS/ED449854.pdf

Aragon, S.R. & Zamani, E.M. (2002). Promoting access and equity through minority serving institutions. In M. C. Brown (Ed.), *Equity and Access in Higher Education: Changing the Definition of Educational Opportunity,* (Readings on Equal Education, Volume 18, pp. 23-50). New York: AMS Press.

Astin, A. W. (1985). *Achieving educational excellence.* San Francisco: Jossey-Bass.

Ayers, D.F. (2010, May–June). Putting the community back into the college. *Academe, 96*(3). Retrieved from http://www.aaup.org/AAUP/pubsres/academe/2010/MJ/feat/ayer.htm

Bailey, T. R. & Alfonzo, M. (2005, January). *Paths to persistence: An analysis of research on program effectiveness at community colleges* [Monograph]. Lumina Foundation for Education New Agenda Series, 6(1).

Bandura, A. (1977). Self-efficacy: Toward a unifying theory of behavioral change. *Psychological Review, 84*(2), 191–215.

Bandura, A. (1997). *Self-efficacy: The exercise of control.* New York: Worth Publishers.

Bandyopadhyay, S. (2008). *Impact of Individual and Institutional Characteristics on Transfer from Two-Year to Four-Year Public Institutions in Ohio.* Athens, OH: Ohio University.

Berger, J. B. & Malaney, G. D. (2003). Assessing the transition of transfer students from community colleges to a university. *NASPA Journal, 40*(4), 1–23.

Bong, M. (1997, March). *Congruence of measurement specificity on relations between academic self efficacy, effort, and achievement indexes.* Paper presented at the Annual Meeting of the American Educational Research Association, Chicago, IL.

Bragg, D. D. (Ed.) (2001). *The new vocationalism in American community colleges: New directions for community colleges.* San Francisco, CA: Jossey-Bass.

Brick, M. (1994). From forum and focus for the junior college movement. In J. L. Ratliff, S.Schwarz, & L. H. Ebbers (Eds.), *Community colleges ASHE reader series* (2nd ed., pp. 43–56). Lexington: Ginn Press.

Brint, S. & Karabel, J. (1989a). *The diverted dream: Community colleges and the promise of educational opportunity in America, 1900–1985.* New York: Oxford University Press.

Brint, S. & Karabel, J. (1989b). American education, meritocratic ideology, and the legitimization of inequality: The community college and the problem of American exceptionalism. *Higher Education, 18,* 725–735.

Brown, M. & Davis, J. E. (2001). The historically Black college as a social contract, social capital, and social equalizer. *Peabody Journal of Education, 76*(1), 31–49.

Cain, M. S. (1999). *The community college in the twenty-first century: A system approach.* Lanham, MD: University Press of America.

Carnevale, A.P., Strohl, J., & Smith, N. (2009). Help wanted: Postsecondary education and training required. *New Directions for Community Colleges, 146,* 21–31.

Christie, R. & Hutchinson, P. (2003). Net effects of institutional type on baccalaureate degree attainment of "traditional" students. *Community College Review, 31*(2), 1–20.

Clark, B. R. (1960). The "cooling out" function in higher education. *American Journal of Sociology, 65,* 569–576.

Clark, B. R. (1973, Winter). Development of the sociology of higher education. *Sociology of Education*, 2–14.

Cohen, A. M., & Brawer, F. B. (1996). *The American community college* (3rd ed.). San Francisco: Jossey-Bass.

Cohen, A. M. & Brawer, F. B. (2008). *The American community college* (5th ed.). San Francisco: Jossey-Bass.

Darity, W.A., Jr. (1982). The human capital approach to black–white earnings inequality: Some unsettled questions. *The Journal of Human Resources, 17*(1), 72–93.

Davies, T. G. & Casey, K. (1999). Transfer student experiences: Comparing their academic and social lives at the community college and university. *College Student Journal, 33*(1), 60–71.

Dougherty, K. J. (1987). The effects of community colleges: Aid or hindrance to socioeconomic attainment? *Sociology of Education, 60,* 86–103.

Dougherty, K.J. (1994). *The contradictory college: The conflicting origins, impacts, and futures of the community college.* Albany: State University of New York Press.

Doyle, W. R. (2006, May/June). Community college transfers and college graduation: Whose choices matter most? *Change, 38*(3), 56–58.

Farmer-Hinton, R. L. (2008). Social capital and college planning: Students of color using school networks for support and guidance. *Education and Urban Society, 41*(1), 127–157.

Farmer-Hinton, R.L. & Adams, T. L. (2006). Social capital and college preparation: Exploring the role of counselors in a college prep school for Black students. *Negro Education Review, 57*(1–2), 101–116.

Flowers, L. A. (2006). Effects of attending a 2-year institution on African American males' academic and social integration in the first year of college. *Teachers College Record, 108*(2), 267–286.

Gabert, G. (1991). *Community colleges in the 1990s.* Bloomington, IN: Phi Delta Kappa Educational Foundation.

Glazer, N. Y. (1991). "Between a rock and a hard place": Women's professional organizations in nursing and class, racial, and ethnic inequalities. *Gender and Society, 5*(3), 351–372.

Gonzalez, K. P., Stoner, C., & Jovel, J. E. (2003). Examining the role of social capital in access to college for Latinas: Toward a college opportunity framework. *Journal of Hispanic Higher Education, 2*(1), 146–170.

Grubb, W. N. (1991). The decline of community college transfer rates: Evidence from national longitudinal surveys. *Journal of Higher Education, 62,* 194–217.

Gurin, P., Dey, E., Hurtado, S., & Gurin, G. (2002). Diversity and higher education: Theory and impact on educational outcomes. *Harvard Educational Review, 72*(3), 330–366.

Hill, J. (1965). Transfer shock: The academic performance of the junior college transfer. *Journal of Experimental Education, 33,* 201–216.

Hunter, L. T. (2007). *Examining attendance patterns of students enrolled in American community colleges.* Athens, OH: Ohio University.

Hurtado, S. (1992). The campus racial climate: Contexts of conflict. *The Journal of Higher Education, 63,* 539–569.

Jackson, G. C., & Healy, C. G. (1996). Career development profiles and interventions for underrepresented college students. *The Career Development Quarterly, 44*, 258–269.

Jimenez, S.S. (2006). *Inspiring academic confidence in the classroom: An investigation of features of the classroom experience that contribute to the academic self-efficacy of undergraduate women enrolled in gateway courses.* Unpublished doctoral dissertation, University of Wisconsin-Madison.

Jovel, J.E. (2008). *Community college transfer: The role of social capital in the transfer process of Chicana/o students.* Doctoral dissertation. Available from ProQuest Dissertations and Theses database. (UMI No. 3332848).

Kerr, K. H. (2006). *The experience of being a transfer student at a four-year university.* CA: California State University.

Kodama, C. M. (2002). Marginality of transfer commuter students. *NASPA Journal, 39*(3), 233–250.

Koenigbauer, L. A. (2006). *Effects of articulation agreements on transfer students of color at predominantly white university.* Bowling Green, OH: Bowling Green University.

Krueger, R. A. & Casey, M.A. (2000). *Focus groups : A practical guide for applied research.* Thousand Oaks, CA: Sage Publications.

Laanan, F. S. (2004). Studying transfer students: Part 1: Instrument design and implications. *Community College Journal of Research and Practice, 28*, 331–351.

Laanan, F.S. & Starobin, S. S. (2004, Summer). Urban community college transfers to a university. *Academic Exchange*, 139–147.

Lee, V. & Frank, K. (1990). Student characteristics that facilitate the transfer from two-year to four-year colleges. *Sociology of Education, 63*, 178–193.

Lent, R.W, Brown, S.D., & Hackett, G. (1994). Sociocognitive mechanisms of personal agency on career development: Pantheoretical prospects. In M. L. Savikas & R. W. Lent (Eds.) *Convergence in Career Development and Theories* (pp. 77–102). Palo Alto, CA: CCP Books.

Levin, J. S. (2002a). In education and in work: The globalized community college. *The Canadian Journal of Higher Education, 32*(2), 47–78.

Levin, J. S. (2002b). Global culture and the community college. *Community College Journal of Research and Practice, 26*(2), 121–145.

Ling, T. J. (2006). *The relation of self variables to transfer student success as measured by academic, psychological, and career functioning.* Latham: University of Maryland.

Mirowski, P. & Hands, D.W. (2006). *Agreement on demand: Consumer theory in the twentieth century.* Durham, NC: Duke University Press.

Morgan D.L. (1997). *Focus groups as qualitative research* (2nd ed.). London: Sage Publications.

Mundell, R.A. (1961). A theory of optimum currency areas. *The American Economic Review, 51*(4), 657–665.

National Center for Education Statistics (2001). *Digest of Education Statistics: 2000.* Washington, DC: U.S. Department of Education.

Palmer, R. & Gasman, M. (2008). "It takes a village to raise a child": The role of social capital in promoting academic success for African American men at a black college. *Journal of College Student Development, 49*(1), 52–70.

Parajes, F. (2002). Self-efficacy beliefs in academic contexts: An outline. Retrieved from http://www.des.emory.edu/mfp/efftalk.html

Pascarella, E.T., Pierson, C.T., Wolniak, G.C., & Terenzini, P.T. (2004). First-generation college students: Additional evidence on college experiences and outcomes. *Journal of Higher Education, 75*(3), 249-284.

Pascarella, E.T., & Terenzini, P. (2005). *How college affects students: A third decade of research* (2nd ed.). San Francisco: Jossey-Bass.

Pincus, F. & Archer, E. (1989). *Bridges to opportunity: Are community colleges meeting the transfer needs of minority students?* New York: Academy for Educational Development and College Entrance Examination Board.

Putnam, R.D. (1995). Bowling alone: America's declining social capital. *Journal of Democracy, 6*(1), 65–78.

Rice, T. J. (2008). *Riding out the waves: Community college transfers graduating with bachelor's degrees.* Bowling Green, OH: Bowling Green State University.

Richardson, R.C. & Bender, L.W. (1987). *Fostering minority access and achievement in higher education: The role of urban community colleges and universities.* San Francisco: Jossey Bass.

Romano, R.M., & Dellow, D.A. (2009). Technological change, globalization, and the college college. *New Directions for Community Colleges, 146,* 11–19.

Schaefer-McDaniel, N. J. (2004). Conceptualizing social capital among young people: Towards a new theory. *Children, Youth and Environments, 14*(1), 153–172.

Schlossberg, N. K. (1995). *Counseling adults in transition: Linking practice with theory.* New York: Springer Publishing Company.

Schultz, T. W. (1961). Investment in human capital. *The American Economic Review, 51*(1), 1–17.

Smith, H. M., & Betz, N. E. (2000). Development and validation of a scale of perceived social self-efficacy. *Journal of Career Assessment, 8*(3), 283–301.

Stanton-Salazar, R. D. (1997). A social capital framework for understanding the socialization of racial minority children and youths. *Harvard Educational Review, 67*(1), 1–40.

Strayhorn, T.L. (2008). The role of supportive relationships in facilitating African American males' success in college. *NASPA Journal, 45*(1), 26–48.

Strayhorn, T.L. (2010). When race and gender collide: Social and cultural capital's influence on the academic achievement of African American and Latino males. *The Review of Higher Education, 33*(3), 307–332.

Tatum, B.D. (2000). The ABC approach to creating climates of engagement on diverse campuses. *Liberal Education, 86*(4), 22–30.

Townsend, B. K. (1995). Community college transfer students: A case study of survival. The *Review of Higher Education, 18*(2), 175–193.

Townsend, B. K., McNerny, N., & Arnold, A. (1993). Will this community college transfer student succeed? Factors affecting transfer student performance. *Community College Journal of Research and Practice, 17,* 433–443.

Townsend, B. K. & Wilson, K. B. (2006). "A hand to hold for a little bit": Factors facilitating the success of community college transfer students to a large research university. *Journal of College Student Development, 47,* 439–456.

Vaughan, G. B. (1997). The community college's mission and milieu: Institutionalizing community-based programming. In E. J. Boone & Associates (Eds.), *Community leadership through community-based programming* (pp. 21–58). Washington, DC: Community College Press.

Wechsler, H. (1989). *The transfer challenge: Removing barriers, maintaining commitment.* Washington, DC: Association of American Colleges.

Wells, R. (2008). The effects of social and cultural capital on student persistence: Are community colleges more meritocratic? *Community College Review, 36*(1), 25–46.

Wells, R. (2009). Social and cultural capital, race and ethnicity, and college student retention. *Journal of College Student Retention, 10*(2), 103–128.

The White House. (2009, July 14). *Excerpts of the president's remarks in Warren, Michigan today and a fact sheet on the American Graduation Initiative.* Washington, DC: Office of the Press Secretary. Retrieved from http://www.whitehouse.gov/the_press_office/excerpts-of-the-presidents-remarks-in-warren-michigan-and-fact-sheet-on-the-american-graduation-initiative/

Wyatt, M. (1992). The past, present and future need for college reading courses in the U.S. *Journal of Reading, 36*(1), 10–20.

Zamani, E. M. (2001). Institutional responses to barriers to the transfer process. *New Directions for Community Colleges, 114,* 15–24.

Zamani-Gallaher, E.M., Green, D.O, Brown, M.C., & Stovall, D.O. (2009). *The case for affirmative action on campus: Concepts of equity, considerations for practice.* Sterling, VA: Stylus Publishing.

PART II

EDUCATIONAL CONTEXT AND THE PRODUCER ASPECTS OF CAPITAL

CHAPTER 5

CAPITAL GAINS AND LOSSES

The Roles of Political, Social, and Cultural Capital in School Reform and School Access

Sheneka M. Williams
University of Georgia

Robert W. Gaines, II
University of Georgia

School reform efforts rarely formulate from top-down governance structures. Instead, they often promulgate from the pressures of grass roots efforts, or in some instances, interest group politics. Regardless of how school reform efforts initiate, most reform efforts are formed by those who possess capital—either political, social, or cultural capital. Following the work of Bartee and Brown (2007), this chapter defines capital as exclusive assets containing the capacity to reproduce profitable, meaningful rewards. More specifically, this chapter will focus on the producer aspects of capital in school reform and access.

Contemporary Perspectives on Capital in Educational Contexts, pages 135–149

Bourdieu and Passeron (1977) argued that the knowledge of the upper and middle classes are considered capital valuable to a hierarchical society. As such, the voices of upper and middle class parents are most often heard in terms of school reform efforts. As the power of the middle class pushes reform efforts forward, the needs of high-poverty students are often left unmet. This, in turn, may give rise to the achievement gap between high-poverty and low-poverty students. Yosso (2005) notes that there is an assumption that people of color and impoverished people lack the social and cultural capital required for social mobility. Additionally, Valenzuela (1999) offers that schools often work from this assumption in structuring ways to help "disadvantaged" students whose race and class background have left them lacking necessary knowledge, social skills, abilities, and cultural capital. For example, Walker and Gutmore (2002) examined the role of civic capacity, or political capital,[1] in urban educational reform in New Jersey. Looking at the state's 30 poorest districts, they sought to

> (a) establish the degree of civic capacity in the districts and determine the factors that explain differences among the districts' abilities to build cross-sector support for the reforms; (b) determine the impact of civic support on the districts' willingness to embrace the remedies proposed by the court; and (c) measure the relationship between civic support and the perceptions of resource problems. (p. 66)

At the conclusion of the study, they found that a district's civic capacity was directly tied to its level of poverty. Districts with less poverty showed higher levels of support for reform efforts in the community. Further, communities with strong histories of political involvement tended to support reform efforts more than those without such histories. Lastly, they found a strong link between districts' civic capacity and access to key groups like the State Department of Education. This is not to say that poor people do not want to be involved in reform efforts. This is also not to suggest that middle class parents intentionally speak for their children only. However, it must be noted that "voice" matters, and middle class parents use their voice as capital. This, in turn, often produces change in terms of school reform and school access.

The racial and social class achievement gap call for reform efforts to improve student achievement for all students, but for students of color, in particular. Given the need for school reform, efforts for leveraging capital come to the forefront as a means to improve our nation's schools, and in turn, improve student achievement for all students. This chapter will focus on capital- political, social, and cultural- and how individuals utilize capital either to influence school reform efforts or to gain access to "better" schooling opportunities. More specifically, this chapter will present cases in which capital—political, social, and cultural—produces profitable ends in terms of school reform and access.

THE INFLUENCE OF POLITICAL CAPITAL ON SCHOOL REFORM

Brazilian intellectual and educator Paulo Freire is lauded as one of the early thinkers who theorized the connection between education and politics, a critical nexus rooted in liberation and responsibility. He saw how methods of separating power, education, and politics "[remind] us that education is a political activity, and that any serious political activity is educational" (Torres, 1998, p. 10). The integrity of any democratic institution and its trek towards democratic utopia, he believed, would depend on its ability to produce an intellectually responsible citizenry dedicated to fulfilling its duty as civic agents (pp. 10–11). Further, he posited the notion that without political revolution, there existed no possibility for educational revolution. Freire's position that politics and education are inseparable establishes a context in which to explore and understand political will and civic capacity as they relate to school reform.

Hammergren (1998), in an examination of Latin American government reform efforts, examines thoroughly the term *political will*, though from a non-educational point of view. She contends that not only is the term difficult to define and identify, but it is often the on-hand "explanation for every policy failure despite the fact that so many programs are undertaken where it certainly does not seem present" (p. 12). Hammergren says that the concept of political will is severely complicated by questions like, "Whose political will?", "How much [political will] is enough?", "Does it have to be government sanctioned?", or "Is it determined by financial contributions?" In light of such questions, it is much easier to recognize the absence than the presence of political will, complete political opposition to reform. Further, she argues that the term is more rhetorical than analytic, leaving reform strategists to look more closely at "the relevant elements of the political environment" (Hammergren, 1998, p. 13). Hammergren also ties political will to constituency building and public support, two concepts she feels are related to but are more advanced than political will.

Clarence Stone (2001), in conjunction with the National Science Foundation, conducted a study on the relationship between civic capacity and school reform in urban cities. Civic capacity, he says, "concerns the extent to which different sectors of the community—business, parents, educators, state and local office holders, non-profits, and others—act in concert around a matter of community-wide import" (Stone, 2001, p. 596). Within the context of education, civic capacity is about achieving a collective mindset about a community issue in a way that is not in line with the normal way of approaching issues. Because building civic capacity is an inherently public endeavor, it is highly volatile and likely to collapse. This means that civic capacity is not easily transferred between major community issues. The challenge then is to engage not only the community's political elites, but also the ordinary citizens in order to maximize community investment and trust.

Marschall and Shah's (2005) research echoes many of Stone's sentiments about the challenge in achieving collective agreement. They find that "the politics and institutions of urban education hinder the emergence of civic capacity because of the diverse interests represented, the difficulty in identifying and employing appropriate selective incentives, and the limited role of policy entrepreneurs" (p. 164). The variety of stakeholders involved in urban school reform makes change a much more difficult task since everyone has different educational goals and interests. Even when changes are implemented, if all stakeholders are not satisfied with the reform, then there is a chance for policy churn, a steady cycle of adopting and purging of policies. Further, Marschall and Shah argue that civic capacity is strongest when stakeholders are equally visible to one another; they agree on strategies for achieving mutual policy goals; and the mayor operates as the chief stakeholder in the reform effort, setting the reform agenda in a way that encourages other stakeholders to coalesce around mutually beneficial ideas (p. 175).

Similarly, Feuerstein (2002) explores the nexus between politics and education as he examines the democratic nature of public education as evidenced through school board elections. He says, "Voting for school board members or school referenda is an important form of civic participation that links citizens to their schools.... It gives individuals an opportunity to express their support or discontent for the school program" (p. 16). In particular, Feuerstein discusses theoretical models of governance that seek to explain the civic influence on school boards. The models are all built on an adversarial view of community politics, which assume that political stakeholders, by nature, do not agree on the major issues. Because the perceived likelihood of community collaboration is minimal, civic issues must be settled through the voting process. Deliberative democracy, on the other hand, suggests that citizens engage in reciprocity and dialogue about their political differences in an effort to understand one another's positions and to establish common goals; such engagement improves the chances for democracy to prevail (p. 30).

In an effort to demonstrate how local school board elections are impacted by a community's political will, we offer the case of Wake County, North Carolina. Wake County Public Schools are often studied due to the nature of the district's successful schools. Many tout that the district's student assignment plan plays a major role in the quality of the district's schools. This vignette on Wake County, North Carolina, exemplifies the role of community leaders' exercise of political will in school reform.

THE CASE OF WAKE COUNTY, NORTH CAROLINA

On January 10, 2000, the Wake County Board of Education officially altered its student assignment policy, shifting from race-based to socioeconomic and performance-based criteria. The resulting policy shift reflected an intellectual trend towards socioeconomic, rather than race-based, integration of public schools through the use of student assignment policies. Wake's original race-based student assignment policy had been in effect since 1981, and was known as a 15/45 policy because it mandated that no school's African American population fall below 15% or rise above 45% (Wake Education Partnership, 2003).

It can be argued that the Wake school system itself was born out of an impulse towards school integration. The system was formed in 1976 by the merger of the greater Wake County system with the Raleigh City Schools. At the time, the Wake County system was comprised of majority white students, and Raleigh City Schools was comprised of majority African American students. One important dynamic of this merger that sets it apart from myriad others in the South during the 1960 and 1970s is that the merger was voted down by public referenda before it was engineered by civic leaders with the help of the state legislature. This narrative—of school and community leaders possessing foresight to take progressive action on behalf of children in the face of community opposition—frames much of the tenor of current controversies over Wake's new SES-based student assignment plan (The Century Foundation, 2001).

In the case of Wake County, suburban population growth hampered implementation efforts of the socioeconomic student assignment policy. Additionally, those who believed in maintaining socioeconomically balanced schools may have become lackadaisical in enforcing the importance of balanced schools. A city administrator noted, "You've got to keep telling your story over and over again. We're not working hard at sustaining that culture." Perhaps political voices that were active during the recent school board election will force district leaders who support balanced schools to tell the story as a means of sustaining the current student assignment policy (Williams & Houck, in press). District advocates of the socioeconomically based assignment policy find themselves fighting to maintain the policy, while a majority of newly elected school board members seek to abolish it. In May 2010, a relatively new school board majority voted to reverse the SES-based assignment plan and develop a policy based on geographic proximity. This vote is viewed by many as a twenty-first century mechanism of resegregating the district's schools. If this were to happen, then Wake County Public School System, which has been lauded as one of the highest performing districts in the nation, might see a change in overall student performance.

Datnow (2000) notes that systemic reform approaches refer to the development of clearly defined goals and intended outcomes that (1) promote sustainability to engage in continuous improvement and (2) build capacity in and around school systems. The success of reform initiatives, whether large-scale, system-wide, or school-level, is contingent upon individuals' and groups' ability to continually reevaluate and enhance practices tied to specific policies. Additionally, it relates to the interactions between various stakeholders in the organizations as they develop an understanding of: What does the reform mean? What is the purpose of the reform? How will it impact my current practices? In essence, it relates to stakeholders' ability to utilize political capital in ways that benefit students and not simply themselves.

Dorothy Shipps (2003) examines civic capacity in urban school reform, particularly in Chicago, and how different geographic contexts impact the political capabilities of a community. She builds on Stone's (2001) work and tackles her analysis through the theoretical lens of urban regime theory, which "focuses on the agency of local urban actors who come together in coalitions around reform ideas and bring their independent political, organizational, and economic resources to bear on these commitments" (p. 842). Further, the theory explains how different political groups in a community are able to coalesce around a specific reform effort in spite of their ideological differences and identifies the necessary components for sustaining educational change. Ultimately, she found that certain types of civic capacity were more easily developed than others. Coalitions that operated within a narrow, materially focused way were more effective than broad, socially driven coalitions that lacked foundational support. She also found that small changes in civic capacity were capable of altering reform efforts drastically. Lastly, she found that multiple reform coalitions, regardless of political strength, may compete for the same resources and goals.

As school district officials and community members work to further shape district schools, it is imperative that they understand that political capital within the context of school reform emerges from community members' endeavors. The extent to which members in a community can coalesce around and work towards achieving collective goals for educational change will determine the extent to which they can achieve their reform goals. According to Stone, Henig, Jones, and Pierannunzi (2001), the primary obstacles in school reform are political in nature; they are rooted in the fact that various groups have distinct interests that often lead them to work against one another in ways that dissipate energies and blunt reform efforts. Thus, in order to produce reform and gain access, stakeholders must develop a common purpose and see it through implementation.

The Use of Social Capital in School Reform Movements

Social capital generally refers to intangible and abstract resources derived from interactions among individuals and the social structures that frame them (Coleman, 1988). As a result, social capital may be produced through social interaction. Social capital consists of three main components: (1) social trust; (2) channels of communication; and (3) norms, expectations, and sanctions (Coleman, 1988, 1990; Smylie & Hart, 1999). While we argue that all three components are necessary for groups to engage each other and evoke change, we also argue that the three ties must be strong and positive in order to impact school reform.

A number of studies have examined the nature of school relationships with external change agents in the implementation of reform. For example, Miles (1993) argued that a key variable in change agents' success was their ability to develop rapport and trust relationships with schools. Additionally, Honig's (2004) study showed how intermediary organizations promote social capital by forming relationships with schools, community agencies, and district offices through meetings and other convening strategies (Smylie & Evans, 2006).

Thinking back on the case of Wake County, NC, whereas the status quo might not have the political capital to maintain the district's current student assignment policy, "newcomers" to the district created social capital through social relationships and used it to secure four seats during the latest school board election. A vignette from Williams & Houck (in press) explains: Although long-term residents attribute public school success to the current student assignment plan, newcomers to the district view the current plan as a nuisance. As such, there is a question of whether or not the current SES-based student assignment plan is sustainable. As the district's population continues to grow, strength and power in the community may tip to newcomers. Given that, long-time residents of Wake County worry that the commitment to diverse schools may diminish. A community leader commented,

> I worry as a long-time resident of the county, that when the generation of leaders that we've had in this community are no longer here leading and we enter this selfish era of me, myself, and I, we will lose this sense of community because we are very different.

A city administrator added,

> The new people don't know what the old people did. The reason why tradition exists is because of re-telling of the story. There's always this vulnerability that enough people will get unhappy at a particular point in time, and the political infrastructure and the community infrastructure are not in tune with each other. Although population growth makes district supporters question the policy's sustainability, adaptations (as opposed to abolishment) to the current student assignment policy may appease both long-term supporters and disgruntled parents.

The case of Wake paints a picture of social capital that may result as a negative or positive case, depending upon which side wins. Research suggests that the influence of social capital on school reform may be situational, depending upon the strength and content in particular settings.

The Influence of Cultural Capital on Students' Schooling Experiences

Cultural capital is a term often used in sociological contexts to describe the tangible/intangible elements in society that provide advantages and disadvantages to certain individuals living in that society. Pierre Bourdieu is most often credited for coining the term and developing the concept's foundational principals during the 1960s, though it has been challenged and reshaped by a number of scholars over the years. Bourdieu explains the roots of the concept in his 1986 work, *The Forms of Capital.* He states:

> The notion of cultural capital initially presented itself to me, in the course of research, as a theoretical hypothesis which made it possible to explain the unequal scholastic achievement of children originating from the different social classes by relating academic success, i.e., the specific profits which children from the different classes and class fractions can obtain in the academic market, to the commonsense view, which sees academic success or failure as an effect of natural aptitudes, and human capital theories. (p. 17)

Specifically, Bourdieu argues that cultural capital can manifest itself in three states: the embodied state, the objectified state, and the institutionalized state. The embodied state, as he describes it, encompasses one's physical disposition and sense of being and is usually the result of unconscious cultivation and inculcation via cultural exposure. The objectified state, on the other hand, works in tandem with the embodied state, as it is more focused on material items and their capacity to transmit culture via sale and acquisition. Lastly, the institutionalized state is one in which academic educational qualifications are used to legitimate one's cultural capital, ultimately providing powerful institutions another tool by which to of differentiate between "desirable" and "undesirable" persons.

In a 1982 article, Paul DiMaggio employs the ideas of Weber and Bourdieu to examine the relationship between cultural capital and school success, particularly high school students' grades. His primary goal was to determine the cause for variation in students' grades when looking outside of measured ability and family background. Working in light of assertions about positive correlations between parental educational attainment and cultural capital, DiMaggio (1982) found that "educational attainment is a very imperfect proxy for cultural capital" (p. 199). He did conclude, however, that cultural capital does have a significant impact on high school grades, especially in non-technical areas of study.

In an effort to further explain the role of cultural capital and how it impacts the schooling experiences of black and white adolescent girls, we consider the case of girls who attend a magnet school[2] in the Southeastern United States.

FRIENDSHIPS AND CLASS: THE CASE OF GIRLS ENROLLED IN A MAGNET MIDDLE SCHOOL IN THE SOUTHEASTERN U.S.

Students enrolled in Handy Magnet Middle School perceived that educational programs at a magnet middle school, although not academically selective, were more rigorous than the program at a zoned public school. Magnet schools, of course, are also public schools, but the girls saw them as two different types of schools. In fact, students viewed this magnet middle school as similar to a private school. They believed that attending a magnet middle school provided them access to an academically selective magnet high school, which in turn, increased their chances of being awarded scholarships to attend college (Williams, 2010).

Not only did students recognize the educational benefits of attending Handy, but they also acknowledged the social benefits of attending Handy. The school's diverse population allowed them to interact with students who were different from students in their neighborhoods. A student discussed the long-term benefits of attending a racially mixed middle magnet school:

> I'll be able to get along and communicate, cooperate better with those of different races, so I just won't belong to the African American race. It will prepare me for the future, because hopefully there won't be segregation again.

Another student commented:

> If it was just one school with mostly white kids and one school with mostly black kids, then one race would never get to talk or converse with another, and then that would probably cause segregation later on. I have gone to schools where the majority has been a race other than I am; it has opened my mind.

Yun and Kurlaender (2004) found that in a survey of high school juniors and seniors across the nation, Caucasian students value interracial experiences and report that their school experiences better prepared them to live, work, and participate in multi-racial communities. Researchers have also found that White students in integrated settings tend to exhibit more racial tolerance and less fear of black peers than in segregated environments (see Braddock et al., 1994; Kurlaender & Yun, 2005; Schofield, 1995; Strefling, 1998). In addition, numerous studies since the *Brown vs. Board of Education* decision have shown how social relations and the social environment of the school affect the attitudes of students from one racial group toward students of other racial groups (e.g., Damico, Bell-Nathaniel, & Green, 1981; Pettigrew, 2004; Schofield & Hausmann, 2004; St. John, 1975). Data from this study reveal that overall educational options at the magnet middle school (e.g., classroom activities and extracurricular activities) may have positively influenced students' educational and social experiences while influencing their cross-racial interactions.[3] Thus, the cultural capital owned by each of the girls enhanced their schooling experiences and friendships, which may later impact their cross-racial friendships and attitudes in adulthood.

In 1987, Annette Lareau published an article entitled "Social Class Differences in Family-School Relationships: The Importance of Cultural Capital" that summarized a qualitative study focused on the relationship between families and school with white working-class and middle-class communities. Ultimately, Lareau's data suggested "that social class position and class culture become a form of cultural capital in the school setting" (1987, p. 82). She found that more often than not, middle class parents have stronger social networks and acquire valuable information more easily than their working class counterparts. Further, whereas working-class parents entrusted the bulk of their children's education experience to the school, middle-class parents were more engaged in the schooling process and complied more readily with the school requests regarding desirable student behavior. These differences Lareau attributes to differences in cultural capital.

In 1999, Roscigno and Ainsworth-Darnell published an article entitled, "Race, Cultural Capital, and Educational Resources: Persistent Inequalities and Achievement Returns," which sought to distinguish between cultural capital gains for blacks and whites and determine the cause for differences in student performance. From their findings, they concluded that cultural capital and educational resources do not explain fully the disparities in student achievement. They suggest that a portion of the disparities may be explained by micropolitical assessments of students that rely heavily on race and social background, which decreases the rate of return on educational experiences.

Paul W. Kingston's (2001) article, "The Unfulfilled Promise of Cultural Capital Theory," essentially is a critique of the shortcomings of the Bourdieu's widely accepted sociological explanation of the differences in student achievement. Kingston rejects the notion that an individual's level of achievement is the result of exclusionary practices of the elite or can be explained simply by assessing a family's social status. Rather, he focuses on impact of domestic experiences such as intellectually stimulating conversations and family reading sessions. Further, he argues that whatever behaviors are most beneficial to student achievement should be embraced, not for any presumed class linkage, but purely because of their efficacy.

While research informs us that a significant portion of students' cultural capital is acquired outside of the formal school context, we also understand that the value of their cultural capital is assessed within schools. Therefore, schools must be socially, culturally, and economically safe spaces in which all students and their respective experiences are valued.

CONCLUDING THOUGHTS

Political, social, and cultural capital function as a fluid tripartite strategy for influencing school reform and increasing school access. Each component is unique, but they must not, and often do not, operate independently of one another. Political capital serves as the foundation of a successful school reform effort, primarily because political capital gives a collective voice to individual community members invested in advancing a shared vision for educational improvement. When individual constituencies in a community mobilize as a unified body for the purpose of educational change, they are able to increase exponentially their political power and formally engage the education policy arena by obtaining political positions that directly shape education policy.

Similarly, social capital emerges from and operates within communities, though it may be within the more personal and intimate recesses of those communities. It operates within the context of trust, open communication, and shared norms in order to foster informal social networks and partnerships among constituents and local organizations, all in an effort to gain influence in matters of education policy. While social capital often lacks the visibility and strength of political capital, it is sometimes the catalyst for development in political capital.

Cultural capital, perhaps the most nebulous of the three, influences school reform in ways more individualized and contextual than political and social capital. In terms of education reform and school access, cultural capital empowers parents to seek and take advantage of high-quality educational opportunities for their children. It is the driving force behind parents securing their children's enrollment in high-quality schools and providing rigor through academically challenging courses.

Throughout this chapter, we bring cases to light in which political, social, and cultural capital influence the schooling of students. More specifically, this chapter examines the role that capital (political, social, and cultural) plays in producing student outcomes. Regardless of varying degrees of capital, stakeholders must organize and formalize to implement reform in schools. If change is not sustained in the short term, then students might miss the opportunity to interact cross-racially, thus limiting their long-term producer capital. Long-term consequences that result from school reform and access to educational opportunities might result in a society segregated by class and race, which also limits individuals' access to producer capital. Although school board elections and magnet school options, for example, may not appear to correlate directly with student outcomes, there are lifelong consequences related to the students' wins and losses. Producer aspects of capital assist students' short-term and long-term educational endeavors. In essence, this chapter calls for parents and communities to exercise capital, whether political, social, or cultural, to improve the educational future of our nation's children.

NOTES

1. Researchers note that political capital is often difficult to define; therefore, we use the term interchangeably with civic capacity.
2. Magnet schools have been used as a desegregation tool since the 1970s.
3. This excerpt was originally published in the lead author's dissertation, titled: Dynamics of Adolescent Friendships: An Investigation of Schools, Classrooms, and Peer Groups: Implications for Educational Policy.

REFERENCES

Bartee, R. D., & Brown, M. C., II (2007). School matters: Why African American students need multiple forms of capital. *Counterpoints, Studies in the Postmodern Theory of Education, 312.* New York: Peter Lang.

Bourdieu, P. (1986). *Forms of capital.* In J. Richardson (Ed.) *Handbook of theory and research for the sociology of education* (pp. 241–258). Westport, CT: Greenwood.

Retrieved from http://home.iitk.ac.in/~amman/soc748/bourdieu_forms_of_capital.pdf

Bourdieu, P., & Passeron, J. C. (1977). *Reproduction, culture, and society.* Beverly Hills, CA: Sage.

Braddock, J. H. (June, 1987). *Segregated high school experiences and black students' college and major field choices.* Paper presented at the National Conference on School Desegregation, Chicago.

Braddock, J. H., Dawkins, M. P., & Trent, W. T. (1994). Why desegregate? The effects of school desegregation on adult educational occupational segregation of African Americans, Whites, and Hispanics. *International Journal of Contemporary Sociology, 31*(2) 271–283.

The Century Foundation. (2001). *Public school choice and integration. Session at the National Press Club.* Retrieved from http://www.tcf.org/Events/02-22-01/transcript.pdf

Coleman, J.S. (1988). Social capital in the creation of human capital. *American Journal of Sociology, 94,* (Suppl.), 95–120.

Coleman, J.S. (1990). *Foundations of social theory.* Cambridge, MA: Harvard University Press.

Damico, S.B., Bell-Nathaniel, A., Green, C. (1981). Effects of school organizational structure on interracial friendships in middle school. *Journal of Education Research, 74,* 388–395.

Datnow, A. (2000). Power and politics in the adoption of school reform. *Educational Evaluation and Policy Analysis, 22*(4), 357–374.

DiMaggio, P. (1982). Cultural capital and school success: The impact of status culture participation on the grades of U.S. high school students. *American Sociological Review, 47*(2), 189–201.

Feuerstein, A. (2002). Elections, voting, and democracy in local school district governance. *Educational Policy, 16*(1), 15–36.

Hammergren, L. (1998). Political will, Constituency building, and public support in rule of law program. Center for Democracy and Governance Bureau for Global Programs, Field Support, and Research. Washington, DC: U.S. Agency for International Development.

Honig, M.I. (2004). The new middle management: Intermediary organizations in education policy implementation. *Educational Evaluation and Policy Analysis, 26*(1), 65–87.

Kingston, P. W. (2001). The unfulfilled promise of cultural capital theory. [Extra issue] *Sociology of Education, 74,* 88–99.

Kurlaender, M. & Yun, J.T. (2005). Fifty years after Brown: New evidence of the impact of school racial composition on student outcomes. *International Journal of Educational Policy, Research and Practice, 6*(1), 51–78.

Lareau, A. (1987). Social class differences in family-school relationships: The importance of cultural capital. *Sociology of Education, 60*(2), 73–85.

Marschall, M. & Shah, P. (2005). Keeping policy churn off the agenda: Urban education and civic capacity. *Policy Studies Journal, 33*(2), 161–180.

Miles, M.B. (1993). Forty years of change in schools: Some personal reflections. *Educational Administration Quarterly, 29*(2), 213–248.

Pettigrew, T.F. (2004). Justice deferred: A half century after *Brown v. Board of Education. American Psychologist, 59*(6), 521–529.

Roscigno, V. J. & Ainsworth-Darnell, J.W. (1999, July). Race, cultural capital, and educational resources: Persistent inequalities and achievement returns. *Sociology of Education*, 72(3), 158–178.

St. John, N.H. (1975). *School desegregation: Outcomes for children.* New York: Wiley.

Schofield, J.W. (1995). Review of research on school desegregation's impact on elementary and secondary school students. In J.A. Banks & C.A.M. Banks (Eds.), *Handbook of Research on Multicultural Education* (pp. 597–616). New York: Simon & Schuster Macmilllan.

Schofield, J.W. & Hausmann, L.R.M. (2004). School desegregation and social science research. *American Psychologist, 59*(6), 538–546.

Shipps, D. (2003). Pulling Together: Civic Capacity and Urban School Reform. *American Educational Research Journal, 40*(4), 841–878.

Smylie, M.A. & Evans, A.E. (2006). Social capital and the problem of implementation. In M. Honig (Ed.), *New directions in education policy implementation: Confronting complexity* (pp. 187–208). Albany: State University of New York Press.

Smylie, M.A. & Hart, A.W. (1999). School leadership for teaching learning and change: A human and social capital development perspective. In J. Murphy & K.S. Louis (Eds.), Handbook of research on educational administration (2nd ed., pp. 421–441). San Francisco, CA: Jossey-Bass.

St. John, N. H. (1975). *School desegregation: Outcomes for children.* New York: Wiley.

Stone, C. N. (2001). Civic capacity and urban education. *Urban Affairs Review, 36*(5), 595–619.

Stone, C.N., Henig, J.R., Jones, B.D., & Pierannunzi, C. (2001). *Building civic capacity: The politics of reforming urban schools.* Lawrence, KS: University Press of Kansas.

Strefling, A.F. (October, 1998). *The Influence of integrated and de facto segregated schools on the racial attitudes of White students toward African Americans.* Paper presented at the University Council of Education Administration. St. Louis, MO.

Torres, C. A. (1998). Introduction: The political-pedagogy of Paulo Freire. In *Paulo Freire, Politics and education UCLA Latin American studies 83* (pp. 1–15). (P.L. Wong, Trans.). Los Angeles: UCLA Latin American Center Publications. (Original work published 1995)

Valenzuela, A. (1999). *Subtractive schooling: US–Mexican youth and the politics of caring.* New York: SUNY Press.

Wake Education Partnership. (2003). *Making choices: Diversity, student assignment and quality in Wake's schools.* Retrieved from http://www.wakeedpartnership.org/publications/d/Making_Choices_report.pdf

Walker, E. M. & Gutmore, D. (2002). The issue of civic capacity in urban educational reform: The case of New Jersey's thirty poorest districts. *Journal of Negro Education, 71*(1), 60–76.

Williams, S.M. (2010). Through the eyes of friends: An investigation of school context and cross-racial friendships in racially mixed schools. *Urban Education, 45*(4), 480–505.

Williams, S. M., & Houck, E. A. (May, 2010). *"To turn back would be a huge mistake": Race, class, and student assignment in Wake County Public Schools.* Paper presented at the American Education Research Association Conference, Denver, CO.

Yosso, T. J. (2005). Whose culture has capital?: A critical race theory discussion of community cultural wealth. *Race Ethnicity and Education 8*(1), 69–91.

Yun, J.T. & Kurlaender, M. (2004). School racial composition and student educational aspirations: A question of equity in a multiracial society. *Journal for Students Placed At Risk, 9*(2), 143–168.

CHAPTER 6

MATHEMATICS MATTERS

Polices and Practices that Impact Access to and Outcomes in the K–12 Pipeline

Lecretia A. Buckley
Jackson State University

INTRODUCTION

Historical and current research in mathematics education reveals that mathematics matters. Mathematics matters for all students in that it serves as a filter of educational and economic opportunities. In many ways, success in mathematics is a form of currency providing students with access to educational opportunities and economic participation. High achievement in mathematics opens doors to science-, technology-, and mathematics-based majors and careers; while low achievement prevents students from not only science, mathematics, and technology disciplines, but it may prevent access to higher education, in general, via college entrance examinations. Mathematics also serves as an entry point to a host of other jobs that do not require post-secondary education (e.g., a postal worker). This function of mathematics has been characterized as a filter or pump.

Contemporary Perspectives on Capital in Educational Contexts, pages 151–166

In this chapter, I examine mathematics education, considering it as the K–12 pipeline in particular, and how it serves as a form of capital that is too often a scarcity for African American, Latina/o, poor, and urban students. Specifically, I consider mathematics education and its potential as a producer of capital. In addition to this conceptual discussion, I offer insights from my research as well as national reports. Finally, I suggest considerations for policymakers, educational researchers, and other stakeholders who are engaged in efforts to address equity issues in mathematics education and who are trying to improve students' lives by increasing their access to capital.

MATHEMATICS AND CAPITAL

Having been in the field of mathematics education for over a decade, I must admit that the combination of mathematics and capital is a novel one with respect to academic inquiry. However, as I consider historical arguments about mathematics education, who should engage in its study, and the benefits for doing so, it becomes clearer that many of these arguments and discussions are ultimately rooted in the nexus of these two concepts. For the sake of clarity, I briefly outline definitions of key terms.

Capital is a primary concept that frames this discussion. The definition of capital and its related terms are informed by the work of Bartee and Brown (2007). There are four types of capital: (1) economic, (2) human, (3) cultural, and (4) social. Economic capital refers to financial currency and includes assets that may be physical assets. Human capital refers to the potential of an individual (e.g., academic potential) and views individuals as resources. Potential, here, increases with degree attainment as well as the quality of the degree or the institution from which the degree was obtained. Cultural capital includes acquired knowledge, value systems, language patterns, and visible dispositions. Social capital is the form of capital obtained as a result of networks of influence. Each of the aforementioned forms of capital provides access to material and non-material resources. Moreover, one form of capital may positively impact one's attainment of another. And, while each form of capital may be thought of independently, it is recognized that they are interrelated and influence each other.

Capital, and specifically each form of capital, may take on various functions. For the sake of this discussion, the specific context for this consideration is mathematics education. Moreover, capital may assume the function of (1) consumer, (2) producer, or (3) regulator. I examine the role of mathematics education as a producer of capital. This function of capital has been well-articulated for economic capital, human capital, and cultural capital (see Bartee & Brown, 2007), and I briefly describe them. Economic capital considers the role of higher education and its capacity to contribute to local economies through increased earnings. Contributions include job creation, increased productivity, and the generation of taxes. These benefits to society or individuals characterize the producer function of economic capital. The producer function of human capital includes those investments in oneself, investments that increase an individual's opportunities through increased knowledge acquisition or the capacity to analyze problems. The producer function of cultural capital considers how cultural capital, in turn, produces more cultural capital as individuals obtain and utilize knowledge, thereby creating or perpetuating hierarchies.

MATHEMATICS: THE GREAT DIVIDER

Mathematics can easily be characterized as the "great divider." John Volmink (1994) describes mathematics as

> more than any other subject, [mathematics has] been cast in the role of an 'objective' judge, in order to decide who in society 'can' and who 'cannot.' It therefore serves as a gatekeeper to participation in the decision making processes in society. To deny some access to participation in mathematics is then also to determine, a priori, who will move ahead and who will stay behind. (pp. 51–52)

With respect to this argument on capital, education, in general, divides or at least sets up a hierarchy in society. In the K–12 school system, one's mathematics achievement becomes critical early. Standardized tests scores begin to define one's place as early as second grade. This is especially true given the atmosphere of accountability that followed the No Child Left Behind Act of 2001. As such, mathematics performance becomes a conduit to further one's education and obtain capital. This is true for both a school system as well as for individual students. At the school level it divides the high achievers from the low achievers, oftentimes yielding a self-fulfilling prophecy and an unfortunate cycle as school ratings impact potential residents' likelihood to move into and eagerness to move out of a given neighborhood. For individual students, mathematics often becomes one of the deciding factors in whether students will have access to post-secondary education. The process of tracking, which has been debated for decades, often begins in the middle grades with the determination of when students will take algebra—a course that has historically been identified as the entry point for the college-bound track. Being placed in an algebra course in the middle grades is almost a certainty that students will be in the college-bound track upon entry in high school. However, a non-placement in algebra in the eighth or ninth grade is likely to yield the exact opposite. It is this early decision that puts students on a trajectory that is hard and almost impossible to redirect once the course has begun.

The aforementioned depiction of mathematics as a filter, gatekeeper, and divider is supported by decades of research and was likewise identified decades ago. In particular, the landmark report *Everybody Counts: A Report to the Nation on the Future of Mathematics Education* (National Research Council, 1989) acknowledges the function of mathematics as a filter, and one that had disproportionately and negatively impacted students of color and poor students. *Everybody Counts* helped to bring to the fore issues of educational equity as it reported that mathematics served as a pump for some and a filter for others by propelling students to educational opportunities and economic access, or by limiting their access to numerous careers. In particular, *Everybody Counts* revealed to the nation that mathematics serves as a gatekeeper to science- and mathematics- based majors and careers. It brought into the mainstream discussion the notion that the nation was not benefiting from all of its resources by leaving the potential of so many students untapped.

Given this indubitable classification of mathematics, its impact on African American, Latina/o, and poor students is amplified. Moreover, these underserved students often suffer at the hands of inadequate funding, under-prepared teachers, and an absence of educational and social experiences to prepare them to maneuver educational institutions and society, in general. This inability to maneuver such systems and to actively participate in these "cultures" further perpetuates students' status in societal hierarchies and limits their ability to obtain more capital. The achievement gap in mathematics (Lubienski, 2002; Lubienski & Crockett, 2007; Secada, 1992; Tate, 1997) exposes the differentiated outcomes that result from an inadequate and deprived mathematics education. While there have been some gains over the years for underrepresented students, these gains typically fall into areas of procedural learning as testing and expectations move toward conceptual understanding. Therefore, the gains are in areas that are being viewed as less needed in order to move ahead in society. Indeed, one can argue that the gains are in areas of knowledge that are becoming less and less valued and will ultimately provide students with less potential to acquire economic, human, or cultural capital.

ADDING EQUITY TO THE DISCUSSION

In order to address the role of mathematics in education, I examine it as a producer of capital. I consider three forms of capital for this discussion: economic, human, and cultural capital. Education has been conceptualized as a producer of economic capital that takes into consideration the role that education plays in increasing one's productivity and earning potential. For human capital, education is viewed as a means of self-investment that leads to improved or additional ways of solving problems as well as the overall acquisition of knowledge. Cultural capital is theorized as being an outcome of education since it provides rewards and access to activities and values that have a higher status.

One might ask the question, "What has been or should be done to address this persistent educational inequity?"—which often leads to the perpetuation of class structures. In the field of mathematics education, there have been several efforts to do just that—both small- and large-scale. These efforts include educational research, curriculum development, and professional development programs. Each effort, in its own right, has attempted to make mathematics more accessible, holding that success in mathematics opens doors of opportunity. These efforts have employed various measures to gauge equity. Equitable mathematics instruction has been characterized as the inability to predict one's achievement based on background factors such as ethnicity, socioeconomic status, or gender (Gutierrez, 2002).

Evaluations of mathematics education programs have considered inputs, instructional process, and outcomes. Rousseau and Tate (2003) assert that inputs (e.g., access to courses), processes (e.g., pedagogical practices), and outputs (e.g., student achievement scores) should be considered. Historically, however, efforts have often focused on one of these measures, in exclusion of the others. Examinations of access (or inputs) (e.g., Lee, Croninger, & Smith, 1997; Oakes, 1990) focused on course taking or tracking and whether or not students had access to mathematics courses that would facilitate their success in and access to more advanced mathematics courses. Tracking is taken to be a set of practices for which it is attempted to place students in homogeneous groups based on prior achievement or some other measure. An underlying assumption is that teachers can be more effective if students have similar achievement levels. Yet, even the proponents of tracking admit that the outcomes are often undesirable. Consequently, this body of work yielded a perspective on the nation's shortcomings in providing a high-quality mathematics education for all students. This national outlook transpired around the same time as did the Second International Mathematics Study (SIMS) study, which also revealed that a lack of access to mathematics courses accounted for low achievement (McKnight et al., 1987). The SIMS further suggests that mathematics holds a critical role for all students; however, its function as a gatekeeper is exacerbated for students who already belong to lower classes. The trend has continued with results from the Third International Mathematics Study (TIMS) as well as with the Seventh Mathematics Assesses of the National Assessment of Educational Progress (Kilpatrick & Gieger, 2000). A merit of the international and national exam is that they offer data to analyze both inputs and outputs in order to gauge equity.

Smaller-scale studies often focused on the processes of mathematics teaching and learning or pedagogy. Research programs were built around promoting equity. For example, the QUASAR Project (Silver & Stein, 1996), also a professional development program, focused on building teachers' capacity to teach students in urban settings. Individual research studies identified policies and practices that promoted high achievement (e.g., Gutierrez, 2000; Gutstein, Lipman, Hernandez, & des los Reyes, 1997). Achievement was viewed as a means to continued learning in mathematics, which thereby provided students with opportunities for furthering their education. For example, taking a calculus course in high school is viewed as desirable since it opens one's access to high-status careers such as doctor or engineer because students are positioned to do well on college entrance exams and to major in science- or mathematics-oriented disciplines.

Other small-scale studies include the work on culturally relevant pedagogy (Gutstein et al., 1997; Ladson-Billings, 1995), which asserts that building on students' culture can provide a richer context and thereby improve learning. This work is grounded in the notion that students' pre-existing cultural norms should be honored as students participate in education and ultimately acquire additional norms that are valued in schooling. From this perspective, there is a quest for the acquisition of capital, and efforts in this body of work often support being explicit when teaching students so that they are aware of the goal of acquired "sanctioned" knowledge that will allow them to ascend social hierarchies.

Another significant area of research is that on course taking. From as far back as the SIMS (McKnight et al., 1987), we learn that low student achievement could be accounted for based on student course taking. Students do not learn what they are not taught. Evaluations at the national and international level bear out the fact that student achievement is improved by taking higher-level courses (Kilpatrick & Gieger, 2000; Lee, Croninger, & Smith, 1997). Consequently, policies and practices that promote taking more and higher-level mathematics classes are preferred. It is critical to note that taking more mathematics classes may not lead to improved achievement if those courses are not more advanced. Gutierrez (1996) found that a rigorous and streamlined curriculum was more successful at promoting high achievement. The content, or what is taught in terms of mathematical concepts, is examined. Certain levels of content are used as gatekeepers to most career options. Exams for common jobs and college and graduate school entrance exams include mathematics. Thus, school mathematics programs that do not lead to student success negatively impact students' opportunities to acquire capital. Alternatively, success in mathematics is believed to provide access to further one's education, thereby positively impacting their earning potential (i.e., economic capital), increasing their knowledge acquisition and problem-solving skills (i.e., human capital), and increasing their understanding of and ability to enjoy the benefits of social norms and values (i.e., cultural capital).

Additionally, more recent work in mathematics education has taken a socio-cultural perspective as a means to challenge traditional modes of educational inquiry and the teaching of mathematics in the school mathematics curriculum. The work of Danny B. Martin (2007) is an exemplar of this work, and he challenges an achievement-based approach to evaluating mathematics education. Rather, Martin argues that mathematics education should be considered from an experiential perspective in which research on the teaching and learning of mathematics is centered on the experiences that students, their family members, and community members have as they learn mathematics. Martin argues that this "experience lens" will add to our understanding of how African-American students learn mathematics and makes it "possible to interrogate previously veiled racist assumptions about who and what may be responsible for differential outcomes" (p. 12).

The studies described above and most of the studies conducted in the area of equity issues in mathematics education were conducted, primarily, in the last twenty years. Within the United States, the mood began to change and more attention was given to the performance of African-American, Latina/o, and poor students after *Everybody Counts* and the near simultaneous *mathematics for all* movement. Smaller research efforts—theoretical and empirical, focused on equity issues (e.g., Gutierrez 2000, 2002; Gutstein et al., 1997; Tate, 1995)—were conducted; grant calls began to include equity-oriented priorities, and the National Council of Teachers of Mathematics' (NCTM) focus on equity increased over the decades (NCTM, 1989, 2000) adding equity to mainstream discussions.

The NCTM is the largest professional organization of practicing mathematics teachers and other mathematics education-related stakeholders such as administrators and mathematics teacher educators. It sets the tone for most states' visions of mathematics programs or the school mathematics curriculum. Most states have adopted NCTM standards. State curricular standards are often a near duplication of the NCTM standards, and textbook publishers rush to include the language of NCTM in order to promote book sales.

NCTM's history of increasing its focus on equity issues can be summarized as we consider several of its major documents. NCTM described equity as a societal need for economic stability in the 1989 *Curriculum and Evaluation Standards for School Mathematics* (NCTM, 1989). In its new standards document, *Principles and Standards for School Mathematics*, equity was identified as one of six guiding principles (NCTM, 2000) among curriculum, teaching, learning, assessment, and technology; these principles are identified as fundamental to ensuring excellence in mathematics education. Specifically, the equity principle states, "Excellence in mathematics education requires equity—high expectations and strong support for all students" (p. 12). NCTM explicates this principle with three statements:

1. Equity requires high expectations and worthwhile opportunities for all.
2. Equity requires accommodating differences to help everyone learn mathematics.
3. Equity requires resources and support for all classrooms and all students.

In the early 2000s, NCTM published a series of yearbooks entitled *Changing the Faces of Mathematics*, which examine successful practices in teaching students who are traditionally underrepresented (Hankes & Fast, 2002; Jacobs, Becker, & Gilmer, 2001; Secada, 2000; Strutchens, Johnson, & Tate, 2000). A few years later, this book series was followed by a position statement published by its research committee aimed at setting an agenda for examining the achievement gap and ways to decrease it (NCTM Research Committee, 2005). The Research Committee called for the incorporation of an equity component into mathematics education research and advocated two approaches: (1) emphasizing equity as a research focus in mathematics education and (2) using a "critical equity lens" to examine research efforts.

NCTM has led the way in bringing equity issues into the mainstream discussion. It asserts that there should be high expectations and adequate support for all students and seeks to "challenge a pervasive societal belief in North America that only some students are capable of learning mathematics" (NCTM, 2000, p. 12). I, too, hold that high expectations and adequate resources and support are necessary requirements to advance students in urban settings in mathematics. These are necessary requirements, but they, alone, are insufficient.

RECONCEPTUALIZING MATHEMATICS EDUCATION

Improving equity in mathematics education in K–12 schools is essential to preparing students for full participation in society. The notion of full participation goes beyond success in mathematics courses, taking higher-level mathematics courses before graduation such as calculus, or achieving high outcomes on standardized exams—whether they are college entrance exams, state tests, or national exams such as the National Assessment of Educational Progress (NAEP). Rather, it prepares students not only for access to mathematics-, science-, or technology-based majors and careers; it positions them for democratic participation as opposed to simply economic participation. Achieving these goals of mathematics education will require a reconceptualization of the power or utility of mathematics as well as the foci of teaching and learning mathematics.

The foci of teaching and learning mathematics have drastically changed over the years. This change is often labeled as the "reform movement." The reform movement places a premium on strategies for teaching and learning activities that promote conceptual understanding as opposed to past efforts which focused primarily on procedural knowledge. Basic assumptions of this movement hold that simply being able to execute procedures is insufficient and that students must acquire a deeper understanding of concepts. A deeper understanding of concepts may be evidenced by students' ability to represent mathematical objects in multiple ways, explain their thinking to others—both verbally and in writing, and to reason and construct valid arguments around mathematical objects or quantitative situations.

There is little debate that that there is added value in the reform approach to mathematics education. However, scholars in the field caution that reform-oriented teaching may negatively impact students of color, poor students, and students in urban settings. Secada and Berman (1999) highlight the creation of Sesame Street, which was originally intended to help underprivileged children learn to read; however, the program yielded a larger achievement gap between these kids and their white, middleclass counterparts. My own research revealed how such unintentional outcomes may occur (Buckley, 2009b).

Consequently, a deeper look of the function of mathematics is required lest an oversimplified explanation results. Teachers' and policymakers' aims and ideas about the role of mathematics matter. One must not only be concerned with what is taught and to whom, but one must also be concerned with the ends for which mathematics teaching is employed. A view of mathematics as a means to understand personal banking or as an end unto itself (e.g., a graduation requirement) yields a much different curriculum and different pedagogical approaches than one that is aimed at modeling complex phenomena (e.g., the spread of disease) and equipping students to critique societal inequities or make sense of complex financial situations (e.g., selecting from various mortgage options or retirement plans).

I conducted a one-year study of a secondary mathematics department redesigning its curriculum in order to address high failure rates and restricted access to higher-level mathematics courses among African-American and poor students (Buckley, 2009b). The members of the department met frequently to discuss the changes and implemented multiple efforts simultaneously. A noteworthy change was the elimination of a four-semester sequence of algebra that was disproportionately taken by African-American students. This course fulfilled the state's mathematics requirement for graduation and allowed a significant number of students in the school to graduate with algebra as their most advanced mathematics course. Eliminating this course was certainly a move in the right direction. However, other changes neutralized the positive impact. In particular, a newly designed geometry course became the new ceiling for students who had been enrolled in the eliminated algebra course. While access to geometry was an improved circumstance, allowing students to be taught fundamental mathematical concepts that they had not previously been taught and positioning them for improved achievement on state tests which included geometry content, it was a relatively low ceiling since most post-secondary admissions standards would require at least a third mathematics course. Moreover, the content knowledge from a first-year algebra course and a geometry course alone would be insufficient to adequately prepare students to obtain good scores on a college entrance exam. Consequently, the mathematics department that had begun curricular redesign to address equity had, in the end, done little to produce higher yields.

Having highlighted some of the negative, and perhaps, unintentional outcomes that may result from well-intended efforts, one must add that access is necessary, but not sufficient in preparing students to obtain the currency that is mathematics in our society. A multi-pronged approach is necessary in achieving equity—one that considers inputs or access, processes, and outputs (Rousseau & Tate, 2003). The mathematics department's efforts did not address the processes of teaching and learning such as pedagogical approaches or the impact on long-term achievement that would be a part of and result from the implemented changes. Without this holistic approach to gauging how equitable a mathematics program is, unintended outcomes are likely. Analogously, multiple forms of capital are needed if students are to enjoy multiple benefits.

Mathematics as a Producer of Capital

This reconceptualization of mathematics can be informed by a simultaneous consideration of capital and the role of mathematics as a producer of capital. Mathematics is clearly a gatekeeper in education and for many careers. Understanding or being able to do mathematics permits students to further their education, and consequently to obtain higher-paying jobs. In this way, it acts as a producer of economic capital. As mathematics positions individuals for continued learning in high-status institutions to obtain high-status careers, it can also be viewed as a producer of human capital. Matriculation and degree obtainment from these institutions is viewed as an investment in oneself that, in turn, adds capital. Finally, mathematics and particular ways of knowing or habits of the mind are valued in higher education. Learning these often implicit standards of the discipline further positions individuals to access other social institutions and benefits. For example, a student who does well in mathematics in high school and is able to demonstrate the types of mathematical understanding valued on college entrance exams has greater access to higher-status institutions. Success at a higher-status institution in turn positions the student for better, higher-status jobs for which the individual enjoys increased income and access to higher-status social networks.

REPRESENTATIONS OF POWER: RECOGNIZING THE UTILITY OF MATHEMATICS

Viewing mathematics as a form of capital is not a fanciful undertaking, as mathematics is often used as a gatekeeper to economic participation. Yet, economic participation is not the sum of the worth that mathematics adds to the lives of students. Beyond economic participation, mathematics is advocated as a means to democratic participation (Buckley, 2009a; Malloy, 2002). Such participation empowers students to think critically and analyze situations in ways that allow them to make complex and complicated decisions. It is here that it especially matters what one views as the role of mathematics education. For some that role is to be able to get through school and to be able to solve relatively routine tasks such as creating a budget, balancing a checkbook, or making purchases such as calculating the area of a room in order to purchase carpet. Such basic skills, however, will not prepare students for full participation. Moreover, these isolated activities do not engage students in significant, everyday activities that are a part of the lived experiences of the middle or upper class. Thus, clinging to the traditional ways of doing mathematics yields a deprived understanding of mathematics and limits students access to the ways of knowing that characterize a more technological and global society.

An alternative view of mathematics as a discipline that empowers students to think might involve modeling real-world situations such a swine flu epidemic or determining when or if a three-year arm or a 30-year fixed-rate mortgage is the preferred option. This alternative view prepares students to think critically about quantitative data in order to make informed decisions or to analyze an argument in order to identify faulty logic. A frequent refrain in the mathematics education community is that mathematics education ought to be relevant, including real-world experiences. The challenge for mathematics teachers and mathematics education researchers is to embrace relevancy while promoting "real-world" applications that are not restricted to one's current "world." If mathematics education is to be a producer of capital, then the teaching and learning of mathematics must open doors of opportunity, moving students up societal hierarchies. It is not enough to simply prepare students to make sense of their world; rather, they need to be prepared to participate in other settings. Applications of mathematics must go beyond students' experiences, presenting them with a vision for both what mathematics can do and for the situations that one is expected to encounter in their futures. Engendering an atmosphere that embraces this power of mathematics requires a change in beliefs and expectations about who can learn mathematics. While our nation, in general, suffers from the view that mathematics can only be learned by some, there is a more dismal expectation for students of color and poor students, and these low expectations impact what teachers are willing to teach as well as the courses that a department is willing to offer (Buckley, 2009b).

Thus, it is important that one's view of mathematics encompasses understanding, modeling, or representing one's world through quantitative means. An additional purpose of mathematics goes beyond these goals of democratic participation and includes transformative work. Rather than understanding one's current state (or plight) in life, one may view mathematics as a means of empowerment that allows one to change one's situation. A body of research on teaching and research from this perspective has been collecting over the past two decades. In the mid-1990s, William F. Tate (1995) studied the work of a middle school mathematics teacher who led her students in addressing a disproportionate number of liquor stores in their neighborhood, and Eric Gutstein and his colleagues (Gutstein et al., 1997) also engaged students in mathematics-based social activism. In his recent book, *Reading and Writing the World with Mathematics: Towards a Pedagogy for Social Justice,* Gutstein (2006) tackles topics such as social justice, sociopoltical consciousness, and social agency and their contributions to implementing mathematics instruction in ways that allow students to transform their circumstances. These examples illustrate an awareness of the power of mathematics to change the larger context in which we live as opposed to a satisfaction of achievement by individual or subgroups of students.

If more students are to reap the benefits of high achievement in mathematics, then one must be concerned about larger societal issues in addition to the curriculum and student outcomes. A deeper look at and engagement in efforts to change society and schooling also must be a part of our efforts; otherwise, the system is perpetuated, allowing a few "exceptions" to achieve while the vast majority of students are "left behind."

MATHEMATICS TEACHER EDUCATION

One cannot escape the history of mathematics as a discipline primarily comprised of white males. Also, one cannot deny the political ramifications that are involved in changing the face of mathematics. Doing so is complicated by long-standing views about who can do mathematics, making it difficult to raise student expectations and to view mathematics as a discipline in which culture and values do matter. Typically, mathematics is regarded as a value-free discipline, a set of procedures, or methods of abstracting ideas. Consequently, teachers, mathematicians, or mathematics teacher educators may not recognize the need to address equity issues in their everyday practices. For some, mathematics is a pure discipline; the teacher teaches and the student learns. This oversimplification, however, denies the complexity of schooling, teaching, and learning, and it certainly denies the complexity of rethinking and changing a system that has steadily disenfranchised far too many students.

As stakeholders plan, engage in, and revise efforts to address equity issues in mathematics education, there are important considerations that ought to be taken into account. Efforts must be multidimensional, focusing on access (or inputs), processes, and outcomes. It is insufficient to obtain high enrollment in calculus courses. Instead, that high enrollment must be accompanied by a pedagogy that prepares students to deeply understand the content in ways that they will be (1) assessed, (2) expected to perform, and (3) prepared to take more advanced mathematics courses in the future. Additionally, students enrolled in such courses should ultimately experience success.

Professional development for mathematics teachers must maintain equity as a primary focus. Doing so may allow teachers to challenge basic assumptions about who can learn mathematics as teachers collaborate through an inquiry-oriented approach to examine and change teaching practices to ensure student achievement (Crockett & Buckley, 2009). Finally, the preparation of new teachers must begin the ongoing process of preparing teachers to be successful in teaching diverse students. This goal, may at times appear daunting, given that many teacher education candidates report feeling inadequately prepared to address the learning needs of a diverse student body (Dee & Henkin, 2002). Teacher education programs are also challenged to prepare teachers for a student population that is becoming more diverse; yet, the teacher population remains fairly homogenous (Sleeter, 2001). This issue prompted Martin (2007) to ask the question "who should teach mathematics to African-American children?" Martin's question challenges conventional knowledge about teacher expectations and the role of viewing mathematics education, primarily through an achievement lens.

Success in mathematics increases students' access to higher-paying jobs, higher-status careers, and higher-status networks. It positions students for acceptance to institutions of higher education and provides them with problem-solving skills that are applicable in multiple areas of their lives.

Indeed, it has the potential to produce multiple forms of capital. However, to facilitate this production, mathematics educators in particular must expand the aims of mathematics education for all students to include not only economic participation via economic capital, but to also include the acquisition of human and cultural capital to maximize students' opportunities to move up the societal ladder.

REFERENCES

Bartee, R. D., & Brown, M. C., II (2007). *School matters: Why African American students need multiple forms of capital.* New York: Peter Lang.

Buckley, L.A. (2009a). Equitable mathematics education as a means to democratic participation. In M.C. Brown II, R.D. Bartee (Eds.), *The broken cisterns of African American education* (pp. 195–210). Charlotte, NC: Information Age Publishing, Inc.

Buckley, L.A. (2009b). Unfulfilled hopes in education for equity: Redesigning the mathematics curriculum in a US high school. *Journal of Curriculum Studies, 42*(1), 51–78.

Crockett, M.D., & Buckley, L.A. (2009). The role of coflection in equity-centered mathematics professional development. *Equity & Excellence in Education, 42*(2), 169–182.

Dee, J.R., & Henkin, A.B. (2002). Assessing dispositions toward cultural diversity among preservice teachers. *Urban Education, 37,* 22–40.

Gutiérrez, R. (1996). Practices, beliefs, and cultures of high school mathematics departments: Understanding their influences on student advancement. *Journal of Curriculum Studies, 28*(5) 495–530.

Gutierrez, R. (2000). Advancing African-American, urban youth in mathematics: Unpacking the success of one math department. *American Journal of Education, 109*(1), 63–111.

Gutierrez, R. (2002). Enabling the practice of mathematics teachers in context: Toward a new-equity research agenda. *Mathematical Thinking and Learning 4*(2–3), 145– 187.

Gutstein, E. (2006). *Reading and writing the world with mathematics.* New York: Routledge.

Gutstein, E., Lipman, P., Hernandez, P., & de los Reyes, R. (1997). Culturally relevant mathematics teaching in a Mexican American context. *Journal for Research in Mathematics Education, 28*(6), 709–737.

Hankes, J.E. & Fast, G.R. (Eds.) (2002). *Changing the faces of mathematics: Perspectives on Indigenous people of North America.* Reston, VA: NCTM.

Jacobs, J.E., Becker, J.R., & Gilmer, G.F. (Eds.). (2001). *Changing the faces of mathematics: Perspectives on gender.* Reston, VA: NCTM.

Kilpatrick, J., & Gieger, J.L. (2000). The performance of students taking advanced mathematics courses. In E.A. Silver, & P.A. Kenney (Eds.), *Results from the seventh mathematics assessment of the national assessment of educational progress* (pp. 377–409). Reston, VA: NCTM.

Ladson-Billings, G. (1995). Toward a theory of culturally relevant pedagogy. *American Educational Research Journal, 32*, 465–491.

Lee, V.E., Croninger, R.G., & Smith, J.B. (1997). Course-taking, equity, and mathematics learning: Testing the constrained curriculum hypothesis in U.S. secondary schools. *Educational Evaluation and Policy Analysis, 19*(2), 99–121.

Lubienski, S.T. (2002). A closer look at black–white mathematics gap: Intersections of races and SES in NAEP achievement and instructional practices data. *The Journal of Negro Education, 71*(4), 269–287.

Lubienski, S.T. & Crockett, M.D. (2007). NAEP findings regarding race/ethnicity: Mathematics achievement, student affect, and school/home experiences. In P. Kloosterman & F.K. Lester (Eds.), *Results from the ninth mathematics assessment of NAEP* (pp. 227–260). Reston, VA: NCTM.

Malloy, C. (2002). Democratic access to mathematics through democratic education: An introduction. In L.D. English, M. B. Bussi, G.A. Jones, R.A. Lesh, & D. Tirosh (Eds.), *Handbook of international research in mathematics education* (pp. 17–25). Mahwah, NJ: Lawrence Erlbaum Associates.

Martin, D.B. (2007). Beyond missionaries or cannibals: Who should teach mathematics to African American children? *The High School Journal, 91*(1), 6–28.

McKnight, C., Crosswhite, F.J., Dossey, J.A., Kifer, E., Swafford, J.O., Travers, K.J., & Cooney, T.J. (1987). *The underachieving curriculum: Assessing U.S. school mathematics from an international perspective.* A national report on the Second International Mathematics Study, International Association for the Evaluation of Education Achievement. Champaign, IL: Stipes Publishing Company.

National Council of Teachers of Mathematics. (1989). *Curriculum and evaluation standards for school mathematics.* Reston, VA: Author.

National Council of Teachers of Mathematics. (2000). *Principles and standards for school mathematics.* Reston, VA: Author.

National Council of Teachers of Mathematics Research Committee. (2005). Equity in school mathematics education: How can research contribute? *Journal for Research in Mathematics Education, 36*(2), 92–100.

National Research Council. (1989). *Everybody counts: A report to the nation on the future of mathematics education.* Washington, DC: National Academy Press.

Oakes, J. (1990). *Multiplying inequalities: The effects of race, social class, and tracking on opportunities to learn mathematics and science.* Santa Monica, CA: RAND.

Rousseau, C. & Tate, W.F. (2003). No time like the present: Reflecting on equity in school mathematics. *Theory Into Practice, 42*(3), 210–216.

Secada, W.G. (1992). Race, ethnicity, social class, language, and achievement in mathematics. In D.A. Grouws (Ed.), *Handbook of research on mathematics teaching and learning* (pp. 146–164). New York: Cambridge University Press.

Secada, W.G. (2000). *Changing the faces of mathematics: Perspectives on multiculturalism and gender equity.* Reston, VA: NCTM.

Secada, W.G., & Berman, P.W. (1999). Equity as a value-ladden dimension in teaching for understanding in school mathematics. In E. Fennema & T.A. Romberg (Eds.), *Mathematics classrooms that promote understanding,* (pp. 33–42). Mahwah, NJ: Lawrence Erlbaum Associates.

Silver, E.A. & Stein, M.K. (1996). The QUASAR Project: The "revolution of the possible" in mathematics instructional reform in urban middle schools. *Urban Education, 30*(4), 476–521.

Sleeter, C. E. (2001). Preparing teachers for culturally diverse schools: Research and the overwhelming presence of whiteness. *Journal of Teacher Education, 52,* 94–106.

Strutchens, M., Johnson, M.L., & Tate, W.F. (Eds.). (2000). *Changing the faces of mathematics: Perspectives on African Americans.* Reston, VA: NCTM.

Tate, W.F. (1997). Race-ethnicity, SES, gender, and language proficiency trends in mathematics achievement: An update. *Journal for Research in Mathematics Education, 28*(6), 652–697.

Tate, W.F. (1995). Returning to the root: A culturally relevant approach to mathematics pedagogy. *Theory Into Practice, 34*(3), 166–173.

Volmink, J. (1994). Mathematics by all. In S. Lerman (Ed.), *Cultural perspectives on the mathematics classroom* (pp. 51–67). Dordrecht, The Netherlands: Kluwer Academic Publishers.

PART III

EDUCATIONAL CONTEXT AND THE REGULATOR ASPECTS OF CAPITAL

CHAPTER 7

EXPLORING CAPITAL WITHIN COLLEGE CHOICE

High Achieving, Low-Income African American Student Perceptions of Selective Colleges

Phillis L. George
Jackson State University

Selective, four-year colleges and universities play a disproportionately small and regulating role in the educational pathways of minority and socioeconomically disadvantaged students (Bowen & Bok, 1998; Bowen, Kurzweil, & Tobin, 2005; Gerald & Haycock, 2005). Collectively, these private and public institutions have the shared attribute of being academically selective, given the average ACT and/or SAT scores and cumulative grade point averages of entering classes.[1] Undergraduate admission tickets and/or degrees from such institution are, in fact, highly regarded because of their selectivity and the embedded networks that provide multifaceted forms of human, social, economic, and cultural capital (Pope, 2007). As a result of their selective practices, notable faculty, and rigorous programs, these institutions receive

Contemporary Perspectives on Capital in Educational Contexts, pages 169–186

thousands of applications annually for limited spots in their freshman cohorts. Surprisingly, only 12% of those applicants are underrepresented racial and ethnic minorities and/or low-income students (Bowen et al., 2005).

Nationally, minority and disadvantaged students account for roughly 9% of students who are admitted to selective, four-year institutions, and an estimated 11% of those enrolled (Bowen et al., 2005). These figures, by any measure, are daunting and paint a rather perplexing picture of the college-going practices of high-achieving, low-income and minority college aspirants. Further, they shed much-needed light on the regulating role of capital within integral processes of college choice and access, as the limited number of minority and disadvantaged applicants and matriculants results in limited access to varied forms of normalizing currency or currency-building capital.

In a 2007 report published by the Jack Kent Cooke Foundation titled "Achievement Trap: How America is Failing Millions of High Achieving Students from Lower Income Families," it was noted that minority and disadvantaged students are far less likely to attend selective, four-year colleges and universities and indeed are more likely to attend the least selective institutions. These disconcerting patterns of college choice and enrollment have not gone unnoticed. In response, selective institutions across America have opened their doors and adopted aggressive strategies to recruit and retain high-achieving, minority and disadvantaged collegians. Their efforts have proven fruitful, as the number of academically outstanding minority and disadvantaged applicants and matriculants has slowly but surely increased.

With a series of unprecedented financial-aid measures, Princeton University increased its low-income, African American student yield (i.e., the percentage of low-income, African American students accepting the university's offer of admission) from 49% in 1997 to 65% in 2001, thereby boosting the total number of African American students in its entering Class of 2001 to 112 (JBHE Foundation, 2001). As a result, African American students comprised 9.5% of Princeton's entering Class of 2001—which was impressive given that it was the largest percentage of African American first-year students at Princeton in 22 consecutive years (JBHE Foundation, 2001). In 2001, Johns Hopkins University boasted of a two-year increase of 134% in African American freshman enrollment (JBHE Foundation, 2003). In 2003, institutional representations of African-American, low-income students at Johns Hopkins rose to 8% of the freshmen cohort (JBHE Foundation, 2003).

Richard Spies (2001) provides data in support of these 21st century increases in minority and low-income student yields. In his study titled "The Effect of Rising Cost on College Choice," Spies reports that an estimated one-third of high-achieving, low-income students now apply to one or more of the nation's most selective institutions (Spies, 2001). While a one-third increase among low-income applicants is impressive, what is perhaps even more impressive is that minority students with competitive SAT scores are now more likely to apply to selective colleges than majority students with similar scores (Bowen et al., 2005).

Based on these figures, it is apparent that great strides have been made concerning efforts to develop and sustain equity in access to selective, four-year institutions nationwide; however, despite increases among high-achieving minority and socioeconomically disadvantaged applicants, the number of applications from high-achieving majority and socioeconomically advantaged students continues to grow (Bowen et al., 2005; Spies, 2001). To date, more than half of high-achieving students from socioeconomically advantaged and majority backgrounds apply to selective colleges and universities (Bowen et al., 2005).

With such consistent gaps, it is vitally important that these institutions become even more aggressive when seeking to reduce the regulating role of capital in college choice by recruiting academically talented and high-achieving minority and disadvantaged students (Jack Kent Cooke Foundation, 2007). Beyond recruitment, further insight is needed concerning students' decisions to apply to selective institutions—so too is an express understanding of students' perceptions of selective colleges and universities along with their perceived ability to access and excel at the aforementioned institutions. These research efforts will help demonstrate how students from the specified backgrounds can build normalizing currency and successfully navigate the college choice process, relative to other groups (Bowen et al., 2005).

This study aims to assist in the normalization of these currency-building endeavors by examining the perceptions of high-achieving African-American high school students from socioeconomically disadvantaged backgrounds concerning the accessibility of America's most selective four year-institutions. The assumption is that students' perceptions (be they positive or negative) drive their college choice impulses and actions and ultimately influence the selectivity of their college choices. Additionally, students' perceptions are influenced by their immediate social and school environments, and they can serve as normalizing or regulating currencies and/or sources of high- or low-status capital during the college choice process (McDonough, 1997). If high-achieving minority and socioeconomically disadvantaged students perceive selective, four-year institutions as inaccessible (from their social vantage point), it is likely they will not include such institutions in their college searches and will self-select out of competitive applicant pools—which subsequently effects the higher education pipeline.

To guard against such maladaptive thought processes and college choice behaviors, this study highlights factors that play a capital-regulating role within the college choice process and thus have an adverse impact on students' perceptions of their ability to access and excel at selective colleges and universities as well as their decisions to search for and apply to selective four-year institutions. The following questions help guide the inquiry: (1)

What are the perceptions of high-achieving, low-income African-American high school students concerning the accessibility of selective four-year colleges and universities? and (2) What factors shape students' perceptions of selective four-year institutions while navigating the college choice process?

LITERATURE REVIEW

The College Choice Process

The college choice process is a series of stages in which an aspiring collegian devotes critical time and thought to his or her future postsecondary aspirations and selections. College choice theorists have noted that students formally enter the process during the latter portion of their high school careers (McDonough, 1997). As demonstrated in the Hossler Model, there are three distinct stages of the college choice process: predisposition, search, and choice (Hossler, Braxton, & Coopersmith, 1989; Hossler & Gallagher, 1987). The predisposition stage is perhaps the most critical as it is the initial stage in which students begin to ponder notions of attending college. The search stage is undoubtedly the lengthiest and includes (1) varied searches for institutionally specific forms of college knowledge, (2) the creation of a short list of desired and preferred schools, and (3) specialized consideration and re-evaluation of institutions included on the short list. The choice stage occurs after an aspirant applies and gains admission to institutions on his or her short list and results in the selection of a single college or university. Regardless of the ability grouping, racial/ethnic background, or socioeconomic status, the college choice process remains the same for all who express interests in pursuing a post-baccalaureate degree.

College Choices of Minority and Disadvantaged Students

When it comes to issues of access and persistence within the higher education pipeline, scholars recognize that many barriers still exist for minority and socioeconomically disadvantaged students (Bowen & Bok, 1998; Jencks & Phillips, 1998; Phillips, Brooks-Gunn, Duncan, Klebanov, & Crane, 1998). In efforts to dismantle these barriers, they have begun to investigate the college choices of racial minorities and low-income students. Much of the existing research on college choice explores what is known about majority and socioeconomically advantaged students and how they fare in the college choice process to determine similarities and differences among other student groups (Alwin & Otto, 1977; Anderson & Hearn, 1992; Boyle, 1966;

Hearn, 1991; Hossler & Gallagher, 1987; Hossler & Vesper, 1993; Litten, Sullivan, & Brodigan, 1983; McDonough, 1994; McDonough, Antonio, & Trent, 1997; Mortenson, 1991; Stage & Hossler, 1989).

Research on African-American college choice has found that students perceive many obstacles, including a lack of dissemination of college knowledge, increased costs, and feelings of intimidation (Freeman, 1997, 1999, 2005). Other research highlights low standardized test scores and a lack of academic preparation as obstacles that many African-American students must overcome (McDonough, Antonio, & Trent, 1997; Perna, 2000). School faculty and staff as well as parental involvement are also recognized as key variables in helping African-American students from socioeconomically disadvantaged backgrounds navigate the college choice process, as students are less likely to receive important information in a timely fashion (Gonzalez, Stoner, & Jovel, 2003; Horvat, 1995; Smith, 2001).

This study expands upon existing yet limited knowledge of African American college choice, as it uncovers key aspects that are crucial to understanding gaps in the application and matriculation rates of high achieving, African American students from disadvantaged backgrounds at selective, four-year colleges and universities. Specifically, it affords researchers a rare and unique opportunity to hear student voices concerning their perceptions of these institutions as well as their ability to access them and to perform at levels commensurate with those of their high achieving, majority and socioeconomically advantaged peers.

METHOD

Research Design and Site Selection

Qualitative methods (i.e., interviews and a focus group session) were used to investigate questions raised in the study. These methods, when used properly and responsibly, provide breathtaking clarity and insight concerning college choice processes across and within student groups (Bogdan & Biklen, 2007). The aforementioned also allows researchers to capture the voices and perspectives of marginalized groups in education (Freeman 1997, 1999, 2005; Tierney, 1993). To date, the voices of high-achieving African-American high school students from socioeconomically disadvantaged backgrounds remain absent from educational debates and dialogues about their academic achievement (Kaplan, 1999; Lattimore, 2001).

In conducting the study, the author was very careful to select a site that fit the problem at hand. The search was concentrated in the southeastern region of the U.S., as the southeast is heavily populated by African Americans and has been historically plagued by racial and economic discrimination.

Also, the southeast is traditionally characterized as a rural region, and the selective colleges and universities referenced within this study traditionally recruit minority and disadvantaged students from urban regions of the U.S. To cast a wider recruitment net, to gain insight on the perceptions of minority and disadvantaged students (i.e., rural and urban), and to break new ground in understanding how all minority and disadvantaged students fare in the college choice process, the researcher elected to conduct the study within the state of Mississippi.

Student Participants

Student participants hailed from a public school district, where approximately 90% of the students identified as African American, and 86% benefited from the Free and Reduced Price Lunch Program (U.S. Census Bureau, 2000).[2] To the extent possible, this study employed purposive sampling and included a total of 16 African-American students ranging in age from 16 to 18. Ten of the participants were females, and six were males. Three of the participants were high school juniors, and the remaining 13 were seniors.[3] Each of the participants self-identified as low-income (i.e., family income of less than $50,000 annually) and held cumulative grade point averages (GPA) of 3.5 or above on a 4.0 scale; the average GPA was 3.89.

Data Collection and Analysis

Participants were asked a series of closed and open-ended questions regarding the following: (1) perceived academic and intellectual abilities, (2) perceptions of selective four-year institutions, (3) postsecondary aspirations and selections, and (4) strategies and resources used during the college choice process. Interviews were 60 to 90 minutes in duration, and the focus group session was approximately two hours in duration. Student responses were recorded, transcribed, and coded for content analysis.

FINDINGS

Lowered Academic Self-Efficacy

Overwhelmingly, students were very forthcoming with their postsecondary aspirations and plans. One by one, they shared personal testimonies and truths—which collectively spoke to their perceived values and deep-seated desires to attend college and obtain a postsecondary degree. When asked why, one student quickly responded, "To further our education." Another retorted, "You can't get good jobs without education, without a degree in something, or a trade, or some higher form of education. Diplomas don't make you money. You gotta make that money."

As seniors, the majority of the student participants were in the final stages of selecting colleges and universities. The juniors were initiating their college searches. While students recognized the inherent value of attending college and obtaining a degree, such value and recognition did not always transfer to seeking admittance and obtaining degrees from selective colleges and universities. When such transference did occur, the high-status values and recognition associated with named institutions like Harvard, Princeton, Stanford, Tulane, Vanderbilt, and Duke were often trumped by a collectively lowered sense of academic self-efficacy.

This was in fact a recurring theme throughout the study. Although gifted and talented in their own right, students were fearful and intimidated by what they regarded as the high academic and intellectual standards of selective four-year institutions. Many felt that admission to select institutions was solely reserved for students within the upper echelons of America's intellectual elite. In their own words and depictions, students painted portraits of academic geniuses in faraway lands conquering bodies of knowledge that were superior to those immediately accessible to them. As one senior stated, "I mean I've never really considered any of those major colleges or whatever because it's just, you know, the way they're portrayed... you have to be a genius or get straight A's." During a one-on-one interview, that same student shared:

> Over the years, I always believed those were the colleges for geniuses, and that, you know, only a certain amount of people out of the minority were eligible to get into those colleges. Me, at the time, I honestly didn't believe I was qualified or educated enough to enter into those [selective] colleges.

Another senior stated, "When I was younger, I learned about them [selective colleges] then... but I was like, no, I'll never get into that. They're real smart or whatever." Other students shared the same sentiments. During the focus group session, students consciously and willingly pitted themselves against seemingly more qualified students and in so doing cast themselves as less qualified and capable, thus birthing into existence psychosocial barriers of intellectual inferiority and academic intimidation.

Intellectual Inferiority

Whether engaged in an interview or a focus group session, students' responses to questions concerning their ability to access and excel at selective colleges and universities were strikingly similar. As a whole, students feared not being able to handle the academic workloads and rigor of selective four-year institutions due to feelings of intellectual inferiority. As one senior commented, "You have to think about it. It's a little scary thinking of going to Harvard. Can I keep up with Harvard coursework? That's a question, a big question." When asked if he had considered applying to Ivy League institutions, one senior stated:

> To be honest, until recently, I haven't considered them at all... I don't know. I guess I didn't think I could compete academically with the people who are there or could handle the rigorous class work that those schools have.

Another senior was asked if he could gain admission to any college of his choosing. After a moment's hesitation, he responded in the most solemn of voices:

> For me, it's not really whether I can get into any college I want to but rather whether I can handle the workload. We're told that as a [high achieving] group that we're expected to do this and we're expected to do that.... Now, check this out. Let's say I wanted to go to Harvard or what not. I have to ask myself, since I grew up in Mississippi, could I hold up at Harvard? Maybe. Could I do the work at Harvard? You know what I'm saying? I could say that I'm not concerned about that, but it's in the back of your head all of the time... it's scary. You know what I'm saying? It's scary.

This student was not alone regarding his fears and anxieties of applying to and enrolling at selective four-year institutions. One by one, students gave riveting and arguably disheartening accounts of how they self-selected out of competitive applicant pools because of their feelings of intellectual inferiority and subsequent fears of failure. When asked if she included selective institutions in her college search, this senior stated:

> No because I felt like, you know, I didn't want to be overwhelmed when I got to college. You tell me that you're interviewing high-achieving students, but I doubt myself sometimes. And that's why I really didn't consider those colleges.

With the exception of one, each of the students offered testimonies in which they felt overwhelmed and consumed by their fears during the college choice process. The lone student who did not succumb to her fears was a junior. Quietly confident yet unassuming, this young woman spoke bold and awe-inspiring truths that her peers only dared to utter. When asked why she did not share the same sentiments as her high achieving peers, this junior humbly responded:

> Well, I'm going to be real with you. Like when I first took my ACT . . . I sent my scores to Harvard. . . . I mean hey, nothing beats a failure but a try. I didn't really want to say that around the other kids because you know they'd probably look at me crazy, but I did. And a lot of stuff they were talking about, I was like, well, I did that. That's why I was being kind of quiet or whatever. Because I believe I can do it. You know you can do anything you put your mind to. . . . I figure, if I can make all of these good grades, the kind of person I am, I know I'm high achieving. I just got that attitude. If you think you're high achieving, then you're high achieving. I can't describe it, but you just know. . . . That's just the kind of attitude I have towards school. I can do anything I want to do.

Unlike her peers, this junior possessed positive images of her academic and intellectual self. She did not question her capabilities and thus did not allow self-doubt and fears of inferiority to consume her. In fact, she made no mention of these self-deprecating behaviors and thought processes. As the prototype of all high-achieving minority and low-income college aspirants, the real and obvious distinction between this student and her peers was a heightened sense of academic self-efficacy, which in turn positively influenced her perceptions of her ability to access even the most selective, four-year institutions.

Lack of Academic Preparedness

In addition to fears of failure and intellectual inferiority, students voiced concerns of a lack of academic preparedness. Through no fault of their own, students believed their academic instruction, advising, and public school curriculum were inferior to that of more affluent and private high schools with direct pipelines into selective four-year institutions. Because of the perceived lowered status of their schools and academic preparation, students felt limited during the college choice process and were extremely hesitant to qualify themselves as nationally high-achieving. When asked if she considered herself to be a high-achieving student, one senior stated, "Well, according to my school, yes, but not . . . in the top of the nation." While commenting on whether he would be able to compete nationally with other academically outstanding college aspirants, a junior said, "I just feel like I wouldn't be the highest achieving. I guess. . . . I would probably lag behind."

Others voiced similar concerns. During the focus group session, the following student was very vocal about his concerns of competing nationally:

> You have to ask yourself if the curriculum at a private high school [with pipelines into selective colleges and universities] is the same as the curriculum here. We're already told that we're not qualified to handle those [rigorous] types of workloads or whatever.

When asked as a group if they considered themselves to be high achieving and able to access any school of their choice, a senior had this to offer:

> It's high achieving at this school. I mean like we don't really know. I know I'm smart, and I know that I can do it. But at this school, I'm not challenged. I can still do so little and pass and still get an A out of a class. I wouldn't just want to jump out there if I didn't think I was ready to go to a school like that.

In this particular instance, the student was specifically referring to selective, four-year institutions. Although high achieving within the direct and immediate confines of her school environment, she was not nearly as confident in her abilities to compete nationally with other high achievers.

During the group session, another student shared, "I don't think I would do that [attend a selective college] because of the simple fact that... those schools have classes that are really hard, and I don't think this school has prepared us." Others quickly chimed in. One senior commented:

> I'm a perfectionist, personally. And all my life I've been accustomed to being the top this and the top that. And I don't want to go to a school where I'm just a C or D student, you know just an average student. I want to go somewhere where I can still be what I'm accustomed to being.

Surprisingly, students were not alone in their assessments of their academic preparation and abilities to compete nationally in selective, college applicant pools. During the focus group session, students made startling revelations about the nature of the guidance and instruction received from counselors and teachers alike during the college choice process. One senior shared:

> At our school, they always say we're the most high achieving and we're so smart, we're this and that, but in the back of their minds, I think they really think, "Well, they're limited to only so much." Because they don't tell us about Harvard and Princeton and all of this. They say Jackson State and all of that. They don't even... they barely say Ole Miss [the state flagship]. Because it's like, one of my counselors, in so many words, she said, "You're not prepared." So they say we're high achieving, but they're kind of putting us down too.

Based on these responses, it is painstakingly clear that students adhered to rational yet limited ways of being, doing, and ultimately existing in their academic worlds. Their postsecondary aspirations and college choices were directly influenced by the lowered expectations of their teachers, counselors, and society. In turn, students' expectations of themselves, their academic curriculum, and their college prospects were rationally bound by a lowered sense of academic self-efficacy.

Financial Barriers

Beyond barriers of academic intimidation and intellectual inferiority, students perceived financial barriers such as the cost of attending selective colleges as more threatening when undergoing the college choice process. There were in fact many themes that emerged during the course of this study regarding students' perceptions of the accessibility of selective institutions; however, the most salient was financial constraints.

Many of the students hailed from socioeconomically disadvantaged backgrounds and resided in households of four or more with combined incomes of less than $50,000. In fact, many participated in the Free and Reduced Price Lunch Programs. Because of their economic backgrounds, students were very cognizant of the financial barriers of accessing selective colleges and universities.

When discussing these constraints, students were remarkably candid in their responses, as evidenced by a senior finalizing his college choices:

> The thing is, let's use Harvard since that's a prestigious university. Let's say that I got accepted into Harvard by any chance. Now, the next question is, "How am I going to pay for school at Harvard?" Well, let's say they give me $3,000... but I have to pay this other $40,000 on my own. I can take out a loan, and pay the $40,000 if I wanted to. But let's check this out. Alcorn wants to give me an academic scholarship. They want to pay for everything, nothing out of my pocket. Now, I have to ask myself. I can go here and pay back these loans for the rest of my life, over forty years, or I can go to Alcorn, and they're paying for me to go there. And then I'll be an honor student there. You have to ask yourself if it would be the same at Harvard.

Another student commented, "I believed that I could get accepted into the [selective] colleges, but as far as scholarships and aid and paying for my education, I believed that I would have little to no assistance." Based on these responses, it is clear students were very pragmatic during the college choice process and favored financially accessible schools. When asked during the focus group what mattered most when selecting colleges and universities, students responded (in a united, forceful, and unapologetic voice), "Money!" In their rational minds, money was the precursor to accessing and excelling at selective colleges and universities. A junior shared she had recently received correspondence from Princeton University because of her exceptionally high standardized test scores. When asked about the correspondence, she stated:

> I really didn't look at it [the correspondence]. I don't have the money to go to Princeton. I don't want my parents to have to pay for my college education.... I

> used to say I wanted to go to Harvard when I was in middle school. Then I realized when I got to high school, Harvard might not be such a good idea.

This particular student resided in a household with six children and a family income of $40,000, and would have greatly benefited from aggressive recruitment strategies for minority and disadvantaged students recently implemented by Princeton, Harvard, and other select institutions—strategies that replace student loans with grants and scholarships. However, this student was unaware of the financial opportunities for outstanding minority and disadvantaged students at selective colleges and universities. Upon completion of the interview, the researcher shared information concerning these financial opportunities, to which the student responded, "I did not know that. I wish I would've known that. I would've had more choices, more options." She was not alone. Another student commented, "I really would have made that my priority to apply to all of those colleges because I was unaware of the financial aid opportunities at that time." As evidenced, there is a need for greater dissemination of college-going knowledge regarding new and improved financial packages for socioeconomically disadvantaged students, particularly those residing within rural areas. Such knowledge would have been expressly beneficial to these college aspirants, as it would have allowed them to choose from a greater variety of institutions.

DISCUSSION

Interpreting Diminished Factors of Academic and Intellectual Worth

This study's findings pose an interesting set of challenges for higher education administrators, researchers, and policy makers who seek to level the playing field by allowing equal access and opportunity to high-quality instruction and education for all students. By focusing on notions as abstract as students' perceptions along with academic self-efficacy and illustrating both the importance and capital-regulating role of such novelties on the selectivity of students' college choices, this study has helped qualify the type and scope of barriers to increased minority and socioeconomically disadvantaged participation in select higher education circles. Furthermore, it has codified various types of normalizing currencies that should be immediately accessible to all college aspirants in order to combat and reduce the effects of capital-regulation within the college choice process.

While the study confirms what college choice and economic theorists have known for sometime about financial barriers or the regulating role of economic capital, namely that expected costs and finances are primary considerations that negatively influence students' perceptions of the value of higher education (Anderson & Hearn, 1992; Becker, 1975; Cohn, 1979), it introduces a new finding regarding psychosocial barriers for high-achieving minority and disadvantaged students in accessing highly selective institutions. Specifically, positive outlooks and perceptions coupled with high expectations for personal and academic excellence (that are reinforced by one's immediate social environment) greatly assist in the obtainment of psychosocial capital (a normalizing currency)—which ultimately influences one's attitudes, preferences, norms, outlooks, and behaviors. In so doing, possession of psychosocial capital helps neutralize or normalize the regulating impact of economic capital on integral processes relating to college choice and access. Based on findings presented within this study, the effects of such currency-building practices and normalization efforts will greatly benefit aspiring collegians from underrepresented minority and low-income backgrounds, as it will help level the college choice playing field and allow for equal access and opportunity within selective higher education circles.

As witnessed within this study, aspirants (who are not in possession of psychosocial capital and other normalizing currencies) can easily fall prey to the all-consuming and regulating role of capital via diminished factors of academic and intellectual worth. In turn, this lowers students' academic self-efficacy and ultimately fuels their fears and misconceptions of selective four-year institutions along with their accessibility. The resulting college choice behavior is disadvantageous, particularly to minority and low-income students, and directly impedes the growth, development, and diversification of higher education pipelines—which is why educators, researchers, and policy makers must further their efforts to reduce capital-regulating roles in college choice and to provide normalizing currencies and/or high-status forms of capital to all college aspirants, regardless of their social and ethnic origin.

Previous research on African American perceptions of the value of higher education suggests that students (e.g., across achievement types) are intimidated by college-going factors such as diversity and climate, or the lack thereof (Freeman, 1997, 1999, 2005). However, the intimidation factors referenced within that body of research do not holistically address the perceptions of the 16 students presented within this study. These high-achieving, low-income college aspirants (and others like them) performed well on traditional and national measures of aptitude, but (1) they were unaware of their high achieving status and abilities to compete nationally with other outstanding, college aspirants, and (2) they qualified their high achieving status as existing solely within their social surroundings. As predicted, this contributed to maladaptive college choice behaviors, which exacerbated the regulating role of capital, regarding the selective nature of students' postsecondary selections. Unfortunately for the students, the result was all too costly. Individually and collectively, students shared disheartening accounts of their self-selection out of competitive applicant pools to selective institutions that offered a rigorous and demanding curriculum that was on par with their levels of academic preparedness and intellectual abilities.

These college choice behaviors and negative outlooks are attributable to Bourdieu's concept of habitus—which he defined as deeply internalized, permanent systems of outlook, experiences, and beliefs about the known world that are birthed from a person's or persons' immediate social environments (1977). Habitus is thought to generate practices in accordance with the structural principles of the social world (Bourdieu, 1977). In this study, habitus refers to the interactive web of perceptions held by high-achieving, low-income aspirants regarding college choices that are deemed appropriate and fitting (given one's background, values, and socioeconomic class) (Gándara, 1995; Gonzalez et al., 2003; Horvat, 1995; McDonough et al., 1997).

The concept of habitus is used here to explore the regulated capital of African American students with respect to perceptions and values of attending selective colleges and universities. Prior research examining the roles of race and class in educational decisions show that minority students employ elements of a unique cultural capital and habitus when choosing colleges (Freeman, 1997, 1999, 2005; Gonzalez et al., 2003; Horvat, 1995; McDonough, 1997). Researchers have also found the college choice behaviors of socioeconomically advantaged and disadvantaged students differ (McDonough, 1997). Here, college knowledge, attitudes, preferences, perceptions, and behaviors that acknowledge the value in attending selective colleges are types of high-status capital. Conversely, the regulation and/or lack of this high-status (and arguably normalizing) capital places high-achieving minority and socioeconomically disadvantaged students at a grave disadvantage in the college choice process. It leads them to employ strategies and thought processes that prohibit access to selective four-year institutions and furthers the regulating role of capital in college choice and access.

Conclusion and Directions for Future Research

Student voices can sometimes serve as tools that help shed light on emerging issues of the day, but within this study, student voices transcended traditional modes of employment and served as a looking glass into the future of select higher education pipelines. Suffice it to say, the future does not look bright, in part because selective, four-year institutions have only recently placed welcoming mats in front of their ivy crests and centuries' old doors, but also because students have been denied the normalizing currencies and opportunities needed to step outside of their known social worlds and expand upon existing notions of rational college choices.

Collectively, this academically outstanding group of college aspirants painted a very grim portrait of stagnant and oppressive cycles of social and economic inequality. Note the intentional use of the word "inequality." As long as underrepresented students perceive certain types of high-status educational attainment as inaccessible to them because of financial constraints or diminishing factors such as academic intimidation and intellectual inferiority and adversely act on those perceptions, educators and researchers alike are forced to reconcile notions of inequality with how select student groups fare in the college choice process relative to other groups. In essence, there is still work to be done.

Further research is needed to expound upon (1) the regulating role of capital in college choice and access, and (2) the nexus between high-achieving minority and disadvantaged students' perceptions of select colleges and universities and their resulting college choice behaviors, with special emphasis placed upon their postsecondary selections. By all means, researchers should continue to reference students during their investigation, for nothing can undermine the power of student voices; however, to ensure high quality and integrity in this line of research, researchers must also reference parents, counselors, teachers, and quite possibly recruiters from selective colleges and universities. In doing so, they will help create a more composite portrait of perceived and actual barriers that regulate currency-building and normalizing efforts within the college choice process and prohibit academically outstanding students of all sorts from accessing select doors.

NOTES

1. Academically selective private and public institutions included in the Andrew W. Mellon Foundation's College and Beyond (C&B) database are used here as indicators of the types of colleges and universities included among the nation's top four-year institutions. Institutional members of the Association of American Universities (AAU), Committee on Institutional Cooperation (CIC), the Consortium on Financing Higher Education (COFHE), and the National Association of State Universities and Land-Grant Colleges (NASULGC) are also used as indicators.
2. While any number of school districts within Mississippi could have been chosen, the author selected this specific district—which for anonymity purposes shall be referred to as College Station Municipal School District—due to issues of access and its demographic make-up.
3. The researcher focused specifically on juniors and seniors, as those are the grades in which students are more likely to have formed perceptions about

the value and worth of investing in a postsecondary education and will have given ample thought to preferred types of postsecondary institutions.

REFERENCES

Alwin, D. & Otto, L. (1977). High school context effects on aspiration. *Sociology of Education, 50,* 259–273.

Anderson, M. & Hearn, L. (1992). Equity issues in higher education outcomes. In W. Becker & D. Lewis (Eds.), *The economics of American higher education* (pp. 301–334). Norwell, MA: Kluwer Academic Publishers.

Becker, G. (1975). *Human capital* (2nd ed.). New York: Columbia University Press.

Bogdan, R. & Biklen, S., (2007). *Qualitative research for education: An introduction to theory and methods* (5th ed.). Boston: Allyn & Bacon.

Bourdieu, P. (1977). Cultural reproduction and social reproduction. In J. Karabel & A. Halsey (Eds.), *Power and ideology in education* (pp. 487–511). New York: Oxford University Press.

Bowen, W. & Bok, D. (1998). *The shape of the river.* Princeton, NJ: Princeton University Press.

Bowen, W., Kurzweil, M., & Tobin, E. (2005). *Equity and excellence in American higher education.* Charlottesville, VA: University of Virginia Press.

Boyle, R. (1966). The effect of the high school on students' aspirations. *The American Journal of Sociology, 6,* 628–639.

Cohn, E. (1979). *The economics of education.* Cambridge, MA: Harper & Row.

Freeman, K. (1997). Increasing African Americans' participation in higher education: African American high-school students' perspectives. *Journal of Higher Education, 68,* 523–550.

Freeman, K. (1999). The race factor in African Americans' college choice. *Urban education, 34*(1), 4–25.

Freeman, K. (2005). *African Americans and college choice: The influence of family and school.* Albany, NY: State University of New York Press.

Gándara, P. (1995). *Over the ivy walls: The educational mobility of low-income Chicanos.* New York: State University of New York Press.

Gerald, D., & Haycock, K. (2005). *Engines of inequality: Diminishing equity in the nation's premier public universities.* Washington, DC: The Education Trust.

Gonzalez, K., Stoner, C., & Jovel, J. (2003). Examining the roles of social capital in access to college for Latinas: Toward a college opportunity framework. *Journal of Hispanic Higher Education, 2,* 146–170.

Hearn, J. (1991). Academic and nonacademic influences on the college destinations of 1980 high school graduates. *Sociology of Education, 64,* 158–171.

Horvat, E. (1995). *Getting in: A case study analysis of college admission and the organizational structure of postsecondary access.* Unpublished doctoral dissertation, University of California, Los Angeles.

Hossler, D., Braxton, J., & Coopersmith, G. (1989). Understanding student college choice. In J. C. Smart (Ed.), *Higher education: Handbook of theory and research* (Vol. 5, pp. 231–288). New York: Agathon Press.

Hossler, D., & Gallagher, K. (1987). Studying student college choice: A three-phase model and the implications for policymakers. *College & University, 62*(3), 207–221.

Hossler, D., & Vesper, N. (1993, April). *Consistency and change in college matriculation decisions: An analysis of the factors which influence the college selection decisions of students.* Paper presented at the annual meeting of the American Educational Research Association, Atlanta, GA.

Jack Kent Cooke Foundation. (2007, September 10). *Achievement trap: How America is failing millions of high achieving students from lower income families.* Retrieved from http://www.jackkentcookefoundation.org/jkcf_web/Documents/Achievement %2T rap.pdf

JBHE Foundation. (2001). How Princeton University has captured top Black students. *Journal of Blacks in Higher Education, 33*(Autumn), 54–55.

JBHE Foundation. (2003). How Johns Hopkins increased Black enrollments by 134 percent in two years. *Journal of Blacks in Higher Education, 42*(Winter), 42–43.

Jencks, C. & Phillips, M. (1998). The black-white test score gap: An introduction. In C. Jencks & M. Phillips (Eds.), *The black white test score gap* (pp. 1–51). Washington, DC: Brookings Institution.

Kaplan, E. (1999). "It's going good": Inner-city Black and Latino adolescents' perceptions about achieving an education. *Urban Education, 34*(2), 181–213.

Lattimore, R. (2001). The wrath of high-stakes tests. *Urban Review, 33*(1), 57–67.

Litten, L., Sullivan, D., & Brodigan, D. (1983). *Applying market research in college admissions.* New York: The College Board.

McDonough, P. (1997). *Choosing colleges: How social class and schools structure opportunity.* New York: State University of New York Press.

McDonough, P. (1994). Buying and selling higher education: The social construction of the college applicant. *Journal of Higher Education, 65*(4), 427–446.

McDonough, P., Antonio, A., & Trent, J. (1997). Black students, Black colleges: An African American college choice model. *Journal for a Just and Caring Education, 3,* 9–36.

Mortenson, T. (1991). *Equity of higher educational opportunity for women, Black, Hispanic, and low income students* (ACT Student Financial Aid Rep. No. 91-1). Iowa City, IA: American College Testing, Educational and Social Research. (ERIC Document Reproduction Service No. ED328133)

Perna, L. (2000). Differences in the decision to attend college among African Americans, Hispanics, and whites. *Journal of Higher Education, 71*(2), 117–141.

Phillips, M., Brooks-Gunn, J., Duncan, G., Klebanov, P., & Crane, J. (1998). Family background, parenting practices, and the black-white test score gap. In C. Jencks & M. Phillips (Eds.), *The black white test score gap* (pp. 103–145). Washington, DC: Brookings Institution.

Pope, L. (2007). *Looking beyond the Ivy League: Finding the college that's right for you.* New York: Penguin Books.

Smith, M. (2001). Low SES African American parents: Playing the college choice game on an unlevel field. *Journal of College Admissions, 171,* 16–21.

Spies, R. (2001). *The effect of rising cost on college choice.* (Research Report Series No. 117). Princeton, NJ: Princeton University.

Stage, F., & Hossler, D. (1989). Differences in family influences on college attendance plans for male and female ninth graders. *Research in Higher Education, 30*(3), 301–315.

Tierney, W. (1993). Introduction: Developing archives of resistance: Speak, memory. In D. McLaughlin & W. Tierney (Eds.), *Naming silenced lives* (pp. 1–5). New York: Routledge.

U.S. Census Bureau, Population Division, Education and Social Stratification Branch. (2000). *American community survey.* Washington, DC. Retrieved from http://factfinder.census.gov/home/saff/main.html?lang-en

CHAPTER 8

BRIDGING THE GAP BETWEEN THEORY AND PRACTICE

An Intra-Educational Analysis of Capital and Its Diverse Forms for Educational Opportunity and Attainment

Susan S. McClelland, Ph.D.
University of Mississippi

Historically, educational research has taken place within the confines of the educational institutions of schools and colleges as if they operated as an autonomous social system. This approach to educational research has been identified as an "intra-educational analysis" (Anderson, 1961, p. 2). In many ways, the reciprocity linkages between the theoretical conceptions and practical viewpoints of capital and its diverse forms (i.e., economic, social, human, cultural) have not been examined using this intra-educational analysis approach to demonstrate their implications for the pursuit of educational opportunities and attainment. An intra-educational analysis elicits a framework for understanding the relationship between social capital as embedded in various communities and economic and human capital as

Contemporary Perspectives on Capital in Educational Contexts, pages 187–201

well as understanding how capital serves to regulate various processes. In effect, the intra-educational analysis provides insight into how educational opportunities and educational attainment become a byproduct of internal and external factors (i.e., parent–child relationships, home–school relations, and teacher expectations).

The No Child Left Behind Act of 2001 fails to account for these factors that relate to capital. While NCLB places emphasis on standards-based instruction and student achievement, it fails to address the essential elements that contribute to failing schools: lack of resources within the schools, the communities in which the schools are located, parental educational levels and incomes, and how these factors influence student achievement. NCLB was enacted in an effort to address enormous disparities in student achievement. Proponents of NCLB claim that setting high academic standards, establishing measurable goals, and holding schools accountable would improve individual student achievement as measured by yearly standardized tests. If a school repeatedly fails to meet the yearly set standard for student growth, or Adequate Yearly Progress (AYP), on the tests, it can face punitive measures. According to Christopher Knaus (2007):

> Because NCLB ignores the social context that shapes opportunity for many African American youth, it shifts conversation about educational equity away from what really matters.... NCLB ignores how the surrounding community, parental income and education levels, language and cultural barriers, teacher awareness of student cultural context, and pedagogical approaches influence academic engagement of all students. (p. 3)

Knaus goes on to say that NCLB favors teaching methods and curricula that cannot have a meaningful impact on African American student achievement nor does it prepare those attending failing Title I schools for college. Thus, NCLB fails to acknowledge that parents' financial and social capital affect student achievement as well as educational opportunity. The act approaches education as though it operates in an autonomous social system without addressing the broader contexts of how various forms of capital within communities serve to regulate educational opportunities for children attending schools in those communities.

This chapter seeks to examine the relationship between social capital, embedded in various communities or social structures, and economic and human capital, and how when used collectively, individuals or agencies serve as regulators (Bartee & Brown, 2007) of educational opportunity. The links between capital, specifically social capital, and educational attainment, may be drawn from the works of Pierre Bourdieu (1984, 1990) and James Coleman (1965, 1987, 1988, 1990).

THEORETICAL CONCEPTIONS OF CAPITAL AND ITS DIVERSE FORMS

Bourdieu's conception of capital reflects his "positioning of actors in social space according to economic, social and cultural characteristics" (McClenaghan, 2000, p. 568). Economic capital is generally seen as a form of currency, assets, or property. It may be referred to as physical capital or financial capital; however, it often connotes financial assets and one's ability to acquire additional assets. Cultural capital refers to values, behaviors, dispositions, or habits "acquired in the socialization process or accumulated through investment in education and training" (McClenaghan, 2000, p. 568). Throsby (2001) asserts that cultural capital exists in two forms: "(1) tangible—occurring in the form of buildings, locations, sites . . . and (2) intangible—occurring as intellectual capital in the form of ideas, practices, beliefs, and values which are shared by a group" (p 46). Social capital refers to influential networks, resources associated with memberships in organizations both formal and informal. Bourdieu emphasizes the importance of group membership and the need for creating and maintaining social networks. His broader theoretical model is detailed in *Distinction: A Social Critique on the Judgment of Taste* (1984), where he uses *habitus* as a set of internalized dispositions that operate in social arenas. He writes that, *habitus* "is a general, transposable disposition which carries out a systematic, universal application—beyond the limits of what has been directly learnt—of the necessity inherent in the learning conditions" (Bourdieu, 1984, p. 170). He discusses the *habitus* primarily in terms of members of a social class or as a part of a culture.

However, later, Bourdieu (1990) describes how each social class will have different *habitus.* He writes:

> The singular *habitus* of members of the same class are united in a relationship of homology, that is, of diversity within homogeneity reflecting the diversity within homogeneity characteristic of their social conditions of production. Each individual system of dispositions is a structural variant of the others, expressing the singularity of its position within the class and its trajectory. (p. 60)

He notes that differences in *habitus* provide individuals with varying social connections, cultural skills and resources, and educational opportunities, all of which lead to different forms of capital—social, cultural, and economic. "In Bourdieu's analysis, social and cultural capital are never completely reducible to an economic form but they are still fundamentally rooted in it, since all types of capital can be derived from economic capital through various efforts of transformation" (McClenaghan, p. 568). Building on the notion that all types of capital evolve from economic capital, Bourdieu posits that privileged groups have a sort of symbolic power, which can be used to regulate their capital uncontested (Bourdieu, 1993).1 Thus, society accords privileged groups status, certain advantages, and membership into exclusive groups or communities.

Within these networks, Bourdieu demonstrates conflict, change, and systemic inequality as it highlights the nature of the relationships between structure and agency (Lareau, 2003). He argues that based on where a person lives or the community in which one is reared, people are socialized differently. "This socialization provides children, and later adults, with a sense of what is comfortable or what is natural (*habitus*). These background experiences also shape the amount and forms of resources (*capital*) individuals inherit and draw upon as they confront various institutional arrangements (*fields*) in the social world" (Lareau, 2003, p. 275). People are empowered or dispossessed based on a number of factors, including geographic locale, resources, and opportunities.

Notwithstanding, James Coleman (1988) is responsible for bridging the inquiry of social capital and education. He defines social capital in terms of its function where two key elements exist: "they all consist of some aspect of social structure, and they facilitate certain actions of actors—whether personal or corporate actors—within the structure" (Coleman, 1988, p. S98). Thus, social capital is a "social structural resource" that serves as a capital asset for individuals and "facilitates certain actions and outcomes" for individuals in various social settings (Coleman, 1990, p. 302). Social capital is not owned or acquired individually, but rather it exists in the relationships between individuals and is characterized by mutual trust.

Social capital has roots in both the economists and sociologists' definitions of capital. In summarizing Coleman (1988), Ackerman, Kiron, Goodwin, Harris, and Gallagher (1997) say that most sociologists view human behavior as the "product of a social environment governed by social norms, rules, and obligations" while economists view humans as "independently motivated by rationally determined, wholly self interested goals" (p. 213). The social capital concept is an integration of both views. It assumes that rationality is a primary motivating force for human behavior both at the level of individual action and of social organization (Ackerman et al., 1997). Thus, individuals possessing social capital are advantaged through and by the various social organizations to which they belong.

Coleman (1988) goes on to say that social capital plays an important role in creating human capital within families as well as their extended communities. This role not only affects human capital for the current family members but for generations to come. Coleman asserts there are three different types of capital within the family structure that affect the educational achievement of children: financial capital (often referred to as economic capital), human capital, and social capital. Financial capital is often measured by the parents' wealth or income. Human capital is often measured in two ways: the level of the parents' education and their potential to create an environment that stimulates and enhances their children's learning. When families do not have particularly high human capital, the type of social capital that they exert may be found in the extra time and effort they provide their children to instill in them learning and discipline (Coleman, 1988). Chin and Phillips (2004) found that social capital, which they defined as social networks, crossed social-class lines and often served to compensate for a lack of financial resources for economically disadvantaged families.

PRACTICAL VIEWPOINTS ON CAPITAL AND ITS DIVERSE FORMS

Understanding the theoretical conception of the various forms of capital provides educational researchers with a framework to utilize intra-educational analysis in which they may explore how the various forms of capital function to regulate educational opportunity and attainment. Research has shown that a nexus exists between education and capital. Bartee and Brown (2007) introduced the notion that within institutional structures are factors that influence how various forms of capital are manifested as a consumer, regulator, and producer. In the field of education, schools have often been viewed as producers of social capital because of their goals and functions. Yet, given Coleman's conclusions, education becomes a regulator of social capital because the greater the influence of parents and community, the better students will perform. However, the quality of the influence also significantly impacts the quality of the performance, and thus the educational experience as a whole. Bartee and Brown (2007) assert that "social capital is highly predicated upon resource access and/or distribution" (p. 37). Then, if social capital is a resource to be used and distributed through networks, some groups will benefit and advance while others will not.

In a study that examined parental networks as a type of social capital and their impact on children's schooling, Horvat, Weininger, and Lareau (2003) detail the characteristics of parental networks across different classes. They examine the ways in which parents access networks when confronted with a problematic school situation. Specifically, they note how informal parental networks differ by class and how parents utilize those networks in resolving problems at school. Their data suggest that there are important "class-specific differences in the architecture of parental networks... and in parents' capacity to effectively intervene in school matters" (p. 320). They found that middle-class parents were able to access resources or utilize network ties to benefit their children, while working-class families or families from low socioeconomic background did not have the connections or resources to utilize.

This action supports Stanton-Salaza's (1997) definition of social capital as the "degree and quality of middle-class forms of social support transmitted through social ties" (p. 5). The authors contend that their results demonstrate the power of middle-class parents to "harness social capital in their interactions with schools" (Horvat et al., 2003, p. 326). For the working-class families and families from low socioeconomic background, "network ties had little relevance to the enhancement of schooling" (p. 341).[2] Their ties were more within their extended families and centered on issues of transportation and childcare. Thus, the parental involvement and intervention in problematic issues with the school function as a source of power. The parents were able to mobilize their social networks to exert authority over school officials. The success of the parents' use of social capital served to regulate or perpetuate their own advantage, which ultimately facilitated the transmission of advantage for one group over another.

In a closer examination, Annette Lareau (2003) conducted an investigation of 12 families, examining the ways in which social capital (or social class) influences the daily lives of people and children. This study resulted in a book entitled *Unequal Childhood: Class, Race, and Family Life*, a provocative yet stirring analysis of class differences. Lareau takes particular care in her examination of four families from each of the three social classes: middle class, working class, and low socioeconomic background. She begins her narrative with a description of conversations between two middle-class families, one white, and the other black. She points out that "discussions between parents and children are a hallmark of middle-class children rearing," not of race (p. 1). Middle-class parents view themselves as "developing" their children through the conversations they have, the organized leisure activities they schedule, and the various other structured events that give their children a robust sense of entitlement. By ensuring their children engage in these experiences, middle-class parents engage in a process that Lareau calls *concerted cultivation* (p. 2). Through this process and sense of entitlement in concerted cultivation, Lareau contends that middle-class children learn to question adults and address them as equals.

Conversely, working-class parents and parents from lower socioeconomic status facilitate what Lareau terms the *accomplishment of natural growth.* Because working-class families and families from low socioeconomic background have fewer resources to negotiate the demands of rearing their children, these parents approach the task differently. These parents do not view leisure time as their responsibility, nor do they view themselves as responsible for intervening in their children's schooling. Lareau draws from Bourdieu's theory of social capital as she defines the child-rearing context to include "the routines of daily life, the dispositions of daily life, or the 'habitus' of daily life" (pp. 289–290). Therefore, while the children have more free time to play independently or in an unsupervised, small group, they are not being socialized into organized groups or structured events.

In her analysis, Lareau (2003) is careful to state that all parents are caregivers, desire the best for their children, and want them to do well in school. However, the varying strategies and beliefs regarding how these play out are due to "cultural repertoires" that are associated with social class. "Because these guidelines are so generally accepted and because they focus on a set of practices concerning how parents should raise children, they form a *dominant set of cultural repertories* about how children should be raised" (p. 4). While middle-class parents are determined to help their children get ahead and not be excluded from any opportunity that could ensure their advancement, they engaged in a pattern of concerted cultivation to stimulate their children's cognitive and social skills. Working-class and families from lower socioeconomic status are committed to providing food, clothing, shelter, and other basic needs that, at times, present economic challenges. As a result, these differences in philosophies and abilities lead to "the *transmission of differential advantages* to children" (p. 5).

Building on Coleman's conceptual framework of social and human capital, Kevin Marjoribanks (1992) conducted a study that examined the relationships between family educational capital—that is, the parents' aspirations for their children as well as their academic socialization—and measures of their children's individual attributes and academic achievement. In this context, Marjoribanks views human capital as not only the amount of education parents have acquired, but also the avenue through which parents provide a learning environment for children in their home. Social capital is related to the relationships between the parents and children. Marjoribanks concluded that "within family opportunity structures, children's individual attributes and family educational capital had modest to moderate associations with measures of academic achievement and that there were family opportunity structure differences in the relationships among family educational capital, children's individual attributes, and their academic performance" (p. 536). This study supports Coleman's (1987) idea that educational outputs may result from the interaction of qualities (characterized as attitudes, effort, and conception of self) children bring from home with qualities of the school. In this sense, a child's academic achievement is not only affected by his/her own attributes and the family educational capital, but also the family opportunity structure or the social capital of the family. Marjoribanks notes that academic achievement would "vary for children from different opportunity structures" (p. 530). In this instance, the different opportunity structures leverage the dominant school or community culture, thereby fulfilling the role of regulator of social capital.

CAPITAL AS A REGULATOR FOR EDUCATIONAL OPPORTUNITY AND EDUCATIONAL ATTAINMENT

When considering how various forms of capital serve as regulators for educational opportunity in schools, educational researchers may glean insights from Coleman's empirical evidence taken from studies on American schools in which he examines educational outcomes. He concludes that the variations in educational attainment and school drop-out rates mirror the variations in levels of parental involvement in schools and community affairs, of family stability, and the quality of shared norms and values within the communities rather than the economic class of the parents (McClenaghan, 2000). Given this, greater educational outcomes should be achieved when parents are involved in organizations such as parent–teacher associations, little league, and reading fairs, and when they attend civic affairs such as political rallies and community theater. Putnam (1993) adds that these associations or networks facilitate coordination and cooperation among the participants for mutual benefit.

Unequal Childhoods (Lareau, 2003) provides evidence to support Coleman's assertion (1988) that social capital exists in at least three forms:

1. The first form is concerned with obligations, expectations, and trust. Members of a social class perform favors for each other. As they perform these favors, they accrue credits from which they can draw. These credits or obligations give members of the social group additional capital to help them meet personal or collective goals. This form of social capital requires a high degree of trust whereby members of the group can retain credit and payment for favors.
2. The second form of social capital is information channels. Actors within a social network rely on social relationships to provide needed and sometimes costly information.
3. The third form of social capital is norms and sanctions. Norms enable various forms of social capital to develop. Many norms are internalized, while others are maintained by an external system of reward for following them and a sanction or punishment for not.

For example, Lareau (2003) describes a situation where a particular middle-class child attempts to gain entrance in the gifted program (an academically advanced program that screens students based on academic achievement and a minimum threshold I.Q. score or entrance exam) at her school. This particular gifted program provides a group of elite students with an enriched and challenging curriculum. The student failed the test by two points. Rather than accepting the results of the test, the mother sought advice from friends and information from teachers (members of her social class) regarding the policies for appeal; she utilized her economic resources; and she used her leverage to appeal the decision and had her daughter privately tested. When the daughter's test score met the school's standard, she was admitted into the program. Although the establishment of a minimum testing requirement served as a regulator for admissions into the program, this parent leveraged her social and economic capital to gain entrance into the program, thus status for her child. This example provides insight into Bartee and Brown's (2007) view that both the educational institution and the parent leveraged various forms of capital to serve as a regulator to control admissions or leverage accessibility. The school required a cut-off test score to regulate student participation in the gifted and talented program. The district also had an appeal process not readily accessible to parents. Nevertheless, the parent utilized her social networks and her financial status to find a legitimate avenue for her daughter to gain access into the program. Both schools and parents recognize the importance of capital, social and economic, and create structures that sustain it.

According to Lareau, educators privilege students who have an extensive vocabulary, knowledge, and reasoning skills, all of which are hallmarks of the middle class. In their daily exchanges with teachers, children discover that those in position of authority value their experiences and opinions. Educators and other professionals "accept (and help to reproduce) an ideology that values... reasoning and negotiating skills, large vocabularies, facility in speaking and working with strangers and time management" (2003, p. 140). This position is supported by Coombs' (1968) assertion that educational systems have a social bias for children whose parents are educated and thereby often provide their children with an extensive vocabulary and a culturally rich environment. Coombs continues that verbal dexterity is largely acquired outside of school, giving these children a head start in school. As the educational system places value on these social and cognitive skills, it functions not only to regulate but also endorse a set of norms and values. While the students within that social network emerge with a sense of entitlement, students outside that social sphere emerge with a "sense of constraint" (Lareau, 2003, p. 140). Children from low socioeconomic background and working-class families lack the language, the vocabulary, and the conversation skills needed in the social institution. Although these students are resourceful at managing their own time and creating games for play and they are respectful and obedient to adults, these skills are "rendered invisible" in the real world or in the daily work at school. These examples further reinforce Bartee and Brown's (2007) assertion that if social capital is a resource to be used and distributed through networks, some groups will benefit while others will not. In this example, educators reinforce or privilege the *habitus* (Bourdieu, 1990) of the middle class over that of the low socioeconomic background and working class. By instilling a set of habitus in their children, the middle-class parents transfer social skills and connections that can be translated into various forms of capital or value. Thus, the opportunities afforded middle-class students as a direct result of their parents' social status and networking ability, coupled with the ideologies of educational institutions, act as regulators of their educational attainment.

In a comprehensive study initiated by Phi Delta Kappa International (Boyd et al., 1999), researchers describe factors that affect children's learning in the Ohio educational system. This team, led by Dr. Richard Boyd, presents factual information from urban and suburban schools that directly reflects student achievement, such as state accountability data, student achievement data, and school/district financial data, as well as factual information that indirectly affects student achievement, such as family income, median housing value, college educational attainment, poverty, and home ownership.

On close examination of the data the researchers note similarities and differences between urban and suburban school-related factors. The similarities were class size, ranging from 17 to 26 students; teacher salaries, from $33,079 to just over $50,000; and local plus state expenditures for schools, a formula developed by the state to "even out" the funds applied to schools. The differences noted were in student achievement, graduation rate, interscholastic sports, and enrollment in advanced academic courses. Other notable differences were that children in the eight largest cities, attending those urban schools, were living among adults "who have less education, lower incomes, less expensive houses, greater poverty, and are on welfare more often" (p. 223). For example, ninth grade children living in Cuyahoga County attending school in East Cleveland School District had a 9% passage rate on the math achievement test, a 46% passage on the reading proficiency test, and a 33% passage on both the writing and the citizenship assessments. The graduation rate in that district was 49.9% and the percent of students enrolled in extra academic subjects was 0. While these statistics are startling, the following data provide a deeper understanding of the problem: children in the East Cleveland School District lived in homes where the median family income was $18,136; 37% of the families owned their own home; 35% of the adults had some college; 36% of the children lived in poverty; and 23% received some type of public assistance (Boyd et al., 1999).

While the purpose of this study is not to discuss theoretical implications of the effects capital on student achievement, it provides evidence that supports Bourdieu's (1992) position that privileged groups (those who maintain economic and social capital) understand how to harness their symbolic power to gain status, certain advantages, and membership into exclusive groups or communities including certain schools in certain neighborhoods. Meanwhile, those who do not possess such capital continue to reproduce social and educational inequality. These data also provide evidence of Coleman's assertion that financial, human, and social capital within the family structure affect the educational achievement of the children (Coleman, 1988). In this case, social capital and economic capital function as regulators to perpetuate the culture of the school and community. Students who live in economically productive communities attend schools that provide rich learning experiences—a variety of educational opportunities—increasing their opportunity for advanced educational attainment.

This point is further supported by Pauline Lipman's (2002) examination of Chicago's public school reform as it relates to urban growth and development. She shows that inequalities in Chicago's housing system relate to inequalities in its educational institutions. The school reform policies actually "exacerbate existing inequalities and create new dynamics of inequality with important implications for students and for the future of the city as a whole" (p. 380). Student access to specialized courses depended on the economic level of their neighborhood. For example, some students had access to specialized college preparatory math and science courses, while others had generalized courses. Students who lived in gentrified neighborhoods or upscale redeveloped areas had access to more specialized college preparatory programs, while the two military academies, which focused on discipline and order, were located in historically African-American neighborhoods. "Chicago's differentiated educational experiences provide different resources for students to draw upon to construct their identities" (p. 407).

While the Ohio study provides student achievement data that support Coleman's (1988) theory that parents' financial and social capital affect student achievement and educational opportunity, Lareau and Horvat (1999) sought to examine the nature of social interaction and the reproduction of inequality by looking at what they call moments of social inclusion and exclusion. While the researchers also draw from Bourdieu's concept of social reproduction, they criticize that he has not been "sufficiently aware of variations in the ways in which institutional actors legitimate or rebuff efforts by individuals to activate their resources" (p. 38). The researchers state that the social setting (or field) dictates the value of capital, that there is a difference between possessing and activating capital, and that the skill with which one uses capital varies. The writers acknowledge that all individuals have some form of social capital that they use in a variety of settings; however, they stress that all social or cultural capital does not have the same value. To be of value in a given field, "social and cultural capital must be activated. The ability to activate social and cultural capital and the way in which it is activated influence its value in a field of interaction" (p. 39). In their study, Lareau and Horvat (1999) examine the parental involvement of 24 students (12 white children and 12 black children) attending a Midwestern elementary school located in the "white and affluent part of town" (p. 40). They define each group as being comprised of middle class ($n = 12$), working class ($N = 7$), and low socioeconomic background ($N = 5$). They find that while educators desire parental involvement, they place value on the "patterns of the dominant ideology in the broader culture" (p. 42). In the context of this particular school community, the parents' cultural and social resources become "forms of capital when they facilitate parents' compliance with dominant standards in school interactions" (p. 42). For example, teachers expect parents' reactions to be supportive and positive, and demonstrate trust in their decisions. When parents respond in this manner, their cultural capital in the school setting increases. However, due to a turbulent legacy of "racial discrimination, black parents are more likely to begin the process" of talking with educators and school officials, being "suspicious and critical of the risk of unfair treatment for their children" (p. 42). Therefore, when black parents seem confrontational—angry or critical—regarding the treatment of black children, their "involvement" is deemed "unacceptable and 'destructive' by the educators" (p. 43).

This application of capital led Lareau and Horvat (1999) to examine the concept of moments of inclusion and moments of exclusion. Moments of inclusion are "the coming together of various forces to provide an advantage to the child in his or her life trajectory" (p. 48). These moments may range from placement in an elite academic program, such as the gifted and talented program, to the use of networks to prepare for admittance into a specific college. Moments of exclusion, however, "may include placement in a low reading group, retention, placement in remedial courses, and the failure to complete college-preparation requirements" (p. 48). Moments of inclusion and exclusion may support Bartee and Brown's (2007) idea that social institutions such as schools serve to regulate the acquisition of capital, in this particular setting, for black parents who lack the human capital skills valued by the dominant culture. This study further demonstrates how parents may leverage social capital to ensure that their children receive the optimal educational opportunities that a school may offer, thus increasing their potential for higher educational attainment. In order to increase leveraging-skill levels of families from low socioeconomic background, educational institutions need to seek practical means for those families to possess and activate capital. This may include listening to the voices of those families in novel ways, seeking to empower them to gain and employ capital more effectively.

CONCLUDING THOUGHTS: WHERE THEORY MEETS PRACTICE IN CAPITAL AS INTRA-EDUCATIONAL ANALYSIS

The works of Bourdieu and Coleman provide a useful theoretical framework in which to build an understanding of the linkages between the theoretical conceptions and practical viewpoints of capital and how they serve as regulators of educational opportunity and attainment using intra-educational analysis. Bourdieu and Passeron (1979) contend that institutions are socially constructed to reproduce existing social classes and economic capital. They are socially constructed "centers of cultural authority, which maintain and disseminate societal standards of value and serve collectively to clarify and periodically revise the cultural currency" (Mohr & DiMaggio, 1995, p. 169). Thus, children whose parents possess social capital are advantaged through the organizations to which they belong and the educational institutions they attend. These social connections and educational opportunities lead to greater opportunities for educational attainment, social status, and economic capital.

Throughout the research, evidence exists of parental utilization of capital to access opportunities for their children. Whether one considers Bourdieu's (1990) *habitus*, Lareau and Horvat's (1999) moments of inclusion, or Coleman's (1988) measure of human capital, parents' ability to understand and leverage capital directly affects their children's educational opportunities. Parents who maintain economic and social capital possess symbolic power; thus they gain status, advantages, and membership into exclusive groups, including certain schools in certain neighborhoods. Meanwhile, parents who do not possess such capital continue to reproduce social and educational inequality. In this sense, the selective nature of this process enables individuals, educational institutions, and other agencies to serve as a regulator of social capital and opportunity for students.

Educational institutions could work to increase the access to information and the educational opportunities for students from low socioeconomic background by attempting to engage parents from that background in diverse ways, working to enable them to access networks to improve their students' mobility. Moreover, educational institutions could strive to broaden parental involvement of parents from low socioeconomic backgrounds by developing communication awareness programs for them, helping them to better understand capital, and empowering them to better employ it for their students' benefit. Finally, given the understanding of capital presented in this chapter, educational institutions need to develop locally based action plans to put that understanding into practice.

NOTES

1. For the purpose of this chapter, "privileged groups" are defined as those to whom society accords status, certain advantages, and membership into exclusive groups or communities. This definition is consistent with Bourdieu's use of it.

2. In several of the research documents included in this chapter, the term "poor" is used. In order to avoid potential negative connotations of this term this chapter uses the term "low socioeconomic background."

REFERENCES

Ackerman, F., Kiron, D., Goodwin, N. R., Harris, J. M., Gallagher, K., (Eds.). (1997). *Human well-being and economic goals.* Washington, DC: Island Press.

Anderson, C. A. (1961). Methodology of comparative education. *International Review of Education,* 7:1, 1 – 23.

Bartee, R. & Brown M. C. (2007). *School matters: Why African American students multiple forms of capital.* New York: Peter Lang.

Bourdieu, P. (1984). *Distinction: A social critique of the judgment of taste.* Cambridge, MA: Harvard University Press.

Bourdieu, P. (1990). *The logic of practice.* Stanford: Stanford University Press.

Bourdieu, P. (1993). *The field of cultural production.* Cambridge: Polity Press.

Bourdieu, P. & Passeron J. C. (1979). *The inheritos: French students and their relations to culture.* (Richard Nice, Trans.). Chicago: University of Chicago.

Boyd, R., Anderson, D., Crosby, E., Cunninghan, L., Frymier, J., Gansneder, B., Roaden, A. (1999). *Are Ohio's urban youth at risk? urban and suburban schools in the buckeye state.* Bloomington, IN: Phi Delta Kappa International.

Chin, T. & Phillips, M. (2004). Social reproduction and child-rearing practices: social class, children's agency, and the summer activity gap. *Sociology of Education, 77,* 185–210.

Coleman, J. S. (Ed.). (1965). *Education and political development.* Princeton, NJ: University Press.

Coleman, J. S. (1987). Families and schools. *Educational Researcher, 16,* 32–38.

Coleman, J. S. (1988). Social capital in the creation of human capital. *American Journal of Sociology, 94* (Supplement), S95–S120.

Coleman, J. S. (1990). *Foundations of social theory.* Cambridge: Harvard University Press.

Coombs, P. H., (1968). *The world educational crisis: A systems analysis.* New York: Oxford University Press.

Horvat, E. M., Weininger, E. B., & Lareau, A. (2003). From social ties to social capital: Class differences in the relations between schools and parent networks. *American Educational Research Journal, 40,* 319–351.

Knaus, C. B. (2007). *Still segregated, still unequal: Analyzing the impact of No Child Left Behind on African American students.* State of Black America. New York: National Urban League.

Lareau, A. (2003). *Unequal childhoods: Class, race, and family life.* Berkely, CA: Univesity of Califonia Press.

Lareau, A. & Horvat E. M. (1999). Moments of social inclusion and exclusion: Race, class, and cultural capital in family-school relationships. *Sociology of Education, 72,* 37–53.

Lipman, P. (2002). Making the global city, making inequality: The political economy and cultural politics of Chicago school policy. *American Educational Research Journal, 39,* 379–419.

Marjoribanks, K. (1992). Family capital, children's individual attributes, and academic achievement. *The Journal of Psychology, 126,* 529–538.

McClenaghan, P. (2000). Social capital: Exploring the theoretical foundations of community development education. *British Educational Research Journal, 26*(5), 566–582.

Mohr, J. & DiMaggio, P (1995). The intergenerational transmission of cultural capital. *Research in Social Stratification and Mobility, 14,* 167–199.

Putnam, R. D. (1993). *Making democracy work: Civic traditions in modern Italy.* Princeton, New Jersey: Princeton University Press.

Stanton-Salazar, R. (1997). A social capital framework for understanding the socialization of racial minority children and youths. *Harvard Educational Review, 67,* 1–40.

Throsby, D (2001). *Economics and culture.* Cambridge: Cambridge University Press.

CHAPTER 9

CAPITALIZING THROUGH LEARNING

Forms of Capital that Affect Graduate School Admissions and Achievement

Saran Donahoo
Southern Illinois University

Illustrated by growing unemployment nationwide, getting a bachelor's degree is no longer enough. Increasingly, people in several fields need to complete some sort of post-baccalaureate degree or training to effectively compete for the limited number of job openings (Stainburn, 2009). However, many minority, low-income, and first-generation undergraduate degree earners are unprepared to pursue education beyond a bachelor's degree because they do not amass the capital needed to go any further than the undergraduate level. Rather than leave their ability to enter graduate and professional degree programs to chance, all prospective graduate students should devote time and effort to identifying, gathering, and redistributing various forms of capital that will allow them to matriculate successfully.

This chapter discusses categories of capital that affect both the ability of students to gain admission to graduate school and the benefits that they

Contemporary Perspectives on Capital in Educational Contexts, pages 203–217

receive in and outside of the collegiate environment as a result of obtaining additional education. Following this introduction, this chapter provides an overview of the graduate school admissions process and a description of common forms of capital that influence graduate school enrollment and success. Next, attention shifts to the concept of hidden capital and how this form affects student experiences within graduate and professional degree programs. Finally, the chapter concludes with some general suggestions for all prospective graduate students about obtaining and expending capital.

GRADUATE SCHOOL ADMISSION

Similar to the admissions process for pursuing a bachelor's degree, programs and institutions require that prospective students provide a range of documentation and proof of readiness. Generally, students must complete applications, provide transcripts for all previous college coursework, submit scores from standardized exams, write essays outlining their goals for obtaining advanced degrees, obtain recommendation letters attesting to their personalities and abilities, and include writing samples or other materials that display skills and talents associated with the programs in which students want to enroll (Kuther, 2010; Pascarella, Wolniak, Pierson, & Flowers, 2004). While prospective students do not begin to gather all of these materials until they decide to pursue additional education, the preparation for this process, i.e., the generation of capital begins and takes place throughout their entire undergraduate training.

COMMON FORMS OF CAPITAL

Higher education is all about capital. In this sense, capital is a general term that refers to the goods, assets, and advantages that individuals acquire and use to improve their political, economic, and social standing. Students must prove that they possess various forms of capital in order to get admitted to, succeed in, and make the most of their graduate education (Aronowitz, 2004; Pascarella et al., 2004; Perna, 2004; Walpole, 2003). Forms of capital that students need to monitor and establish as they look to and participate in post-baccalaureate programs include economic, academic, and social capital.

Economic Capital

Anyone who has ever attended or read any of the literature related to the costs of attending college knows all too well that economic capital is a crucial and vital element. Economic capital refers to the financial standing that students have, their ability to pay for college, and the monetary benefits individuals attain as a result of completing a college degree (Perna, 2005; Perna & Titus, 2005; Schieman & Plickert, 2008; Sissoko & Shiau, 2005; Strayhorn, 2008). According to The College Board (2009), the average annual tuition rate is $7,020 at a public four-year institution and $26,273 at a private four-year institution for the 2009–2010 academic year. Yet, with those identified as African American and Hispanic being three times as likely to live in poverty than Caucasians (Kaiser Family Foundation, n.d.), it is clear that a good number of potential students from this segment of the population generally lack the economic capital needed to pay for a college degree.

Initiated in the 1960s to help make college more accessible to students from low-income families (Hearn, 2001), the federal financial aid system provides many students with the economic capital needed to enter higher education. Recognizing that financial aid in the U.S. now emphasizes student loans above most other forms of aid, students at all levels need to understand what they are borrowing, the terms for repayment, and the impact that this borrowing will have on all forms of capital that they will have available to them now and in the future. At the outset of borrowing, all students at least need the knowledge or social capital that will allow them to navigate the financial aid system and put them in contact with others who know how to do so (Paulsen & St. John, 2002). Without a good understanding of the system, students may borrow too much, neglect to recognize the difference between low-interest federal loans and private loans that include high variable interests rates, turn down aid such as work study that they do not have to repay, or fail to obtain enough education or degrees that will position them to enter careers and fields where they can afford to both live independently and repay their educational debt (Millett, 2003; Paulsen & St. John, 2002; Williams, 2006).

In addition to influencing where and how students work and live during and after pursuing undergraduate degrees, student loan debt also inhibits the economic capital that prospective graduate and professional enrollees have for obtaining additional education. Long touted as the pathway to greater social capital, students who earn large amounts of debt while also earning their degrees must devote much of their financial resources to loan repayment, thus limiting the economic capital that they actually experience as a result of earning a degree (Paulsen & St. John, 2002; Williams, 2006). Related specifically to the issue of post-baccalaureate education, Perna (2004) found that bachelor's degree-holding men of all races who earn relatively low salaries are less likely to go on to attend graduate school than men who earn higher salaries, suggesting that these men feel that they simply cannot afford to pursue more schooling. Likewise, students carrying debt from their undergraduate degrees tend to be less likely to apply for or enroll in graduate and professional degree programs (Millett, 2003), thus doubly limiting their ability to reap economic benefits from their education since many do not earn enough to experience significant gains in capital nor can they afford to seek additional education, which would allow them to expand the fields and opportunities where they might access greater incomes.

Although student loans are often the form of financial aid that it is easiest for most students to access, individuals pursuing graduate education do have other options. Similar to undergraduate education, graduate students can pursue gift aid (financial support that they do not have to repay) in the form of scholarships and fellowships as well as earning money through assistantships. These forms of aid are appealing to most students because money received via scholarship, fellowship, or assistantship does not have to be repaid while or after students complete their degrees. In most cases, students receive scholarships and fellowships to support them as they pursue a degree as a result of demonstrated academic success often as it relates to a particular degree program or field of study (Ehrenberg, 2000; Millett, 2003). On the other hand, students receive assistantships as both academic support and labor compensation for services that they provide to their institutions such as teaching, assisting with research, or helping to fulfill other institutional obligations. While the actual policies vary across states, universities, and programs, the economic assistance provided by graduate-level scholarships, fellowships, and assistantships often covers most of the costs associated with enrollment. Yet, whether they meet the criteria to receive some form of graduate aid or not, many minority and firs-generation college students do not pursue or utilize these opportunities (Millett, 2003). As a result, these students are missing out on both the economic and the academic advantages that come with this aid in addition to the lifelong benefits that an advanced degree can bring.

In many ways, economic capital is both the foundation for pursuing a graduate degree and a gatekeeper controlling access to an advanced education. Recognizing the competition that recent college graduates will face from numerous others who have both more skills and greater professional experiences in an economy that some anticipate will continue to carry high rates of unemployment for at least two more years (Nutting, 2009), matriculating into graduate school may provide the best economic option to weather this recession. Beyond just riding out bad economic times, obtaining a graduate degree will help students to expand their economic capital by making them eligible to enter more and often higher paying careers. However, students also need economic capital to pursue the advanced degrees that will help them to earn more as professionals. While money is not everything, students cannot expect to succeed in graduate school without economic capital.

Academic Capital

Another key element needed to access graduate education is academic capital. Related to knowledge capital, academic capital is a building block of human capital where people attend school to earn degrees and credentials that will allow them to provide more diverse or specialized forms of labor (Paulsen & St. John, 2002; Perna, 2005; Titus, 2009). In turn, possessing strong academic capital can help individuals gain more economic capital by making their labor more valuable.

For students looking to enter and excel in graduate programs, academic capital includes grades, scores from standardized exams needed for graduate school admissions, and strong study skills. Similar to economic capital, students need to succeed at exhibiting academic capital in order to matriculate into graduate school, earn a post-baccalaureate credential, and successfully use their new education to acquire additional forms of capital.

Good grades should be the goal of all students at all educational levels. Outside of the personal sense of accomplishment, earning good grades helps to build a positive foundation for job searching and pursuing additional degrees (Millett, 2006; Walpole, 2008). Sadly, many minority and low-income students do not achieve the grade point averages (GPAs) that will make it easy for them to transition into graduate school. Possibly continuing to feel the impact of their high school academic disadvantages and deficiencies, many of these students do not perform well in college (Aronowitz, 2004; Millett, 2006; Walpole, 2008). Looking specifically at the influence of family economics, Walpole (2008) found that students from low-income backgrounds not only earned lower grades than their higher-income colleagues, but also spent less time studying, making it difficult for them to improve their academic standing. While the Internet is full of people who support the mantra of "Cs get degrees," the reality for students seeking post-baccalaureate education is that those with GPAs lower than a 2.5 (C+/B– average) generally do not get admitted, and those with less than a 3.0 (B average) frequently do not get any aid that does not require repayment. Clearly, students are aware of the consequences of having a low GPA since those who complete a bachelor's degree with a 2.74 or less are 3.5 times less likely to even apply for admission to a graduate program in the first place (Walpole, 2008). Essentially, students who earn better grades are more likely to apply and get admitted to graduate school, which, by definition, tends to limit the matriculation of students who are male, low-income, minority, and/or attend less prestigious undergraduate institutions (Aronowitz, 2004; Millett, 2006; Perna, 2004; Walpole, 2008).

Along with grades, most graduate programs also expect prospective students to take and submit scores from the Graduate Record Examination (GRE) or some other standardized tests focused on assessing the knowledge attained by undergraduates. While research conducted by the Educational Testing Service (ETS), the maker of the GRE, argues that the exam forecasts the ability of students to earn good grades in graduate school (Burton & Wang, 2005), others suggest that the exam is not the strongest predictor of graduate school success (Feeley, Williams, & Wise, 2005; Gardner, 2009; Jacobson, 2003; Lovitts, 2008; Sacks, 2001). While not necessarily a crystal ball for graduate school performance, many graduate programs use these exams to judge the quality of their applicants. Indeed, programs and faculty members tout the high GRE scores of their students as proof of intelligence and readiness for graduate education (Feely, Williams, & Wise, 2005; Gardener, 2009). As such, most students interested in going on to graduate school will have to take and hope to perform well on the GRE or some other standardized exam. Unfortunately, the test scores that many students earn parallel their GPAs, since students who receive low grades in their undergraduate coursework generally perform poorly on standardized tests as well (Feeley et al., 2005). Taken together, having low GPAs and weak exam scores effectively prevent many interested students from getting admitted to a graduate program because they simply cannot prove that they have the academic capital highly prized and sought after by faculty members and institutions.

Although earning good grades and exam scores is an important part of college life for all students, they also need to focus their attention on improving their academic skills. While the assignments, textbooks, and venues may differ, faculty tend to prefer students who communicate well, especially in writing; follow directions; come prepared for class; and know how to work independently (Boyle & Boice, 1998; Gardner, 2009; Weaver & Qi, 2005; Weidman, Twale, & Stein, 2001). Students who spend their time on campus focusing on things other than academics (whether as a result of social interests or financial necessity) generally do not develop these skills. Conversely, even when students earn good grades, the information provided on their transcripts does not prove that these students actually possess the skills that academic programs and prospective employers desire (Atwell, Lavin, Domina, & Levey, 2006; Cuyjet, Longwell-Grice, & Molina, 2009). As such, students with weak academic scores are at a double disadvantage since they lack the documented proof that they can perform well, while also suffering from the general suspicion that they will embarrass or jeopardize programs by failing to actually complete a degree even if faculty members are willing to take a chance by extending an opportunity.

Social Capital

Often the most important form of capital involved in any level of education is social capital. Social capital refers to relationships, group memberships, and networks that give individuals access to information and activities (Aronowitz, 2004; Perna, 2004; Perna & Titus, 2005). Within higher education, social capital involves the amassing of both connections to gatekeepers who control access to resources and an understanding of what it takes to cultivate success in an academic environment. For those seeking admission to graduate school, social capital influences the general preparation they have for entering into an advanced educational program and their ability to obtain favorable letters of recommendation.

The networks and relationships that students establish during their undergraduate years can have a significant impact on their ability to move on to a graduate degree. Compared to getting a bachelor's degree, students really must know people in order to get admitted to and gain the most out of a graduate program. However, many minority, first-generation, and low-income students do not take the time to build up the right capital during their undergraduate years. While many of these students do expand their social networks by making new friends, these students frequently miss out on important academic and pre-professional connections by declining to participate in official collective academic activities and organizations (Cole, 2007, 2008; Fischer, 2007; Walpole, 2003, 2008). Moreover, some social interactions actually hinder students' ability to build capital since studying in groups tends to lead to lower grades for Hispanic students (Cole, 2008); African American students often focus on interacting with people of the same race, which can be particularly limiting, especially at institutions where people of color are underrepresented within the ranks of faculty and staff (Fischer, 2007); and low-income students generally find it necessary to concentrate on maintaining the employment that they need to help pay for a degree, thus preventing them from building the other types of capital that they might gain as participants in student clubs and other on-campus involvement opportunities (Walpole, 2003). Indeed, establishing interracial social networks is of particular importance for minority students who need help and information from faculty members in order to obtain both post-graduate employment and additional education (Cole, 2007, 2008; Walpole, 2003). While not as easy to measure as grades and test scores, the social capital that students gain from interacting positively with a range of people from different races/ethnicities, campus units, and even academic disciplines is crucial for those desiring additional education because it is through these relationships that students learn how to navigate the higher education environment, position themselves to appeal to potential employers, and gain the approval of various gatekeepers that will allow them to move on through the educational pipeline.

Directly related to the social capital that undergraduate students attain are the letters of recommendation that they need to apply to graduate school. The value of recommendations varies depending on the program, institution, number of applicants, number of openings, nature of the program, and other elements of a student's completed application packet. Even so, graduate programs generally require all applicants to submit letters of recommendation with their applications and these letters can be especially influential in deciding whether or not to ultimately admit a student (Halberstam & Redstone, 2005). For students who fail to build social capital with faculty members while attending their undergraduate institutions, obtaining strong, highly favorable letters of recommendation can be very difficult. While writing letters for students is indeed one of the responsibilities that accompany faculty life (Petress, 1999), many professors are unwilling to write letters for students with whom they have had very little interaction. Students who receive faculty mentoring generally find it easier to get letters because these faculty members have a real opportunity to get to know both the work habits and the personalities of these students (Davis, 2007; Strayhorn & Terrell, 2007). As such, students must invest special efforts into building relationships with faculty so that they will have professors who feel that they know them well enough to recommend them for either employment or educational opportunities. It is remarkably important that students generate this type of social capital with faculty who are in either their undergraduate majors (Fehrman, 2009) or the academic areas that they want to study in graduate school since these individuals are best qualified to assess the overall academic skills of a student as well as his or her ability to perform in the future.

Preparing for the Future

Economic, academic, and social capital continuously influences the environment in which undergraduate students both pursue their degrees and prepare for their futures. While the variety of experiences and responsibilities that accompany college life often overshadow the everyday foci of all students, they must be careful not to allow their concerns from the present to prevent them from preparing for what lies ahead. Minority, low-income, and first-generation students must be especially attentive to both their present and future needs by simultaneously building and maintaining capital that will help them to succeed in life and not just the moment. Whether committed or uncertain about their intentions of going on to earn a graduate degree, all undergraduate students would do well to gather the various forms of capital in ways that will allow them to open this door if they desire. Whereas economic, academic, and social forms of capital have a clear and direct impact on the ability of undergraduate students to move on to an advanced education, prospective graduate students also need to discover and acquire currency within the hidden curriculum or hidden capital of their academic disciplines, graduate programs and institutions, and professional fields in order to ascend in the ivory tower.

UNCOMMON FORMS OF CAPITAL

Economic, academic, and social capitals are forms of capital that are routinely apparent in higher education. Requiring students to pay for credit hours, prove their intelligence and scholastic abilities, and attain approval from current members of the academy reaffirms the relationship between these common forms of capital and the process and payoffs associated with higher education. Even so, students also need other forms of capital to enter, succeed in, and complete a college education.

Hidden Capital

As defined in this chapter, hidden capital[1] stems from the hidden curriculum, which is the collection of implicit messages, ideas, and expectations that influence student progress and success in an academic program for which they receive little or no formal instruction (Rennert-Ariev, 2008). Viewed in this way, hidden capital is the intrinsic currency that students earn within an academic environment by responding and performing in ways that make faculty members feel as though students have begun to recognize and learn the hidden curriculum. For the most part, hidden capital functions as a specific form of cultural capital by centering on the characteristics and skills that students can acquire that will allow them to ascend to the top of the academic pecking order. While not clearly visible on transcripts, hidden capital gains in graduate school include those elements of academic and professional development that faculty reserve for only those students whom they consider to be most worthy. Students who earn hidden capital while in school not only have superior academic experiences, but also add items and value to their resumes as they move into their professions.

Hidden Issues in Transitioning into Graduate School

Students who begin to consider going on to graduate or professional school generally find that universities provide basically the same information and structures for advanced degrees as they do regarding baccalaureate education. Utilizing the Internet, students can go to the websites of institutions and programs to learn about the application process, fees, requirements, and submission deadlines (Brunner & Boyer, 2008; Hartley &

Morphew, 2008). Despite the wide range of details available on the Internet, institution websites never tell students other crucial information that they need to know such as the climate experienced by minority students in departments and on campus; the research and other career-related opportunities enjoyed, especially by members of traditionally underrepresented populations; and the degrees of satisfaction that students feel about the program, department, and the faculty regardless of their course grades. Even when institutions or programs attempt to provide a glimpse into these issues, websites generally offer profiles and commentary only from the most successful and, presumably, satisfied students. Prospective students seeking to know more about the reality of attending a program should contact both administrators and faculty members with specific concerns that the website does not address before applying for admission. In addition, they should ask for the contact information of a similarly situated student. For example, only a single parent can truly begin to understand the concerns that another single parent would have about selecting an academic program and potentially locating to a new area. If the program does not have someone who has your exact background, ask the department to provide a couple of contacts so that you can get a range of perspectives. When institutions provide interested parties with these contacts, they still tend to choose those that faculty and administrators believe have had a positive experience. Even so, students tend to be more willing to share both their negative and positive views about their academic programs than professionals associated with an institution. At the same time, students also have the best perspective on what a future student can expect to encounter as they enter a graduate or professional degree program.

Another element of hidden capital related to applying to graduate school is knowing when to apply. Websites provide information on the deadlines that departments use to make their decisions. However, departments do not always post or readily share information about the deadlines used specifically to make decisions about financial assistance. Generally, institutions require applications for aid by early to mid February. Yet, to be eligible for much of this aid, departments must admit students ahead of time. As a result, students who want the best chance of getting the prime scholarships, fellowships, and assistantships must apply for admission to graduate and professional degree programs by late in the fall semester (November or early December). Moreover, much of the aid available to graduate students is not under the direct control of academic departments. Consequently, students will have to identify the various other offices on and even around a campus that offer various forms of financial support. In most cases, this will require students to both search the Internet and make direct contact (phone and email) with the gatekeepers who award this aid.

Hidden in Plain Sight

Once admitted to graduate school, hidden capital continues to influence the experiences of students. Hidden capital has the strongest impact on out-of-class opportunities and interactions that graduate students have with faculty members. Faculty mentoring of graduate students allows the faculty agents to give neophyte students access to elements of the curriculum not covered in class (Heathcott, 2005; Rosen & Bates, 1967). Participating in these mentoring relationships enables students to learn how to present themselves as professionals; the duties, expectations, and ethics of the profession; and how to practice specific skills key to both academic and professional achievement (Davis, 2007; Strayhorn & Terrell, 2007).

Relationships with faculty members are particularly priceless for students who have professional aspirations of remaining in academia. While students may find it possible to perform well in class by putting their heads down and focusing on their coursework, this pattern will not prepare them to win an academic career. Instead, students need to spend time getting to know faculty members both socially and professionally in order to help craft a foundation for mentoring relationships. In addition, prospective academics also need to hone their research skills, learn to write grants, and familiarize themselves with the processes that lead to the publication of research and scholarship (Davis, 2007; Mendoza, 2007; Strayhorn & Terrell, 2007). Living in a climate where several individuals meet the basic qualifications for virtually every open position, student acquisition of this type of knowledge is not just a perk of graduate school life, but an absolute necessity for those interested in academic employment.

Discovering the Hidden Pathway to Success

Although sometimes difficult to name or identify, hidden capital significantly affects the experiences that students encounter while in graduate school. Getting accepted into a graduate degree program is only the first hurdle that prospective students face in their race to recognize and attain hidden capital. Once admitted, learning the nuances of their programs, faculty members, and professions will allow students to develop the hidden capital that they need to succeed in graduate school and beyond.

GENERATING CAPITAL IN EDUCATIONAL CONTEXTS

Life is a culmination of the past, an awareness of the present, an indication of the future beyond knowledge, and the quality that gives a touch of divinity to the matter.

—Charles Lindbergh (1964)

The guy who takes a chance, who walks the line between the known and unknown, who is unafraid of failure, will succeed.

—Gordon Parks (n.d.)

Exhibited throughout their lives, both Charles Lindbergh and Gordon Parks learned and applied tremendous knowledge about generating capital. Both of these men voluntarily entered, worked hard, and eventually succeeded in a variety of careers. In order to achieve in their range of sometimes unrelated fields, both Lindbergh and Parks had to routinely establish, gain, and expend capital. Students looking to pursue an advanced degree should follow the example provided in the lives of these men by recognizing that all forms of capital are renewable resources that require lifelong attention.

In addition to being a lifelong investment, graduate education also has a cyclical structure in relation to capital. Students need capital in order to get into graduate school, so that they can gain more capital in the form of additional education and professional skills, which will allow students to later obtain even more capital after graduation by getting lucrative careers, increased social capital, and access to new forms of capital that might otherwise elude them. Even though gaining admission to graduate school does require a large investment of initial capital, students must continue to invest even more capital in order to receive continual capital as a benefit.

Furthermore, students must also accept that every degree, employment, or any other result of the investment of recognized capital will also involve some form of hidden capital. In any context, acquiring hidden capital will require students to do more than just the minimum, often much more than simply get by. Gaining forms of or circumventing the limitations imposed by hidden capital will involve the investment of more capital simply because it is not always clear what this capital is or exactly what or where students can find it. Essentially, hidden capital, like other forms of capital, is input driven since students who put in more effort to acquire capital are more likely to gain both the capital itself and its benefits. Similar to Gordon Parks and Charles Lindbergh, students must be both diligent and proactive in all of their endeavors if they want to maximize their gains in and advantageous use of capital.

According to the Bureau of Labor Statistics (2010), Americans ranging in ages from mid-40s to mid-60s held an average of 10.8 jobs over the course of a lifetime. Given the recent changes in the economy, younger Americans should learn from the example of Gordon Parks and Charles Lindbergh by preparing to pursue and succeed in several jobs and careers throughout their lives. While attending graduate school will not guarantee that young people can attain every job that they desire, completing a post-baccalaureate degree will better prepare them to weather a life of economic variations.

NOTES

1. The definition of hidden capital used in this chapter differs from the meaning associated with the banking industry. See Woo (2003).

REFERENCES

Aronowitz, S. (2004, Summer). Against schooling: Education and social class. *Social Text, 22*(2), 13–35.

Atwell, P., Lavin, D., Domina, T., & Levey, T. (2006, September/October). New evidence on college remediation. *The Journal of Higher Education, 77*(5), 886–924.

Boyle, P. & Boice, B. (1998, Spring). Best practices for enculturation: Collegiality, mentoring, and structure. *New Directions for Higher Education, 101,* 87–94.

Brunner, B. R. & Boyer, L. (2008). Internet presence and historically black colleges and universities: Protecting their images on the World Wide Web? *Public Relations Review, 34,* 80–82.

Bureau of Labor Statistics. (2010, July 20). *Frequently asked questions: Number of jobs held in a lifetime.* Retrieved from http://www.bls.gov/nls/nlsfaqs.htm#anch41

Burton, N. W., & Wang, M. (2005, April). Predicting long-term success in graduate school: A collaborative validity study. *GRE Board Report No. 99-14A.* Princeton, NJ: Educational Testing Service.

Cole, D. (2007, May/June). Do interracial interactions matter? An examination of student-faculty contact and intellectual self-concept. *The Journal of Higher Education, 78*(3), 249–281.

Cole, D. (2008, November/December). Constructive criticism: The role of student–faculty interactions on African American and Hispanic students' educational gains. *Journal of College Student Development, 49*(6), 587–605.

The College Board. (2009). *Trends in college pricing, 2009.* New York: Author. Retrieved from http://www.trends-collegeboard.com/college_pricing/

Cuyjet, M. J., Longwell-Grice, R., & Molina, E. (2009, January/February). Perceptions of new student affairs professionals and their supervisors regarding the application of competencies learned in preparation programs. *Journal of College Student Development, 50*(1), 104–119.

Davis, D. J. (2007, Fall/Winter). Access to academe: The importance of mentoring to black students. *Negro Educational Review, 58*(3–4), 217–231.

Ehrenberg, R. G. (2000). *Tuition rising: Why college costs so much.* Cambridge, MA: Harvard University Press.

Feeley, T. H., Williams, V. M., & Wise, T. J. (2005). Testing the predictive validity of the GRE exam on communication graduate student success: A case study at University of Buffalo. *Communication Quarterly, 53*(2), 229–245.

Fehrman, C. T. (2009, Summer). Preprofessionalism: Rankings, rewards, and the graduate admissions process. *College Literature, 36*(3), 184–210.

Fischer, M. J. (2007, March/April). Settling into campus life: Differences by race/ethnicity in college involvement and outcomes. *The Journal of Higher Education, 78*(2), 125–156.

Gardner, S. K. (2009, Spring). Conceptualizing success in doctoral education: Perspectives of faculty in seven disciplines. *The Review of Higher Education, 32*(3), 383–406.

Halberstam, B. & Redstone, F. (2005, July). The predictive value of admissions materials on objective and subjective measures of graduate school performance in speech-language pathology. *Journal of Higher Education Policy and Management, 27*(2), 261–272.

Hartley, M. & Morphew, C. C. (2008, November/December). What's being sold and to what end? A content analysis of college viewbooks. *The Journal of Higher Education, 79*(6), 671–691.

Hearn, J. C. (2001). The paradox in growth of federal aid for college students, 1960–1990. In M. B. Paulsen & J. C. Smart (Eds.), *The finance of higher education: Theory, research, policy and practice* (pp. 267–320). New York: Algora Publishing.

Heathcott, J. (2005, Nov./Dec.). Trained for nothing. *Academe, 91*(6), 14–17.

Jacobson, R. L. (2003, March 24). Critics say Graduate Record Exam does not measure qualities for success and is often misused. *The Chronicle of Higher Education, 39*(29), A27.

Kaiser Family Foundation. (n.d.). Poverty rate by race/ethnicity, states (2007–2008), U. S. (2008). Retrieved from http://www.statehealthfacts.org/comparebar.jsp?ind=14&cat=1

Kuther, T. (2010). Graduate admissions 101: Parts of the grad school application. *About.com* [Online]. Retrieved from http://gradschool.about.com/od/admissionsadvice/a/overview.htm

Lindbergh, C. A., II. (1964, July). Is civilization progress? *Reader's Digest, 89.* Retrieved from http://www.brainyquote.com/quotes/authors/c/charles_lindbergh.html

Lovitts, B. E. (2008, May/June). The transition to independent research: Who makes it, who doesn't , and why. *The Journal of Higher Education, 79*(3), 296–325.

Mendoza, P. (2007, January/February). Academic capitalism and doctoral student socialization: A case study. *The Journal of Higher Education, 78*(1), 71–96.

Millett, C. (2003, July/August). How undergraduate loan debt affects application and enrollment in graduate or first professional school. *The Journal of Higher Education, 74*(4), 386–427.

Nutting, R. (2009, December 24). For 2010, little improvement seen in job market. *MarketWatch*[On-line]. Retrieved from http://www.marketwatch.com/story/little-improvement-seen-in-job-market-in-2010-2009-12-24

Parks, G. (n.d.). *Quotations by author: Gordon Parks.* Retrieved from http://www.quotationspage.com/quotes/Gordon_Parks/

Pascarella, E. T., Wolniak, G. C., Pierson, C. T., & Flowers, L. A. (2004, Spring). The role of race in the development of plans for a graduate education. *The Review of Higher Education, 27*(3), 299–320.

Paulsen, M. B. & St. John, E. P. (2002, March/April). Social class and college costs: Examining the financial nexus between college choice and persistence. *The Journal of Higher Education, 73*(2), 189–236.

Perna, L. W. (2004, Sept./Oct.). Understanding the decision to enroll in graduate school: Sex and racial/ethnic group differences. *The Journal of Higher Education, 75*(5), 487–527.

Perna, L. W. (2005, Fall). The benefits of higher education: Sex, racial/ethnic, and socioeconomic group differences. *The Review of Higher Education, 29*(1), 23–52.

Perna, L. W. & Titus, M. A. (2005, September/October). The relationship between parental involvement as social capital and college enrollment: Racial/ethnic group differences. *The Journal of Higher Education, 76*(5), 485–518.

Petress, K. C. (1999, Dec.). Letters of recommendation: Their motive and content. *College Student Journal, 33*(4), 485–487.

Rennert-Ariev, P. (2008, January). The hidden curriculum of performance-based teacher education. *Teachers College Education, 110*(1), 105–138.

Rosen, B. C. & Bates, A. P. (1967, Winter). The structure of socialization in graduate school. *Sociological Inquiry, 37*(1), 71–84.

Sacks, P. (2001, June 8). How admissions test hinder access to graduate and professionals schools. *The Chronicle of Higher Education.* Retrieved from http://chronicle.com/article/How-Admissions-Tests-Hinder/16775/

Schieman, S. & Plickert, G. (2008, September). How knowledge is power: Education and the sense of control. *Social Forces, 87*(1), 153–183.

Sissoko, M. & Shiau, L. (2005, March/April). Minority enrollment demand for higher education at historically black colleges and universities from 1976 to 1998: An empirical analysis. *The Journal of Higher Education, 76*(2), 181–208.

Stainburn, S. (2009, July 26). Up to their ears in debt. *The New York Times.* Retrieved from http://www.nytimes.com/2009/07/26/education/edlife/26spending-t.html?_r=1

Strayhorn, T. L. (2008, January/February). Influences on labor market outcomes of African American college graduates: A national study. *The Journal of Higher Education, 79*(1), 28–57.

Strayhorn, T, L., & Terrell, M. C. (2007), Mentoring and satisfaction with college for Black students. *The Negro Educational Review, 58,* 69–83.

Titus, M. A. (2009, July/August). The production of bachelor's degrees and financial aspects of state higher education policy: A dynamic analysis. *The Journal of Higher Education, 80*(4), 439–468.

Walpole, M. (2003, Fall). Socioeconomic status and college: How SES affects college experiences and outcomes. *The Review of Higher Education, 27*(1), 45–73.

Walpole, M. (2008, May). Emerging from the pipeline: African American students, socioeconomic status, and college experiences and outcomes. *Research in Higher Education, 49*(3), 237–255.

Weaver, R. R. & Qi, J. (2005, Sept./Oct.). Classroom organization and participation: College students' perceptions. *The Journal of Higher Education, 76*(5), 570–601.

Weidman, J. C., Twale, D. J., & Stein, E. L. (2001). Socialization of graduate and professional students in higher education: A perilous passage? *ASHE-ERIC Higher Education Report, 28*(3). San Francisco, CA: Jossey-Bass.

Williams, J. (2006, Fall). The pedagogy of debt. *College Literature, 33*(4), 155-169.

Woo, D. (2003, December). In search of "capital crunch": Supply factors behind the credit slowdown in Japan. *Journal of Money, Credit, and Banking, 35*(6, Part 1), 1019–1038.

ABOUT THE CONTRIBUTORS

Stanley A. Bazile currently serves as the Assistant Dean of the College of Liberal Arts and Sciences at St. John's University. There, he helps provide leadership and strategic assessment of 35 core curriculum programs in collaboration with faculty. He also works closely with administrators and faculty to identify retention initiatives to support and promote successful retention of community college transfer students. Prior to St. John's University, Dr. Bazile worked at Cumberland County College as the Director/ Assistant to the Vice President for Academic Affairs. While there he served as one of the chief administrative officers responsible for the overall planning, coordination, delivery, funding and evaluation of academic affairs programs and services. In addition he delivered administrative oversight for seven on site universities which offered bachelors, masters, and doctoral degrees at the Shirlee and Bernard Brown University Center. Bazile maintains an active research agenda that examines student retention, transfer and success of community college students.

Floyd A. Beachum is the Bennett Professor of Urban School Leadership at Lehigh University. He is also an Associate Professor and program coordinator for the Educational Leadership program in the College of Education. His research interests include: leadership in urban education, moral and ethical leadership, and social justice issues in K–12 schools. He has authored several peer-reviewed articles on these topics in journals such as the *Journal of School Leadership, International Journal of Qualitative Studies in Education, Urban Education,* and the *Journal of Cases in Educational Leadership.* In addition, he is co-editor of the book, *Urban Education for the 21st Century: Research, Issues, and Perspectives* and a co-author of the book *Radicalizing educational leadership: Dimensions of social justice.*

Contemporary Perspectives on Capital in Educational Contexts, pages 219–222

Lecretia A. Buckley is an associate professor of mathematics education in the Department of Mathematics at Jackson State University in Jackson, MS. Her research focuses on equity issues in mathematics education in secondary schools and in pre-service teaching. Her work includes an examination of a high school mathematics department aimed at providing greater access to advanced mathematics for underrepresented students, research in curriculum design for secondary mathematics teacher education aimed at addressing equity issues in mathematics education at a predominately White institution, and the development of an equity-based model for professional development.

Saran Donahoo is an Associate Professor in the Department of Educational Administration and Higher Education and Director of the College Student Personnel Program at Southern Illinois University–Carbondale. She completed her B. A. at the University of Arizona and graduate degrees at the University of Illinois at Urbana-Champaign. Her published works include and articles in *Teachers College Record, Equity & Excellence in Education, Christian Higher Education, Urban Education,* and *Education and Urban Society* as well as an array of book chapters. In 2009, she received both the Joyce Cain Award for Distinguished Research on African Descendants from the Comparative and International Education Society (CIES) and the AERA Division J Outstanding Publication Award.

Robert W. Gaines, II is a third year doctoral student in the Department of Lifelong Education, Administration, and Policy at the University of Georgia. His research interests include the intersection of race, religion, and the history of education. Mr. Gaines completed undergraduate studies in English at Morehouse College and earned his Master of Arts in English from Penn State University. He intends to pursue a career as an academic upon graduating from the University of Georgia.

Phillis A. George is the Assistant Director of Service Learning for the Community Service/Service Learning Center at Jackson State University. She completed a doctorate in Educational Leadership and Policy Analysis at the University of Wisconsin-Madison and a Master's in Sociology at Oxford University, United Kingdom. As a higher education administrator and researcher, Dr. George's research interest include college access, choice and success for high-achieving, low-income and minority students as well as minority retention and graduation within science, technology, engineering, and mathematics (STEM). Dr. George's research and scholarly interests also include college student development, outcomes and engagement through service learning.

Susan S. McClelland joined the School of Education, University of Mississippi (UM) faculty in August, 2005 as Assistant Professor of Educational Leadership. While working at UM she was offered the challenge to lead in the redesign efforts for principal preparation, becoming the Director of the Mississippi Principal Corps. In addition to her professorial role, she administers the 13-month full-time academic program as well as the full time internship placements. Prior to joining the UM faculty, Dr. McClelland served as an Assistant Superintendent, high school principal, assistant high school principal, and a high school teacher where she taught gifted education, special education, and English. In addition to her K–12 administrative and teaching experience, Dr. McClelland has served as Co-Director of the University of Mississippi Writing Project, and Mississippi Teacher Corps English Methods Instructor at the University of Mississippi. She currently serves as a consultant to the National Institute of School Leadership, and North Mississippi Education Consortium. Dr. McClelland teaches courses in instructional leadership, strategic planning, and organizational culture; her research interests are leadership development, school and organizational culture, and issues relating to rural education.

Carlos A. McCray is an Associate Professor at Fordham University in New York at the Lincoln Center where he teaches a seminar on ethics and social justice. Dr. McCray's research interests include Multicultural education and building level leadership. He has also done extensive research on issues surrounding urban education. His work has appeared in journals such as the *Journal of School Leadership*, the *Journal of Cases in Educational Administration*, *Urban Education*, and the *International Journal of Education Policy and Leadership*. Dr. McCray is also co-authoring a book titled, *Cultural collision and collusion: Reflections on hip-hop culture, values, and schools.*

Mario S. Torres, Jr. is an Associate Professor within the Educational Administration program at Texas A&M University, College Station. Dr. Torres obtained his Ph.D. in Educational Administration from Penn State University, University Park in 2003. His research interests include elementary and secondary school law and policy. His legal scholarship has examined administrative, political, and demographic dimensions associated with students' Fourth Amendment rights, while his policy research has focused largely on the ethical and political implications of school reform. Dr. Torres has published in the field's premier journals including *the Educational Administration Quarterly, Journal of Educational Administration, the Journal of School Leadership*, and *Education and Urban Society*. He also currently serves on the summer faculty at Teachers College, Columbia University and is a research fellow with the Mexican American and U.S. Latino Research Center.

Tamara N. Stevenson is a doctoral candidate in educational leadership (higher education administration) and a doctoral fellow with the Department of Leadership and Counseling at Eastern Michigan University. Her research interests include the role of race and gender in higher education participation, critical race theory, community colleges/leadership, faculty/professional development issues, qualitative research methods, adult and continuing education, college student development, and organizational/corporate communication and public relations. She is an adjunct speech instructor in Liberal (Communication) Arts at Schoolcraft College, a public two-year college in the metropolitan Detroit area. She holds bachelor's and master's degrees in journalism and organizational communication from Wayne State University, a specialist of arts in educational leadership and a community college leadership certificate from Eastern Michigan University.

Sheneka N. Williams is an assistant professor in the Department of Lifelong Education, Administration, and Policy within the College of Education at the University of Georgia. A graduate of Vanderbilt University's Peabody College of Education and Human and Organizational Development, her research interests include student assignment policies, school governance, and school-community relations. Her most recent study examines the micro-politics of student assignment policies in four large, urban school districts. Dr. Williams has authored and co-authored journal articles and book chapters concerning her research interests, and she has presented her work at national and state conferences.

Eboni M. Zamani-Gallaher is Professor and Coordinator of the Graduate Certificate Program in Community College Leadership in the Department of Leadership and Counseling at Eastern Michigan University. She holds a Ph.D. in Higher Education Administration with a specialization in Community College Leadership and Educational Evaluation from the University of Illinois at Urbana-Champaign. Her teaching, research, and consulting activities include psychosocial adjustment and transition of marginalized collegians, transfer, access policies, women in leadership, and institutional practices affecting work and family balance. Her most recent scholarship includes co-authorship of The Case for Affirmative Action on Campus: Concepts of Equity, Considerations for Practice (Stylus Publishing 2009) and co-editing The State of the African American Male (Michigan State University Press 2010).

ABOUT THE EDITOR

RoSusan D. Bartee, Ph.D., is currently an Associate Professor of Educational Leadership at the University of Mississippi in University, Mississippi. Dr. Bartee's research interests are K–12 education leadership, organizational culture, and social contexts of schools. Dr. Bartee teaches graduate-level courses in educational leadership, research methods, and cultural contexts of education.

Prior to assuming the Associate Professorship at the University of Mississippi, Dr. Bartee served as the Associate Director at the National Council for Accreditation of Teacher Education (NCATE) in Washington, DC for the Reading First Teacher Education Network (RFTEN). RFTEN, a $4.5 million dollar federal grant focused on restructuring teacher education programs using evidence-based research for minority serving institutions (i.e. Historically Black Colleges and Universities, Hispanic Serving Institution, Tribal Colleges). Dr. Bartee provided administrative leadership, budget oversight, and served as a liaison between the RFTEN project, the respective institutions, and the U.S. Department of Education. Dr. Bartee also previously served as Interim Executive Director at the Frederick D. Patterson Research Institute of the United Negro College Fund (UNCF) in Fairfax, Virginia as well as the Project Coordinator for the Summer Research Opportunities Program at the University of Illinois at Urbana-Champaign. Dr. Bartee has taught at the University of Maryland and the University of Illinois at Urbana-Champaign.

Dr. Bartee is the author or editor of two books—*The broken cisterns of African American education: Academic performance and achievement in the post-Brown era* (2008), *School matters: Why African American students need multiple*

Contemporary Perspectives on Capital in Educational Contexts, pages 223–224

forms of capital (2007). Dr. Bartee is also the author or coauthor of more than twenty journal articles or manuscripts. Dr. Bartee, a 2010 recipient of a Travel Grant to conduct research in Tanzania, Africa from the Office of Research and Sponsored Programs at the University of Mississippi, is also the 2008 recipient of the Researcher of the Year Award at the School of Education at the University of Mississippi. Dr. Bartee is listed as Who's Who of American Women (2008), Who's Who Among Executives and Professionals (2008), Who's Who in America (2007), and is a former Institute of Governmental Affairs Program Fellow (IGAP). Dr. Bartee served as the Director of the National Educational Policy Forum, one of the activities adjoining the 2008 Presidential Debate at the University of Mississippi, which convened nationally recognized educational researchers and public policy advocates from across the country. Dr. Bartee is an active member of the American Educational Research Association, 2008–2010 Chair of the Commission on the Status of Women at the University of Mississippi, and a Board of Examiners Member for the National Council for Accreditation of Teacher Education (both national and state levels). Dr. Bartee has served further in the capacities of an educational consultant, program evaluator, and motivational speaker.

Dr. Bartee received a Doctor of Philosophy in Educational Policy Studies from the University of Illinois at Urbana-Champaign, a Master of Arts in Liberal Studies from Northwestern University in Evanston, Illinois and a Bachelor of Arts in English (*magna cum laude*) from Tougaloo College in Jackson, Mississippi.

Printed and bound by CPI Group (UK) Ltd, Croydon, CR0 4YY

15/09/2026

14962368-0004